Playing for time

Manchester University Press

Playing for time

Stories of lost children, ghosts and the endangered present in contemporary theatre

Geraldine Cousin

Manchester University Press
Manchester and New York
distributed exclusively in the USA by Palgrave

Copyright © Geraldine Cousin 2007

The right of Geraldine Cousin to be identified as the author
of this work has been asserted by her in accordance with the
Copyright, Designs and Patents Act 1988.

Published by Manchester University Press
Oxford Road, Manchester M13 9NR, UK
and Room 400, 175 Fifth Avenue, New York, NY 10010, USA
www.manchesteruniversitypress.co.uk

Distributed in the United States exclusively by
Palgrave Macmillan, 175 Fifth Avenue,
New York, NY 10010, USA

Distributed in Canada exclusively by
UBC Press, University of British Columbia, 2029 West Mall,
Vancouver, BC, Canada V6T 1Z2

British Library Cataloguing-in-Publication Data is available

Library of Congress Cataloging-in-Publication Data is available

ISBN 978 0 7190 6198 1 paperback

First published by Manchester University Press in hardback 2007

This paperback edition first published 2013

The publisher has no responsibility for the persistence or accuracy of URLs
for any external or third-party internet websites referred to in this book,
and does not guarantee that any content on such websites is, or will remain,
accurate or appropriate.

Printed by Lightning Source

For my nephews and nieces, and with gratitude to
Joan, Julia and especially to Kate

But who shall return us the children?
(Rudyard Kipling, *The Children***)**

Contents

	Preface	*page* xi
1	The collapsing house	1
2	Past present: dramatisations of 'return'	9
3	Enter the revenant	28
4	*Nunc Instantis: Arcadia* and *Copenhagen*	55
5	Stories of lost futures	73
6	The Skriker's progeny	93
7	Blood sacrifice	120
8	Daughters' tales	136
9	*Coram Boy*: a final story	161
	Bibliography	166
	Index	169

Preface

Virtually all the plays that are discussed in this book were staged either in London or another English city between 1990 and 2005. Many of them were written during that time, though some are older – in a couple of cases much older. I saw a fair number of the productions and my comments on them derive from memories of performances, to which I have added the responses of reviewers. What struck me forcibly about the productions, despite obvious differences between them, was a recurrent atmosphere of anxiety, a pervasive sense of the imminence of danger.

The book grew out of a preoccupation with this sense of precariousness, which seems currently to haunt our imaginations in various forms. Newspaper headlines warn that we are under threat from an alarming number of different directions, and, though the majority of these dangers fail to materialise, the underlying feeling of anxiety persists. Disaster, it seems, is merely deferred, not averted. The spectres that perturb us are both global and close-at-hand. Danger manifests itself one day in the worryingly innocuous-looking face of a paedophile, the next in the image of a suicide bomber or the melting polar ice cap. It is only the outer shape of our fears that changes, however. An inner core of dread remains constant.

Given theatre's ability to embody our fears and desires, it is hardly surprising that contemporary plays and productions should reflect these anxieties. What *is* noteworthy though is the fact that theatre is ideally suited to the representation of precariousness because the theatrical present moment is itself inherently unstable. Theatre exists here and now, and then – sometimes disturbingly – it is gone. The insistent present tense of the theatrical experience – the sharing of time by actors/characters and audience – is unique. Whereas the events of a novel have happened (the completed book is in our hands to prove it), the events of the play are always happening. The passage of time is built into the occasion, and it is precisely for that reason that time itself can become part of the playwright's game plan. If the continuum that we take for granted in the auditorium is challenged or disrupted on the stage, we are confronted with the disturbing unreliability of the present tense. Our confidence in *nowness* is threatened.

The first chapter of the book begins with a defining stage moment from the 1990s that translated this sense of danger into an image of a devastated world. It occurred during Stephen Daldry's revival of J. B. Priestley's *An Inspector Calls* – one of the key productions of the decade. It was the experience of seeing this production that initially stimulated my awareness of the prevalence of representations of precariousness in the contemporary repertoire. As a number of reviewers pointed out, Daldry's production rescued *An Inspector Calls* from its perceived status as a creaky old repertory 'war-horse', but its huge critical and popular success cannot, I think, entirely be credited to the director, or the equally gifted designer. The longevity of the production, and the lesser (but still notable) success of other recent revivals of Priestley's plays seem to suggest that they have reclaimed a hold on audiences because they tap into the *Zeitgeist* of our age of anxiety.

Though the theatrical present moment is subject to erasure, it also contains the possibility of restitution. The past can be reconstituted within the present, just as the future can be imagined. A key motif in the book is the 'lost child', and these missing or endangered children are markers both of private pain and a profound uneasiness about our communal future. One 'lost child', who was the subject of a recent stage revival, was created by Priestley's contemporary, J. M. Barrie. This was not Peter Pan, literature's most famous lost boy (though he was currently in the news because of the hunt for an author to write a sequel to his story), but his more perturbing dramatic sibling, Mary Rose. Loss, however, can be remedied. Lost children project the possibility of children who are found – as Mary Rose is, for a time. While the book focuses initially on the relationship between past and present, later chapters explore future scenarios, sometimes of danger, but sometimes, too, of hope and redemption. In the final pages, precariousness is countered to some degree by intimations of survival.

1

The collapsing house

On 11 September 1992, Stephen Daldry's production of J. B. Priestley's *An Inspector Calls* opened at the National Theatre in London, nine years to the day before the obliteration of the twin towers of New York's World Trade Centre. With hindsight, the stunning, act-three *coup de théâtre*, when the doll's house on stilts that represented the Birling family's home suddenly pitched forward and collapsed, was to acquire the status of prophecy. Writing a few days after the first night, Jeremy Kingston, in his review for *The Times* newspaper (14.9.92), highlighted the production's contemporary relevance. Two speeches, he wrote:

> are central to [Daldry's] interpretation. One is spoken by Richard Pasco's self-satisfied industrialist, as he surveys his well-appointed home: 'A man has to mind his own business and look after himself and his own.' The other, by Margaret Thatcher, is quoted in the progamme: 'There is no such thing as society. There are individual men and women, and there are families.'

As the production vividly demonstrated, these 'pronouncements' were, Kingston stressed, 'false, corrupting and dangerous'. When the production was revived at the Playhouse Theatre London on 27 September 2001 (following runs in the interim at the Olivier, the Aldwych and the Garrick), recent events had redefined its significance in a terrifying way. On 3 October 2001, John Thaxter wrote in *What's On*:

> At first it was seen as a smack in the eye for Mrs Thatcher's notorious views on 'society'. It then became a parable for single mothers, beggars and rough sleepers. But now, as the building collapses in a cascade of shattered glass and china, Priestley's prophecies of fire, blood and terror take on a horrifying new relevance.

This hugely successful, multi-award-winning production, described by the *Daily Telegraph* reviewer Charles Spencer as 'the defining production of the 1990s' (2.10.01), was still touring in 2005, the year in which the most recent productions I discuss were first performed. I have begun with the spectacular effect of the collapsing house because, as I explained in the Preface, it seems to me that it symbolises a preoccupation with the precariousness of the present moment that is an important characteristic of contemporary theatre. I do not mean to suggest that the plays and productions I explore are a direct response to 9/11 or other traumatic events. The book's address is to the *Zeitgeist* more than to particular events in the real world that have had an impact on the *Zeitgeist*. This is true even with regard to *Frozen*, Bryony Lavery's dramatisation of the murder of a child by a paedophile, which I analyse in Chapter 5 partly in relation to newspaper articles about the killing of Sarah Payne, Holly Wells and Jessica Chapman. Lavery wrote *Frozen* before any of these murders were committed, but, by a dreadful coincidence, a revival of the play was running at the National Theatre when Jessica and Holly were killed. It is for this reason that I draw comparisons between *Frozen* and a selection of journalists' responses to the girls' deaths.

Frozen was first performed in 1998. Productions of another, far older, play that I focus on were also interpreted by reviewers in relation to a horrific, contemporary event. The play was Euripides' *Hecuba*, which portrays the savage revenge killing of children. Though *Hecuba* is rarely performed in this country, during 2004 and 2005 it received three separate productions. The first opened on 14 September 2004, the second at the beginning of October and the third in April 2005. The final production had been scheduled for an earlier performance, but the opening night was postponed because the leading actress, Vanessa Redgrave, was ill. A number of reviewers highlighted the productions' relevance to the massacre of schoolchildren by terrorists that took place in Beslan at the beginning of September 2004. The three productions were in the planning stage, however, before the massacre happened. The decisions to stage the play were taken in the context of public anxiety about international terrorism, but the specific event – like the murder of Holly and Jessica – became coincidentally intertwined with a fictional representation that in some ways resembled it.

While the murdered children in *Frozen* and *Hecuba* had recognisable, if accidental, real-life counterparts, other 'lost' children in the book are more obviously confined to page and stage. They belong sometimes to the realm of memory, where they become signifiers of what can and cannot be retrieved from the past. At other times, they represent our fears for, and of, the future, or our anxieties about an inability to protect the vulnerable, given the precarious state of the world. Precariousness is both a prevalent theme in the plays and a key characteristic of the form in which the theme is communicated to an audience. In theatre it is always the present moment, and yet the moment constantly vanishes. Three of the playwrights I consider – J. B. Priestley, August Strindberg and Caryl Churchill – were/are particularly intrigued by the malleability of theatre time, but a fascination with the fragility, and the fecundity, of the present moment also characterises many of the plays I discuss by other playwrights. In the following chapter, I focus on four of Priestley's plays: *Dangerous Corner, An Inspector Calls* (including Stephen Daldry's long-running production), *Time and the Conways* and *Eden End*. *Dangerous Corner* and *Eden End* were performed as part of a successful Priestley season at the West Yorkshire Playhouse in 2001, following which *Dangerous Corner* transferred to the Garrick Theatre in London. *Time and the Conways* was staged in December 2001 at Manchester's Royal Exchange Theatre, and also by Theatre Royal Bath Productions in 2003. I begin my examination of dramatic representations of the precariousness of the present moment with these four plays partly because of this revival of interest in Priestley's work, but chiefly because the plays explore so effectively key themes of time, culpability and loss that recur throughout the book.

Chapter 2 is entitled 'Past present: dramatisations of "return"', and the return of the past – in some form – underpins pretty well all the plays I address in this, and later chapters. The four examples of Priestley's work have all been described as 'time plays'. *Dangerous Corner* and *An Inspector Calls* are also heavily indebted to a popular narrative form that relies on an investigation of the past in order to bring the present into clearer focus. This is the 'whodunnit'. Priestley dexterously manipulates the whodunnit format in order to construct dramatic narratives which then twist back on themselves and return to an earlier, key, point in the action. In *Dangerous Corner,* he does this, in the main, simply for dramatic effect, but his purpose in *An Inspector Calls* is more serious. His utilisation of the motif of 'return', and appropriation of the whodunnit format have an honourable dramatic heritage. Indeed, one of the most famous characters of all – Sophocles' Oedipus – is both a 'returner' (though he doesn't know this) and a figure in a whodunnit. Unfortunately, Oedipus tragically misinterprets his role in the mystery. After solving the Sphinx's riddle, he is impressed by his own abilities as a detective, when in reality he is the villain. He fails to understand the clues that are offered him because he lacks one vital piece of information. He believes that he has come to Thebes for the first time, when it was actually his birthplace. It is only when he understands this, and correctly aligns past and present, that he is able to name the culprit responsible for the contamination of the city, i.e. himself. At the end of *Oedipus Rex*, Oedipus solves the puzzle that he has wrestled with throughout the play. He is a detective after all, but he is also the murderer, and that duality destroys the seeds of a positive future that might have existed within the present moment. Unlike Oedipus, Inspector Goole in *An Inspector Calls* understands who the culprits are from the beginning. The purpose of his investigation is to offer them a chance to behave differently. As he did in his earlier play *Dangerous Corner*, Priestley twists 'time's tail', but this time for a clear moral purpose.

By returning to an earlier point in the narrative at the end of *An Inspector Calls*, Priestley simultaneously emphasises culpability and opens up the possibility that this time round the characters might be ready to admit their guilt. A number of the plays I discuss in later chapters – notably Tom Stoppard's *Arcadia*, Michael Frayn's *Copenhagen*, and Caryl Churchill's *Far Away* and *A Number* – are also fascinating reworkings of the whodunnit format. *Arcadia* and *Copenhagen*, which are discussed in Chapter 4, use the whodunnit as a framework for complex investigations into the nature of responsibility and of time. Like Priestley in *An Inspector Calls*, Churchill utilises elements of the whodunnit in *Far Away* to pinpoint moments of choice that will have tragic consequences. Priestley is more hopeful, however. He shows us not only the imminence of catastrophe, but also how to avert it. *Far Away* offers no such reassurance. *A Number*, Churchill's response to human cloning, begins as a kind of detective story, and transforms into an exploration of parental responsibility and the fragility of human identity. *A Number* and *Far Away*, both of which, interestingly, were directed, like *An Inspector Calls*, by Stephen Daldry and designed by Ian MacNeil, are discussed in Chapter 6. I have devoted an entire chapter to Churchill's work because she seems to me to be the playwright who best captures our current sense of precariousness.

Dangerous Corner and *An Inspector Calls* are a mixture of a whodunnit and a time play. *Time and the Conways* is an investigation into the nature of time, in which the ghosts of the future disturb the present. *Eden End* is structured around the return of a character who is searching for a lost past. Her re-entry into the other characters' lives unsettles them. Stella herself is in a mental limbo – uneasily marooned between a past she cannot access and a future that is fraught with difficulty. *Eden End* and *Time and the Conways* are both about loss, but they are also about seeing things differently. Even though the future is apparently predetermined in *Time and the Conways*, Priestley's experimentation with time creates a sense of hope. *Eden End* concludes with Stella – the 'returner' – accepting the fact that the past is closed to her, and moving on. A character whose return acts as a hinge between past and present is a kind of ghost. There is something inherently unsettling about the idea of coming back, a sense of uneasiness that Caryl Churchill plays with humorously in *Heart's Desire* (the first part of her double bill, *Blue Heart*), and manipulates with spooky effectiveness in *A Number*. I end Chapter 2 with an analysis of a play about a ghost, J. M. Barrie's *Mary Rose*, which I discuss in relation to *Eden End*. Ghosts are 'returners' by their very nature. Return is what defines them. It is what they do. 'What has this thing appeared again tonight?' Horatio asks at the beginning of *Hamlet*, in relation to dramatic literature's best-known ghost. I explore *Mary Rose* in the context of *Eden End* because both plays were informed by the loss of millions of young lives in the First World War. The year 2004 was the centenary of the first performance of Barrie's more famous 'lost child' play, *Peter Pan* (which took place on 27 December 1904 at the Duke of York's Theatre in London). Two films commemorated the centenary: *Peter Pan*, directed by P. J. Hogan, and *Finding Neverland* with Johnny Depp as Barrie. There was also a high-profile competition to find an author to write a sequel to *Peter Pan*. Barrie gave the intellectual property rights to *Peter Pan* to London's Great Ormond Street Hospital for Children, and the trustees of the Hospital launched the competition because the copyright was due to come to an end in 2007. The name of the winner, Geraldine McCaughrean, was announced in March 2005. *Mary Rose* (a far more disturbing play about a lost child than *Peter Pan*) was revived by Two Colour Theatre Company in 2001, in February and, again, at the end of November. There was also a production of the play at the Nottingham Playhouse in October 2002.

The ghostly *Mary Rose* is followed in Chapter 3 by a discussion of ghost characters in six Irish plays: Conor McPherson's award-winning *The Weir*, *Shining City* (also by McPherson), Stewart Parker's *Pentecost* and three plays by Marina Carr: *The Mai*, *Portia Coughlan* and *By the Bog of Cats*. Apart from *The Mai*, each of the plays was performed in London between 1989 and 2004, concluding with *By the Bog of Cats* at Wyndhams Theatre with Holly Hunter in the leading role. As I note in Chapter 3, the return of a figure from the past is a frequent occurrence in Irish plays. I have chosen to concentrate on these six plays, out of the explosion of Irish dramatic talent on the London stage in the 1990s and the opening years of the twenty-first century, because of the nature of their representation of time.

McPherson's, and, even more obviously, Carr's, investment in the past lives of their characters creates static, liminal, worlds where ghosts multiply. There is more forward momentum in *Pentecost,* because the living reach a greater accommodation with the dead, but the haunted house in which the action takes place has something in common with the two other playwrights' ghost-infested settings. Chapter 3 ends with a description of a ghostly drama that took a less conventional form. *Carnesky's Ghost Train,* which emulated a ride on a fairground ghost train, encapsulated the idea of stasis. The 'audience' was taken on a repetitive, hopeless journey, a circular quest for missing ghost-daughters who would never be found.

Because they belong equally to past and present, it is the nature of ghosts to link these two aspects of time. In a different way, the plays discussed in Chapter 4, Tom Stoppard's *Arcadia* and *Copenhagen* by Michael Frayn (both of which premiered at the National Theatre, to critical acclaim, in the 1990s), also probe the intersection of past and present. So, too, does Michael Frayn's novel *Spies,* which is discussed at the end of Chapter 4. The few novels that are considered in the book are included either because of their relevance to a particular play, or because they were adapted for stage performance. The investigation of the past in *Spies,* which won the Whitbread Prize in 2002, recalls *Copenhagen.* The subject matter of Alice Sebold's highly acclaimed novel, *The Lovely Bones* (see Chapter 5), has links with *Frozen.* In almost all the plays stories and storytelling are important. Often the stories relate to a lost past, as is the case in *Arcadia* and *Copenhagen.* Carr's protagonists attempt to redeem losses that occurred in their childhoods, while both *Frozen* and *The Memory of Water* feature mothers who have lost children. This loss creates, initially, a sense of stasis that is reminiscent of the plays discussed in Chapter 3. Mary still inhabits an emotional winter-land at the end of *The Memory of Water,* but, despite her grief, Nancy in *Frozen* moves finally into a summer landscape.

In addition to the whodunnit, there is another narrative form that I refer to quite often, and that is the fairy story. The dramatists I focus on use fairy stories, as they do the whodunnit, to provide a structure and a set of expectations that can then be either realised or subverted. Dark fairy stories inform Marina Carr's plays. Churchill's *The Skriker* retells traditional fairy tales, in order to construct from them an urgent warning of the proximity of danger. In addition to the whodunnit, act one of *Far Away* is reliant on fairy tales, while Bryony Lavery's *Frozen* is indebted to the story of *Little Red Riding Hood.* The two plays by Euripides that are discussed in Chapter 7, *Hecuba* and *Iphigenia at Aulis,* tell parts of the story of the Trojan War. *Iphigenia at Aulis* is about the ritual killing of Iphigenia, which kick-started that war. *Hecuba* relates the war's horrific consequences. *Iphigenia at Aulis* was staged at the National Theatre in the summer of 2004. Like the three 2004/05 productions of *Hecuba*, it was interpreted by reviewers in relation to the contemporary international situation – in this case, the aftermath of the joint American/British invasion of Iraq. As an introduction to these plays and productions, I briefly consider, in Chapter 7, a key play from the 1990s that encapsulated contemporary violence in images of shocking immediacy. Sarah Kane's *Blasted*, which involves, among other horrors, the eating of a dead baby, was first performed in 1995 at the Royal Court, and revived at the same theatre in 2001. I examine reviews of the two productions, which are markedly different in tone.

Like *Iphigenia at Aulis*, the texts that I discuss in Chapters 8 and 9 (a play and adaptations of novels) were staged at the National Theatre. They were all in performance, at the Olivier Theatre or the Cottesloe, in 2005, and it is for this reason, in addition to the thematic links between them, that I consider them in conjunction. Chapter 7 is about murdered children and vengeful mothers. Chapters 8 and 9 are about the reclamation and survival of children. Chapter 8 is called 'Daughters' tales', and the daughters are Lyra Belacqua, Philip Pullman's child-protagonist in the *His Dark Materials* trilogy, and Strindberg's protagonist, Indra's Daughter (also called Agnes), in *A Dream Play*. A dramatisation of *His Dark Materials* was running at the Olivier Theatre when Katie Mitchell's adaptation of *A Dream Play* opened at the Cottesloe Theatre on 15 February 2005. Katie Mitchell marginalised the Daughter, who is at the centre of Strindberg's play. I have attempted to relocate her – to find a 'lost child' – partly through a discussion of the play, and various productions of it (notably Ingmar Bergman's 1970 adaptation). In addition, I refer to Strindberg's related letters and diary entries, and also to his paintings that were on display at Tate Modern in an exhibition that ran concurrently with the Cottesloe production. My self-imposed task in Chapter 8, therefore, is to tell the Daughter's tale that Katie Mitchell obscured. Lyra Belacqua is herself a storyteller, and her tale has some points in common with the Daughter's in *A Dream Play*. Both protagonists are reworkings of biblical figures – Eve and Christ – and both journey through alternative, parallel, worlds, where space – and also time in *A Dream Play* – is reimagined.

My focus on Strindberg's Daughter in *A Dream Play* in the context of a lost child refound leads, in the final chapter, to a discussion of Jamila Gavin's award-winning story of lost children, *Coram Boy*, an adaptation of which opened at the Olivier Theatre in November 2005. *Coram Boy* completes the exploration of 'return' that I begin in relation to *Dangerous Corner* and *An Inspector Calls*. Like Priestley, Gavin utilises the idea of 'return' to forge a connection between past and present. While Priestley does this in order to question the shape of the future, however, Gavin concentrates on rediscovery and renewal. At the end of her story, a lost child is found and a breach in time is healed.

2
Past present: dramatisations of 'return'

My focus in this chapter is primarily on four of Priestley's 'time plays', each of which is structured either around the return of a character or a reversal to a previous point in the action. The present is inescapably linked to the past. *Dangerous Corner* and *An Inspector Calls* skilfully manipulate the whodunnit format in order to shine a powerful beam of light on moments when choices are made that will have momentous consequences for the future. *Time and the Conways* and *Eden End* are meditations on the nature of loss, but they, too, like *Dangerous Corner* and *An Inspector Calls*, contain seeds of hope. Stella, in *Eden End*, can choose whether or not she will be imprisoned by her past. In *Time and the Conways*, though Priestley's experimentation with time indicates, on the one hand, that the future is already determined, it suggests, too, the possibility that the characters may not necessarily be constrained by temporal linearity. In relation to Priestley's text of *An Inspector Calls*, I explore Stephen Daldry's 1992 production of the play, which linked the time of its composition – close to the end of the Second World War – to our own precarious world. *Eden End*, which was first performed in 1934, depicts a lost, pre-1914, world. Acts one and three of *Time and the Conways* (1937) are set at the end of the First World War. The clever time shift in act two contains pre-echoes of the war to come. Both *Time and the Conways* and *Eden End* portray the fragility of human happiness, while also emphasising the possibility of human resilience. Finally in the chapter, I discuss J. M. Barrie's *Mary Rose*, which, I suggest, is haunted even more obviously than *Eden End* by the lost generation of the First World War. Loss in *Mary Rose* is eventually succeeded by redemption, but the ghostly protagonist can find release only by embracing her dead state. There is no re-entry into life. Partly because she is a ghost, and partly because the island that has such a hold on her resembles the isolated, darkly seductive settings in Marina Carr's plays, *Mary Rose* acts as a bridge to the plays that are explored in Chapter 3. The power of the past, with its terrors and guilts – and sometimes its joys – is readdressed in later chapters, where Priestley's experimentations with the whodunnit, and his exploration of the link between time and loss find new formulations.

Twisting 'time's tail'

When J. B. Priestley wrote his first play, *Dangerous Corner*, he was already a successful novelist, but it looked initially as if his foray into the world of theatre was going to be a flop. The reviews were discouraging, and a few days after the production opened at the Lyric Theatre, London, on 17 May 1932, Priestley was advised that it should be taken off. But then came the Sunday papers and both Ivor Brown in the *Observer* and James Agate in the *Sunday Times* wrote enthusiastic reviews. Agate was particularly complimentary. 'If this is not a brilliant device', he enthused, 'I do not grasp the meaning of either word, and if the plot is not a piece of sustained ingenuity of the highest technical accomplishment, I am not an impercipient donkey but an ass who has perceived too much.' Emboldened by this praise, Priestley decided to 'risk a large proportion' of the profits from his novel *The Good Companions* 'in backing it himself' (Cook, *Priestley*, p. 120). The gamble paid off. *Dangerous Corner* went on to become hugely successful with audiences all over the world. Writing in 1958, David Hughes claimed, 'it would be safe to guess . . . that the curtain has gone up on *Dangerous Corner* more times and in more places than any other play written during the past thirty years' (Hughes, *J.B. Priestley,* p. 200).

Priestley's early confidence in the play's ability to attract audiences initially seems surprising in light of the dismissive comments he made about it in his Introduction to Volume One of his plays, published by Heinemann in 1948:

> It has never been a favourite of mine, for it seems to me merely an ingenious box of tricks, which I constructed to prove – for it was my first play – that I could think and create like a dramatist and not necessarily like a novelist, and also to make use of the device of splitting time into two, thus showing what might have happened, an idea that has always fascinated me. (p. viii)

What is clear from these words, however, is that, like Agate, Priestley understood the source of *Dangerous Corner's* effectiveness as theatre. The play may be largely 'a box of tricks', but the crucial trick, Agate's 'brilliant device', still has the capacity to keep audiences on the edge of their seats.

As I have already noted, *Dangerous Corner* is a whodunnit. The plot revolves around a group of friends who are attending a dinner party at the home of Freda and Robert Caplan. Robert and two of the guests, Gordon Whitehouse and Charles Stanton, are directors of a publishing firm. The other guests are Gordon's wife, Betty, Olwen Peel, an employee of the publishing firm, and a novelist called Miss Mockridge. The play begins in darkness. The muffled sound of a revolver shot is heard, followed by a woman's scream. The lights come up on the four female characters, who are seated in the Caplans' drawing room, and the revelation that the violent sounds the audience has heard were the conclusion of a play called *The Sleeping Dog* that the women have been listening to on the wireless. This revelation is Priestley's first trick, its purpose being to create a sense of instability – things may not be quite as they seem – and to motivate speculation with regard to the nature and desirability of 'truth'. The sleeping dog signifies truth, Olwen decides, and it may be best to let it lie. Charles Stanton agrees with her. 'I think telling the truth is about as healthy as skidding round a corner at sixty', he remarks. 'And life's got a lot of dangerous corners' (ibid., p. 5), Freda adds and then, unwittingly, propels the action towards the dangerous corner around which the characters begin to skid to disaster. She offers Olwen a cigarette from a musical cigarette box that Olwen recognises. Martin, Robert's brother, showed it to her a year ago, she claims, shortly before he killed himself. 'He couldn't have shown it to you, Olwen', Freda replies. 'He hadn't got it when you saw him last' (ibid., p. 6). Even at this point, the corner could be negotiated safely. Olwen backs down. Perhaps she saw the box – or one like it – somewhere else, but Robert insists on pursuing the truth. One discovery leads to another until a whole network of unsavoury relationships connected to the dead Martin is revealed. Robert becomes so distraught about what he discovers that he shoots himself. The sound of a gunshot is heard in darkness, and, when the lights come up, we are back at the beginning of the play. Once again, the women are seen listening to *The Sleeping Dog*. A shortened version of act one follows up the point when Olwen opens the cigarette box, but this time Gordon, who has been trying to tune the wireless, succeeds, and loud dance music is heard. Attention shifts away from the cigarette box. The dangerous corner has been avoided. It is a trick, but a clever one, and the first time one sees it it can be breathtaking.

Though the characters are mostly two-dimensional, *Dangerous Corner* does have one more complex character, and that is Olwen Peel, played in the original production by the gifted Flora Robson. Olwen has glimpses of 'truth' as something beyond the superficial revelations of a whodunnit. 'The *real* truth', she explains, 'is something so deep you can't get at it this way' (ibid. p. 48). Priestley's manipulation of time in the play complicates the idea of 'truth', suggesting that it is dependent on the vagaries of chance. As Gareth Lloyd Evans writes in *J.B. Priestley – The Dramatist* (p. 80), '[i]f the end of the truth-telling is the truth about a dead man whom we never meet, the means become an exercise in the relativity of truth'. Priestley's device of 'splitting time into two . . . showing what *might* have happened' takes the play's final moments onto a more complex and ambiguous terrain. There is, if only briefly, 'a sudden powerful feeling of the strangeness of life, of the softness of the ground we tread' (Hughes, p. 132). Behind the cardboard facade most of the characters present to the world something more disturbing is momentarily evoked.

The sense of disquiet the ending can provoke was enhanced in the production at the West Yorkshire Playhouse in 2001. For the first American production of *Dangerous Corner*, Priestley provided an alternative version of the text in which Freda describes a ghostly white owl that visits the garden at night. Laurie Sansom's production, which opened in the Playhouse's small Courtyard Theatre in Leeds on 7 September 2001, used a hybrid of the British and American texts, which included references to this owl. In the final moments of the performance, a huge white bird, a ghostly manifestation of the owl, appeared to fly directly towards the audience. It was 'an effect', Rhoda Koenig wrote in the *Independent* (25.9.01), 'as beautiful as it [was] terrifying', symbolising 'both avenging truth and Robert's dead brother'.

Like *Dangerous Corner*, *An Inspector Calls* is a 'thriller that closes breathlessly on an unexpected twist of time's tail' (Hughes, p. 198). This play has a serious moral dimension, however, that *Dangerous Corner* lacks. Priestley wrote it close to the end of the Second World War, 'during the winter of 1944–5 . . . in one week flat' (Cook, p. 201). There was no 'vacant theatre' in London for it, so Priestley 'sent the script to his Russian translator in the USSR where it was immediately taken up by two theatre companies – the Kamerny in Moscow and the Leningrad Theatre Company – and had its first performance in two cities at the same time' (ibid., pp. 201–2). It was produced in England at the Opera House, Manchester, on 9 March 1946, and subsequently, with the same cast, at the New Theatre, London, where the opening night was 1 October 1946. As in *Dangerous Corner*, the plot involves the investigation of a suicide. This time, however, in place of the louche, sadistic Martin, the victim is a young, pregnant, working-class woman (known to some of the characters as Eva Smith and to others as Daisy Renton) who has killed herself by swallowing disinfectant. Unlike *Dangerous Corner*, where, in the absence of a detective, all the characters take on this function, the role of investigator is fulfilled by the eponymous caller. Inspector Goole is no ordinary detective. Though his purpose gradually becomes clear, his provenance remains uncertain: 'Is . . . this omniscient inspector Priestley's idea of the angel with the flaming sword?' J. C. Trewin asked in his *Observer* review of 6 October 1946. 'Who can tell? He comes in such a questionable shape. He may be an embodiment of conscience or the representative of a celestial Watch Committee . . .'. Judith Cook writes that *An Inspector Calls* has 'been described variously as a well-constructed thriller, a time play and a morality play' (Cook, p. 202). Inspector Goole is the crucial figure in relation to each of these three aspects, simultaneously a detective, an expression of 'conscience' and the twister of 'time's tail'. The purpose of this twist is not to avoid a dangerous corner, but instead to try to impel the characters to face the truth and take responsibility for their past actions.

In *Dangerous Corner,* the cigarette box is at first simply a clue to the solution of a mystery, but then it takes on 'the role of a sinister *deus ex machina* whose malevolence is inescapable' (Evans, p. 76). In *An Inspector Calls,* the chief clue is a photograph of the dead young woman. The *deus ex machina* is a telephone, which, when it rings, calls the characters to justice. Inspector Goole brings the photograph with him and shows it separately to each of the characters (the members of the Birling family and Sheila Birling's fiancé, Gerald Croft) as a means of inducing them to confess their part in the events that led to the victim's death. The fact that no two characters ever look at the photograph together enables them to attempt to deny their responsibility once the Inspector leaves. How do they know, they ask each other, that they were shown the same photograph? Each of them has treated a young woman badly, but was it the same young woman? Perhaps they are not collectively responsible for Eva Smith's/Daisy Renton's death. Maybe she isn't even dead. Could the Inspector have been an impostor? A telephone call to the Chief Constable establishes the fact that there is no Inspector Goole in the police force, while another to the Infirmary confirms their growing confidence in their innocence. No suicide victim has been brought to the Infirmary. The photograph – the awakener of 'Conscience' – is no longer the clue to their guilt, but evidence of a trick that has been played on them. Then, as they are laughing at themselves for their stupidity in being duped by the Inspector, the *'telephone rings sharply'*, and, after *'a moment's complete silence',* Mr Birling answers it. 'A girl has just died –' he informs the shocked assembly, 'on her way to the Infirmary – after swallowing some disinfectant. And a Police Inspector is on his way . . . to ask some – questions' (Priestley, *An Inspector Calls*, p. 52)

Like the cigarette box in *Dangerous Corner*, the photograph leads to the solution of the whodunnit. The fact that the audience never sees the girl's face is important because Priestley implicates us along with the characters. The name of the dead girl is immaterial. Whether or not the characters mistreated the same young woman is beside the point. They – we – each have a personal 'photograph' that identifies our individual, and collective, responsibility for other members of society. The telephone, the *deus ex machina*, returns the play's action to the beginning. The characters are caught off guard, on the threshold of the moment that will lead, irrevocably, to their being called to account for their actions.

The shrill warning note of the telephone is particularly effective because it isn't heard until this point in the play. The 1948 acting edition of *An Inspector Calls*, published by Samuel French, included two separate furniture and property lists, one using only one set, and the other three sets. At the New Theatre, the dining room of the Birlings' house, in which the action takes place, was shown from a different perspective in each of the three acts. In act one, the back wall was parallel to the audience, and the stage-right wall formed almost a right angle with it. In act two, the set had shifted towards stage left. In act three, the shift had become so pronounced that what had previously been the back wall now formed an acute angle with the stage-right wall, while most of the stage-left wall had disappeared. The effect was to create a sense of constriction and a distortion of perspective in contrast to the openness and regularity of act one. And, for the first time, the telephone was in a prominent position, signalling the important role it would have to play.

The Daldry/MacNeil production of *An Inspector Calls*

The 1992 revival of *An Inspector Calls* directed by Stephen Daldry established a disturbingly distorted atmosphere from the beginning. In Ian MacNeil's expressionist setting, Priestley's domestic telephone was transformed into a large, red telephone box, which indicated the wider, public, consequences of the characters' guilt. The performance began with the sound of an air-raid siren. An old-fashioned, red theatre curtain hid most of the set, but in front of it was a battered, 1940s-style wireless. As the houselights slowly faded, a small boy appeared and struggled unsuccessfully to lift the heavy curtain. Irritated by his failure, he began to kick the wireless, which stuttered briefly into life. The effect, Nicholas de Jongh wrote, was to suggest that the play was being 'relayed from a post-1945 repertory theatre to wireless-listeners' (*Evening Standard*, 25.10.95). The curtain then rose slowly to reveal a bleak, weirdly beautiful stage picture. Rain was falling on wet, glistening, black cobblestones and smouldering bomb craters. At the front of the stage, the little boy, who had now been joined by two small girls, ran to and fro, while the girls stretched out their arms and twirled around in the rain. Centre stage, stood an extraordinary structure: a three-storey house, surmounted by a green cupola. The entire edifice perched precariously on a flimsy, skeletal structure that looked incapable of bearing its weight. Though pretty and picturesque, the house was peculiar. The upper storeys were constructed on a smaller scale than the lower one, though even this had the dimensions of a toy building. Disturbingly large heads could be glimpsed through the tiny windows, creating an additional 'distortion of scale' that transformed the characters 'into ogres inhabiting an Edwardian doll's house' (Robert Hanks, *Independent*, 28.8.93). Upstage right of this 'doll's house on stilts', as a number of reviewers dubbed it, was a tiny replica of the house. The added sense of distortion this created was enhanced by a row of tiny lamp-posts upstage, which echoed a realistically-sized lamp-post downstage right. In contrast to the gleaming blackness of the cobblestones and the lowering sky, the bottom storey of the house was filled with light. It could potentially therefore have suggested a beacon of hope in the surrounding darkness, but the house's strangeness and its over-large occupants were at odds with this. The people resembled 'Lilliputians glimpsed through the wrong end of a telescope', in a house 'precariously perched on a ruined pier at what seem[ed] like the end of the world' (Maureen Paton, *Daily Express*, 12.9.92). It was the children spinning in the rain who appeared, in their innocent enjoyment, to suggest hope.

When they exited, they were replaced downstage by an elderly woman who scuttled around, trying to create order in the ruined landscape. This was Edna, the Birlings' maid, who in this production remained outside the house. Her words, like the Inspector's, were spoken from stage level. Along with a group of servicemen and civilians in 1940s costume who appeared at various points as silent witnesses of events, these two characters, and the children, were distinct from the doll's-house characters. Their separation, the peculiar perspective of the house and the chiaroscuro lighting effect all created a sense of unease.

From the start, there was need of a reference point from which the audience could interpret what they were seeing. When Inspector Goole arrived to provide it, Edna announced his arrival facing not towards her employers in the house, but directly out to the audience. Inspector Goole took up a position close to her, downstage right, between the lamp-post and the phone box. He, too, faced the audience, implicating them from the beginning in the investigation he had come to undertake. His connection with the children, the silent witnesses and the bomb damage was emphasised by his 1940s-style clothes, in contrast to the Birlings who wore Edwardian dress. He belonged, like the children and the witnesses, to the time of the play's composition. Though definitely an embodiment of 'Conscience', he wasn't a representative of Trewin's 'celestial Watch Committee'. He came from the Birling family's future to apportion blame for the devastation they had helped to create. Immediately prior to his entry, Mr Birling had forcibly rejected any belief in social responsibility. '[T]he way some of these cranks talk and write now', he explained to Gerald Croft, 'you'd think everybody has to look after everybody else, as if we were all mixed up together like bees in a hive – community and all that nonsense' (*An Inspector Calls*, p. 7). As Edna announced the Inspector's arrival, the doll's house split open in the middle, and there were its inhabitants, looking like figures in a children's pop-up book as they perched absurdly on child-sized furniture. Inspector Goole manoeuvred a rickety metal staircase into position to enable them to descend, one by one, to ground level in order to answer his questions. There, surrounded by the debris of war, the story of their complicity in Eva Smith's/Daisy Renton's death became linked to a far wider context of self-interest and damage.

Mrs Birling, the final character to leave the house, was also the one who was most resistant to admitting culpability. Prior to her descent, a carpet was spread over the cobblestones, to protect her from touching their dirt, even with her feet. However, when she learned that the young woman whom she had refused to help (in her capacity as a prominent member of a charity organization) had been carrying her son's child, she collapsed onto the cobblestones. The son, Eric, also fell to the ground, and, standing beside them, Inspector Goole delivered Priestley's blistering attack on self-interest straight out into the audience. As he did so the lights in the auditorium came on:

> We don't live alone. We are members of one body. We are responsible for each other. And I tell you that the time will soon come when, if men will not learn that lesson, then they will be taught it in fire and blood and anguish. (ibid., p. 42)

In an unexpected gesture of tenderness, he covered Eric and his mother with a blanket, and then exited. What happened next was awe-inspiring. The house teetered on its stilts and then disintegrated. Walls fell in on one another, shattered china and glass cascaded to the floor. As the dust cleared and the noise died away, all that was left was a distorted shell, and a heap of debris that looked as if it had been created by an explosion.

For a few moments nothing happened. The characters remained motionless, too shocked to move. Then, very slowly, they started to look around, and dust themselves down. More slowly still, they began to sift through memories of what had happened. Gradually, one thing stood out with increasing clarity: the photograph. That was what had started everything off. But was the Inspector genuine, or had they been tricked? As the majority of them reached the conclusion that they were blameless, the house began groggily to reassemble itself. Shaking off dust and broken glass, it shuddered upright, and all the characters apart from Sheila and Eric, who couldn't forget the Inspector's words, went back into it, and closed it up behind them. Giant heads bobbed at diminutive windows as they laughed at the foolish pair who had remained outside. Abruptly, the telephone in the large public phone box began to ring, and Mr Birling came back down – into the Inspector's territory, the place where he had earlier come close to admitting his guilt – to answer it. After his shocked recital of the information that a police Inspector was on his way to question them about a young woman's death, the front curtain began to descend very slowly. It continued downwards until the entire curtain, including the bar to which it was attached, was lying on the stage floor. When the house was revealed, it was open, and, inside it, in place of the Birling family, were the Inspector, the silent Second World War witnesses and the little boy. The doll's house had become a time capsule linking the Edwardian world of the play, Daldry's and MacNeil's 1940s setting, and, by implication, the present-day world of the audience. Priestley's time twist had been replaced by three time frames, superimposed one upon another. The effect was to reinforce Inspector Goole's message that time was running out. If lessons of social responsibility were not learned, the future would be obliterated in 'fire and blood and anguish'. Next time the house's collapse would be final.

'A tear in the fabric of time'

Following two runs at the National Theatre (the first in the Lyttelton auditorium, the second in the Olivier), Daldry's production of *An Inspector*

Calls was revived at the Aldwych Theatre in 1993, and, at the Garrick in 1995, where it ran until April 2001. It was revived again, in September of that year, at the Playhouse Theatre, while, in November, the West Yorkshire Playhouse production of *Dangerous Corner* transferred to the Garrick. In December 2001, a production of Priestley's best-known time play, *Time and the Conways,* opened at the Royal Exchange in Manchester.

Time and the Conways was first performed on 26 August 1937 at the Duchess Theatre in London. On 22 September of the same year another Priestley time play, *I Have Been Here Before,* opened at the Royalty Theatre. 'It must have appeared that Priestley was behaving a shade naughtily', David Hughes commented. '[D]own in the Strand they were nightly mouthing words that carried one theory of time, while at the Royalty in Dean Street the same writer's dialogue was pressing points about the same subject which could only be regarded as contradictory' (Hughes, p. 146). Each of the plays was influenced by a currently popular book on the nature of time, *Time and the Conways* by J. W. Dunne's *An Experiment with Time* and *I Have Been Here Before* by P. D. Ouspensky's *A New Model of the Universe.* The latter play explores the notion of time as endless recurrence. A character called Dr Görtler arrives at the Black Bull Inn on the North Yorkshire moors one Whitsuntide, and asks the landlord whether he lets rooms to visitors. The information he receives about the guests who are staying there leads to his strange remark, 'This must be the wrong year'. He leaves, but returns later, to discover that the expected visitors have rung to say they are unable to come after all. A Mr and Mrs Ormund are now expected instead, and Dr Görtler decides to stay. Dr Görtler's function in the play is to serve as the embodiment of Ouspensky's ideas. Time is circular, not linear, and Görtler is a special individual who is able to use his experience of alternative time cycles to warn the characters of the consequences of their current course of action. He succeeds in preventing a suicide, and the further tragic events that would have been consequent upon it. Circular time has a similar effect to the time twist in *Dangerous Corner* therefore, though, in this case, the crucial decision that changes the course of the future is made deliberately. Reviews of the original production were enthusiastic, particularly of Wilfred Lawson in the important role of Walter Ormund, but the play has dated more than *Time and the Conways* and is rarely performed today.

In *Time and the Conways,* Priestley explores the idea that we only perceive time as a linear progression because of our limited human perspective. In actuality, past, present and future are simultaneous. 'Time is not to be considered as a tape', *The Times* reviewer wrote on 27 August

1937. '[T]he past is not lost, the present is not the only reality, the future is not all that is left to us. The whole of Time is continually ours.' Structurally, Priestley explores this simultaneity through a disruption of narrative chronology. Act one takes place during Kay Conway's twenty-first birthday party in 1919, but the atmosphere of youthful anticipation it evokes is replaced in act two by a bleaker, sourer note. The occasion now is Kay's fortieth birthday and the characters' youthful hopes have given way to a depressing reality. Kay had dreamed of becoming a successful novelist, but instead she now earns a living by writing gossipy pieces for the newspapers about silly film starlets whom she despises. Her sister Madge's earnest socialist beliefs have hardened into a joyless dogmatism, while her brother Robin – a dashing, young RAF officer in act one – is now a shady, unsuccessful businessman who has deserted his wife and children. Hazel, the golden beauty of the family, has married a man she fears and dislikes, and Carol, the youngest Conway, and the one most full of life and belief in the future, died before she reached the age of twenty. Only shy, awkward Alan has gained something of value in the intervening years: 'an inward certainty and serenity' (*The Plays of J.B. Priestley, Vol. One*, p. 153).

Priestley's master stroke is to return in act three to the precise point where act one ended, with the result that members of an audience watch it with the foreshadowing knowledge of what is to come. Most of the characters have no apprehension of what lies in wait for them. Only Kay and Alan have momentary glimmers of something beyond the specifics of here and now. In the midst of a family discussion about their hopes for the future, Kay is suddenly overwhelmed by a sense of foreboding. Though she doesn't know it, she has had a glimpse through a 'tear in the fabric of time' (Ned Chaillet, *The Times*, 26.9.80; review of a production at the Greenwich Theatre). At the end of act two, Alan becomes a spokesman for the play's central idea when he describes time as a 'kind of dream ... [which] merely moves us on – in this life – from one peep-hole to the next'. The result is that, 'at this moment, or any moment, we're only a cross-section of our real selves ... and when we come to the end of this life, all those selves, all our time, will be *us*, the real you, the real me' (ibid., p.117).

Priestley's reordering of linear narrative has been seen as the source of the play's effectiveness from the time of the first production. On 29 August 1937, for example, in his *Observer* review, Ivor Brown described the second act as 'dramatically brilliant'. Reviewing a production of the play at Manchester's Royal Exchange in 1973, Irving Wardle praised the play's 'immensely accomplished' structure (*The Times*, 29.12.73). In 2001, Jeremy Kingston wrote of the current Royal Exchange production, 'the third act takes us to the ominous end of [Kay's] birthday party. But we would hardly register these omens were it not for Priestley's ingenious, and strikingly successful, idea of sandwiching between the 1919 acts a glimpse of the family on Kay's 40th birthday, on the eve of another war' (*The Times*, 17.12.01).

Reviewers, and Priestley himself, have been less enthusiastic about act one. 'I do not like its first act now – it seems to me both fussy and clumsy', Priestley commented in his Introduction to *The Plays of J. B. Priestley* (p. ix). It is true that this act can be irritating in performance if the youthfulness of the characters is overplayed, but it seems to me that it fulfils a couple of important functions in relation to the play as a whole. It conveys the 'bright promise and laughter' (*The Times*, 26.9.80) that act two will destroy, and it establishes from the outset the theatrical nature of Priestley's investigation of time.

The play begins in semi-darkness. Stage left, there is the glow of firelight; stage right, a curtained archway through which light from the hall can be seen. Young voices are heard, 'chattering and laughing and singing' (Priestley, *Plays, Vol. One*, p. 131). There is the sound of crackers being pulled and a piano playing popular music. The audience's attention is focused therefore on both the empty stage and the off-stage activity. The curtained archway is rather like a miniature proscenium arch, and there is a sense of anticipation. Who will enter? What will happen next? What in fact happens is that Hazel dashes in, carrying an armful of dressing-up clothes, and switches on the light. The other young people follow and begin to get into costume for a game of charades. Once the lights come on, the sense of ambiguity created by the opening moments is dispelled, but a new complexity is evoked. The charades are being performed off stage, while the stage itself becomes a kind of dressing room, or green room. Effectively, what we are looking at is happening 'backstage'.

This duality of place – the ability of a stage to depict one location whilst simultaneously evoking another – hints at what is to come in act two. The subdued lighting at the beginning is echoed at the end of the act, when the stage is once again lit only by firelight and light from the hall. Kay, who is alone on stage, goes to the window upstage centre and pulls back the curtains. She '*sits on the window-seat, her head . . . silvered in moonlight*'. Off stage, her mother is singing Schumann's *Der Nussbaum*, and, as Kay sits, motionlessly, listening to the song, she '*seems to stare not at but into something*' (ibid., p. 152). The curtain slowly falls. When it rises on act two, Kay is still in the same position. It is only when Alan enters and switches on the light that we realise that the characters and the room have changed. This change, though, has been prepared for from the beginning of the performance through Priestley's highlighting of theatre's ability to suggest multiple worlds.

The moment of realisation at the beginning of act two that we are witnessing a different Kay is disturbing, as though we are in the presence of her ghostly double. It has a haunting quality, which is recaptured and strengthened at the end of the play. Carol, Hazel, and Robin's future wife, Joan, are sitting together in near darkness. From off stage, the opening bars of Brahms' *Wiegenlied* are heard. Kay is once again by the window, and Alan joins her. '*And then the lights begin to fade, and very soon the three girls are no more than ghosts*' (ibid., 197). The room grows even darker until only Kay's and Alan's faces can be seen, and then they too are gone. The characters slip away, but, in an effective production, a ghostly after-image remains in the minds of members of the audience. In his review in the *Spectator* on 3 September 1937, Rupert Hart-Davis implicitly compared the major theme of *Time and the Conways* to a ghost. 'Those who . . . grasp it', he wrote, 'will be haunted by it long after they have left the theatre.' In 1973 Irving Wardle extended the ghostliness to an image of England. He noted the topicality of references in the play 'to mining and rail strikes', and added:

> The whole portrait of an upper-middle-class family running on the rocks of self-interested improvidence is alive with disturbing echoes: and it follows the '69 Theatre Company's revival of *The Family Reunion* as another reduction of England to a haunted house.

The connections with *An Inspector Calls* are not hard to seek. Another, earlier, review was oddly prophetic of Stephen Daldry's production. In his 1937 *Observer* review, Ivor Brown described the Conways' home in act two as 'a shell of shattered things. Great Expectations had become Bleak House – with the shutters torn away'.

An Inspector Calls and *Time and the Conways* are also linked through the deaths of two of their young female characters. Carol's absence in act two of *Time and the Conways* is framed and emphasised by her vibrant presence in the other two acts. The young woman victim in *An Inspector Calls* never appears, but her death, and that of her unborn – 'lost' – child, is repeatedly referred to. Loss is an important motif in Priestley's work. In *Time and the Conways* and *An Inspector Calls* it is bound up with

Priestley's experimentation with time, and it is also an important element of the structurally more conventional *Eden End*. Priestley doesn't re-assemble chronology in *Eden End*. Instead, he portrays the precariousness of the theatrical present moment in the context of a time of historical instability: the threshold of the First World War.

Eden End and *Mary Rose*

Like *Time and the Conways*, *Eden End* was first performed at London's Duchess Theatre. It opened there on 13 September 1934 with Ralph Richardson (who twelve years later was the first British Inspector Goole) in the cast. The continuing effectiveness of the play in performance was demonstrated by the following comment by a reviewer in 2001. 'The J.B. Priestley season at the West Yorkshire Playhouse concludes with the rediscovery of a beautiful piece of writing – last performed in London in 1974 – evoking the golden days of the Edwardian era, before the First World War blasted a generation's hopes and dreams into dust' (Dominic Cavendish, *Daily Telegraph*, 1.11.01).

Reviewers and other commentators on the play have frequently remarked on its Chekhovian overtones. Gareth Lloyd Evans compared it to *The Cherry Orchard*. 'The poetry of both plays', he wrote, 'lies in the dramatic reconciliation' of apparently irreconcilable responses to time. 'The actualities of the situation are time-bound', whereas 'the valid reality of the characters' consciousness of interdependence in the fragile ebbs and flows of human existence, are preciously timeless' (Lloyd Evans, p. 83). *Eden End* is not as great a play as *The Cherry Orchard*. Priestley's characterisation and dialogue are superficial in comparison with Chekhov's, but, like Chekhov, Priestley understood the ability of the theatrical present moment to express what has gone as well as what is happening now. The title, *Eden End*, captures this, through its evocation of 'a location where mutability and immutability ... meet' (ibid.).

Eden End is the home of Dr Kirby in the north of England, to which his daughter – an actress called Stella – unexpectedly returns, and disrupts the lives of the inhabitants, like Mme Ranyevskaia in *The Cherry Orchard*. Eden End represents childhood innocence to Stella, and a confidence she once had in the future that she longs to rediscover. At the end of the play, Stella accepts that it isn't possible to recapture the past. She must become a 'braver traveller' and journey on. The final moments of *Eden End* are reminiscent of the endings of both *The Cherry Orchard* and *Time and the Conways*. Stella leaves, sorrowfully, to catch a train, and Sarah, an old servant who has spent most of her life at Eden End, is alone on stage. She stands at the window for a few moments, watching Stella go, then goes over to the fire and lights a taper from it. The telephone rings and she '*holds the light close to it for a second, staring at it in bewilderment, then slowly withdraws into her own room*'. The sound of the telephone grows fainter until it dies away completely. The lights fade to darkness, '*and the play has ended*' (*Priestley, Plays, Vol. One*, p. 125). The effect is of a snapshot of a place and time that gradually disappears from view. There is a powerful sense of loss. Sarah's lack of comprehension of the telephone suggests change, the impact of the new, while the unanswered sound of its ringing evokes uncertainty and a lack of completion.

The apprehension of mutability in the play arises in large part from the conscious use Priestley makes of the date of its setting. One of the characters tells Stella that 'things don't change much here', but she disagrees. 'They do. Even in ten years time – in Nineteen Twenty-two . . . we might look back at this year and see it – oh, a thousand years away. In another world, a lost world' (ibid., p. 98). Priestley deliberately uses Stella here as a kind of chorus who speaks outside her naturalistic context. The implied reference is to the First World War, and the lost world that preceded it. From the future vantage point that Stella invokes, Eden End is a paradise on the edge of being lost. And yet, impermanence is the major characteristic of Eden End from the beginning of the play. It is as though the war has cast its shadow into the past, forewarning what is to come.

Loss and the First World War were personally closely linked for Priestley. As a very young man he volunteered for active service and fought in the trenches throughout the war. Judith Cook comments that he 'never recovered from his war experiences', and quotes from his collection of essays entitled *Margin Released*:

> I felt, as indeed I still feel today and must go on feeling until I die, the open wound, never to be healed, of my generation's fate, the best sorted out and then slaughtered, not by hard necessity but mainly by huge, murderous, public folly. (Cook, p. 49)

This unhealed wound underlies the portrayal of loss in *Eden End*, and also in *Time and the Conways*. In *Eden End* loss is embodied in a place, the name of which signifies the unattainability of desire. By contrast, 'The Island that Likes to be Visited', the desired place in Barrie's *Mary Rose, can* be accessed – though with ominous consequences.

The popular success of J. M. Barrie's *Mary Rose*, which was first performed in the immediate aftermath of the First World War, on 22 April

1920, at the Haymarket Theatre in London, was almost certainly due in part to the tragic relevance of its story of a lost child. Barrie was more than thirty years older than Priestley and didn't fight in the war, though his adopted son, George Llewelyn Davies, was killed in action. Barrie's recurrent theme of lost children had a personal inspiration in his own childhood. When he was six, his elder brother David was killed in a skating accident, and this traumatic event affected him greatly. As Peter Hollindale notes in his Introduction to the Oxford World Classics edition of *Peter Pan and Other Plays*, when Barrie wrote *Mary Rose* immediately after the First World War, 'his own awareness of a tragic tension between time and timelessness had become a nation's' (p. xxii). Time and timelessness – mutability and immutability – are Barrie's themes, as they are Priestley's, but, whereas Stella in *Eden End* accepts the inevitability of change and moves on, Mary Rose is a ghost trapped in a timeless limbo who can be released only by forces beyond her control.

As a ghost, Mary Rose is inevitably a 'returner'. Even if she wasn't a ghost in the place she has come from, she has made herself one 'by coming back', Harry tells her (ibid., p. 296). Harry is also a 'returner'. He has fought in the war and survived, and now he has come back to the home he ran away from at the age of twelve. He finds it deserted apart from a caretaker, and Mary Rose's ghost. His return instigates the re-enactment of Mary Rose's story, which can be completed now that he is there 'to provide the end' (ibid., p. 247). When Mary Rose was eleven, she visited the Outer Hebrides with her parents and discovered a small, uninhabited island the name of which in Gaelic meant 'The Island that Likes to be Visited'. The locals avoided the place but Mary Rose became very fond of it, and her father, Mr Morland, often left her there to sketch while he was fishing from his boat. Early one evening, he waved to her from the boat and began to row back to the island. He had his back to her, but the distance was very short, less than a hundred yards. When he reached the island, she had disappeared and, though he searched everywhere, she couldn't be found. Twenty days later, as he was looking towards the island, he saw Mary Rose sitting there, sketching. She had no memory of what had happened, nor any sense of time having elapsed. Occasionally, though, her parents would catch her apparently listening 'for some sound that never came' (ibid., p. 260). Mrs Morland speaks these words to Simon, the young man who wants to marry her. Simon and Mary Rose do marry, and a few years later they visit the island. As they prepare to leave at the end of their visit, Mary Rose bids goodbye to the 'little island that likes too much to be visited'. Simon is busy putting out a fire they have lit, and he doesn't hear the voices, '*at first as soft and furtive as whisperings from holes in the ground*', that begin to call Mary Rose's name. The sound gathers volume until '*in a fury as of storm and whistling winds that might be an unholy organ it rushes upon the island, raking every bush for her*'. Other sounds, '*of an unearthly sweetness*', are heard in contestation, '*seeking perhaps to beat them back and put a girdle of safety round her*'. Mary Rose holds out her arms momentarily to her husband, but then forgets his presence completely. '*Her face is rapt, but there is neither fear nor joy in it*' (ibid., p. 278). When Simon looks up, she has vanished. This is the end of act two. In act three Harry, the returned soldier, is revealed to be Mary Rose's son and his presence eventually allows her to stop searching – for what she doesn't know until this point– and to find peace.

In order to work in performance, the play needs the right actress in the title role. It's not enough simply to choose any good, young actress. As Michael Meyer writes, in his biography of August Strindberg, *Mary Rose*, like Strindberg's *Easter*, requires 'a very special kind of actress', and, if the right actress isn't available, these plays are 'better left undone' (Meyer, *Strindberg*, p. 408). There are some similarities between Mary Rose and Eleanora in *Easter*, in that both characters have an unworldly, childlike innocence, but, whereas Eleanora is unquestionably good, Mary Rose is more ambiguous. Though Simon talks about the holiness of her innocence, Mrs Morland describes her as 'curiously young for her age – as if – you know how just a touch of frost may stop the growth of a plant and yet leave it blooming' (Hollindale, p. 260). Mary Rose was originally played by Fay Compton, and, as Irving Wardle remarked in his 1972 review of a production of the play at the Shaw Theatre, her name is 'for ever identified with the role'. Reviewing the 1920 production in the *Observer*, Ivor Brown praised Fay Compton's 'actress-power of sending what she means speeding out from her, like light from a lamp, as if she had no need of movement or speech for expression' (25.4.20). Fay Compton played Mary Rose again at the Haymarket in 1926. The same theatre revived the play in 1929, this time with Angela Baddeley in the lead role. 'She suggests "the touch of frost" and compels belief in the allurement of the enchanted island', *The Times* reviewer commented (13.5.29). In the 1972 production at the Shaw Theatre, Mary Rose was played by Mia Farrow. Irving Wardle's response to her performance was mixed, but his praise of her 'great eyes and wraith-like appearance' (*The Times*, 14.7.72) emphasised the character's strangeness.

From its first performance, reviewers of *Mary Rose* have found something unnerving about the play. 'What if this were not a ghost, but a still living woman, left behind by a past that was past? It hardly bears thinking of; and yet –' Ivor Brown wrote. 'Something very dark lurks in the background; and it may be that Barrie shrank from it', was Irving Wardle's view. The theme of the lost child had great resonance for reviewers and audience members in 1920, who had witnessed the loss of a generation of young men. Later commentators have also speculated about the relevance of the sleeping-sickness epidemic (*encephalitis lethargia*) which began as the First World War was drawing to a close. Oliver Sacks discusses the epidemic in his book, *Awakenings*. Interestingly, he includes a case study of a woman born in 1905 to whom he gives the name 'Rose R'. The sense of an artificially arrested life is indicated by the fact that, at the age of sixty-one, 'Rose R' looked thirty years younger. In a review of the production of *Mary Rose* by Two Colour Theatre Company in 2001, Nicholas de Jongh suggested that Barrie's play 'eerily foreshadows the theme of Pinter's *A Kind of Alaska*', which was inspired by *Awakenings* (*Evening Standard*, 9.2.01). When Two Colour Theatre Company's production was revived later in the year, Sarah Adams began her review in *Time Out* by asking: 'What is it about J. M. Barrie's tale . . . that chills to the core?' She offers various possible solutions and then asks another question: 'Or is it the creeping suspicion that, beneath that genteel Edwardian veneer, a plethora of gothic monsters (and Gaelic fairies) are sharpening their fangs' (28.11.01).

Whatever meaning we draw from the play, the source of its strangeness is Mary Rose's relationship with the 'island that likes too much to be visited'. Barrie seems to have been fascinated, perhaps too fascinated, by islands. Peter Hollindale notes that Barrie's Preface to R.M. Ballantyne's *The Coral Island* included the words, 'To be born is to be wrecked on an island', and the word 'wrecked' in the context of being born is disquieting. In early drafts of *Mary Rose* the island was identified with Peter Pan's Never Land, but it became more sinister as Barrie worked on the play. Whatever it represents – childlike imagination? an alternative world where the restrictions (and the morality) of the human world don't apply? the abode of the lost dead who can never return? – is uncertain, but its mixture of malevolence and beauty is unsettling. A place outside time, the island is the site equally of good and evil forces. Harry tells Mary Rose, 'it was as if . . . there were two kinds of dogs out hunting you – the good and the bad' (Hollindale, p. 295). What I find chilling about the play is the fact that, the first time Mary Rose vanishes on the island, she is only a child. We never learn what happened to her there, but the 'unholy' voices that call the adult Mary Rose presumably also sought to entrap her when she was a child. In the final moments, voices again call Mary Rose's name, and now there is '*no unholy sound*' (ibid., p. 298). She exits with '*shining*' face, presumably to enter heaven. The sentimentally religious ending poses some difficulties for a present-day, secular audience, but the play's oddity (and its fascination) derives from the dark after-taste it leaves behind. This may be created in part from a sense that, somehow, some part of the child Mary Rose is still on the island.

3

Enter the revenant

> One of the defining features of ghosts is their capacity to return (*Ghosts: Deconstruction, Psychoanalysis, History*, eds, P. Buse and A. Stott, p. 8)

In *Dangerous Corner, An Inspector Calls* and *Time and the Conways*, Priestley manipulates theatrical time in order to offer his characters, and by extension his audience, the possibility of a new relationship with the past, and potentially therefore also with the future. This is particularly evident in *An Inspector Calls*, where Inspector Goole's warning of the dire consequences of a failure to accept communal responsibility for injustices is followed by the crucial twist of 'time's tail'. This moment of return offers the characters the opportunity, at least, to behave differently. While *Eden End* also focuses on a new way of viewing the past, return in this play is shown to be a delusion. Stella can go back to somewhere called Eden End, but it is no longer the place that she once knew. Time has irredeemably changed it. Given that Stella is the central character, her exile from Eden is clearly important, but the play in its entirety is suffused with a longing for a lost Paradise that can never be regained. Only three years separate the first nights of *Eden End* and *Time and the Conways* (both at London's Duchess Theatre), but the difference in atmosphere between the two plays is marked. *Eden End* is set in 1912, before the First World War changed the world for ever. *Time and the Conways* is split between two worlds and times: the immediate aftermath of one war and the threshold of the next.

Eden End is haunted by a vanished past, and the only choice available to Stella is how to accept its loss and journey onwards. Barrie, by contrast, created in Mary Rose a character that is a manifestation of repeated return. When she is alive, she yearns to return to the island. As a ghost, she repeatedly comes back until – a lost child herself – she finds the child for whom she is seeking. Like *Mary Rose*, this chapter is fundamentally concerned with ghosts, and also with lost children. Unlike Priestley, who uses the idea of return chiefly to provide occasions of choice for his characters, the authors of the theatre pieces discussed in this chapter create worlds that are characterised by stasis. The past does not simply inform the present. It holds it prisoner. In addition, while Stephen Daldry's production of *An Inspector Calls* brought the *Zeitgeist* into sharp focus, fear in these pieces is more difficult to define. There is a similar sense of precariousness, but it remains largely amorphous – a ghostly visitation, not an urgent warning of the proximity of the abyss. The chapter is mainly given over to a discussion of six Irish plays: Stewart Parker's *Pentecost; The Weir* and *Shining City* by Conor McPherson; *The Mai, Portia Coughlan* and *By the Bog of Cats* by Marina Carr. The two plays by McPherson both received their premieres in London, *The Weir*, in 1997 and *Shining City* in 2004. The Marina Carr plays were first performed in Dublin, but the initial production of *Portia Coughlan* was seen at the Royal Court only a few weeks after its opening night at Dublin's Peacock Theatre. *Pentecost* is the earliest of the six plays. Set in Belfast during the 1974 Loyalist strike, it was first performed in 1987, at the Guildhall, Derry, by the Field Day Theatre Company. It was subsequently performed by Tricycle Theatre Company, in January 1989, at the Lyric Studio in London, a couple of months after its author's untimely death. The chapter ends with a discussion of *Carnesky's Ghost Train*, which I saw in a tent outside Coventry Cathedral in 2005. The derivation of *Carnesky's Ghost Train* is East European, not Irish, but it depicts a world even more isolated and liminal than the worlds of the Irish plays. It is peopled entirely by ghosts and its action endlessly recurs. It is also haunted, even more obviously than the plays, by lost and endangered children.

The theme of the lost child runs through all seven theatre pieces, as does the notion of 'return'. 'Return' is a prominent motif in Irish dramatic literature, in large part because the emigration and enforced exile of so many of Ireland's sons and daughters created a wound in the national psyche that has yet to be healed. In *Contemporary Irish Drama and Cultural Identity*, Margaret Llewellyn-Jones writes that a 'key figure in Irish drama is the individual who decides on exile, or the family member whose return visit from abroad acts as a catalyst, challenging the identities and lifestyles of those who have stayed at home' (p. 119). The 'returned emigrant is a kind of ghost', Christopher Murray notes. It is his 'incomplete knowledge' of the situation that motivates dramatic revelations (*Twentieth-Century Irish Drama: Mirror up to Nation*, p. 168). The ghosts in this chapter are not returned emigrants, however, except in the sense that death is another country. They are remnants of their troubled pasts, and they are stuck in an emotional hinterland because of their difficulty in reaching an accommodation with the past. Lily, the ghost in *Pentecost*, is an unresolved fragment of Belfast's troubled political history, as well as her own personal unhappiness. A dramatic sibling of Mary Rose, her return is partly motivated by a longing for the child she lost in its infancy. In the Carr and McPherson plays, both the living and the dead characters are emotionally marooned. Parker appropriates biblical imagery in *Pentecost* to provide a resolution – a possibility of redemption. The confessional nature of the two McPherson plays indicates a basis in Catholicism, but, though the characters are in search of absolution, this proves hard to find. Carr largely eschews a Christian context, in favour of a background drawn from folk and fairy tales. From this material, and from Shakespearean and Euripidean references, she creates original mythic narratives of an enchanted, frozen time in which women long for the unattainable. The object of their desire is sometimes a man, but they have other, deeper, desires that originated in childhood. Like Lily Matthews, the protagonists of *Portia Coughlan* and *By the Bog of Cats* have echoes of Mary Rose. Despite their apparent adulthood, they are lost children, and they have a ghostly quality even though they are alive.

A Pentecostal haunting

What is a ghost? Marjorie Garber asks in *Shakespeare's Ghost Writers: Literature as Uncanny Causality*. Her answer: 'It is a memory trace . . . the sign of something missing, something omitted, something undone' (Garber, p. 129). Because a ghost manifests itself by coming back, it is a 'returner' figure par excellence. It is, 'to use Derrida's favoured term, *revenant,* the thing that returns' (Buse and Stott, p. 11). Return however presumes pre-existence – to come back one must have been here before – but each ghostly return is also a first entrance, an 'apparitional debut' (ibid.). Ghosts belong to neither past nor present, because 'haunting, by its very structure, implies a deformation of linear temporality' (ibid., p. 1). Inherently anachronistic, ghosts are also elusive and transgressive. They 'haunt borders' and 'breach . . . boundaries' (ibid., p. 52). They belong nowhere but materialise somewhere, deforming place as well as time.

Because each haunting is an 'apparitional debut', ghosts have an inherent theatricality. 'Plays and ghosts have a lot in common', the late Stewart Parker wrote in the Introduction to his *Three Plays for Ireland*. 'The energy which flows from some intense moment of conflict in a particular time and place seems to activate them both' (Parker, p. 9). The three plays, *Northern Star*, *Heavenly Bodies* and *Pentecost*, form what Parker calls a 'triptych'. Each is a 'history play', from, respectively, the eighteenth, nineteenth and twentieth centuries, and, together, they create 'a continuing comedy of terrors' (ibid.). Each play has a ghost character – or 'uncompleted soul', as Parker terms it. *Heavenly Bodies* in fact has two ghosts: the Phantom Fiddler and the dead Irish Singing Clown, Johnny Patterson, who acts as a 'Mephistophelean sparring partner' (ibid.) for the other central character, the dramatist Dion Boucicault. In contrast to the plays Boucicault writes about 'a never-never emerald Island' (ibid., p. 134), Johnny Patterson's songs recall violence and famine. At the end of act one, Patterson describes the occasion when he sang 'The Garden where the Praties Grow' to an Irish audience in Liverpool. 'Famine', he tells Boucicault, '. . . not a man, woman or youngster in that audience whose destiny wasn't ordained by it' (ibid., p. 113). As he finished the song, he heard, coming from the audience, a 'keen of grief for the phantom generations with [them] there in the tent' (ibid., p. 114).

Lily Matthews, the ghost in *Pentecost*, haunts the Belfast house that is the play's setting. A remnant both of her own unhappy past and the nation's, Lily's lack of completion is symbolised by the *'piece of unfinished knitting still on the needles'* (ibid., p. 155) she left behind when she went into hospital. Lily lived in the house all her adult life, from 1918 to 1974 – the year of her death, and of the play's action. The house is haunted by its violent history, as well as by Lily. Situated in a no man's land between Protestant and Catholic areas of the city, it resembles a ghost that is on the edge of disappearing: 'it's the last house on the road left inhabited! – the very road itself is scheduled to vanish off the map' (ibid., p. 154). A few years after the Protestant Lily and her husband Alfie moved into the house, it was almost destroyed by a Catholic mob, and this, and other acts of violence, along with Lily's personal unhappiness, have deformed the house, as if it, too, were a spectral manifestation. Though the furniture and household objects are realistic, the house's proportions are distorted. The rooms are impossibly narrow, and the walls, with their five layers of peeling wallpaper, reach up high into an embracing darkness.

The angry, grieving ghost of Lily Matthews has a living counterpart in the play in the character of Marian, whose husband inherits the house when Lily dies. A couple of years after the play was first performed (in a ghostly reordering of temporal linearity), Lily also had a spectral counterpart in a real Belfast house. In *Shattering Silence: Women, Nationalism, and Political Subjectivity in Northern Ireland*, Begoña Aretxaga records a story about a violent female ghost, in June 1989, who demanded that a family vacate the Belfast house 'which she claimed was hers' (Aretxaga, p. 40). Sprinklings of holy water, and even an exorcism by the Archbishop, failed to dislodge the ghost, who was rumoured to be a victim of early-twentieth-century violence by the Black and Tans, and eventually the family was driven out. Lily Matthews isn't violent, but she, too, claims the house as hers and she tries to frighten Marian out of it. Marian stands her ground, however. She learns the ghost's story, which connects with her own in that both she and Lily lost a child in the first months of its life. Lily's baby was the result of an adulterous affair, and, knowing that her husband could never accept it, she left it in the porch of a Baptist church. Marian discovered *her* little boy dead in his cot. Through listening to Lily's story she is able to help the ghost to find peace, and, at the end of the play, she comes to an accommodation with her own loss. She called her child Christopher because to her 'he was a kind of Christ . . . he brought love with him . . . the truth and the life . . . a future' (Parker, p. 207). When he died, she felt that the whole ugly Northern Irish history of bigotry and brutality had conspired to kill him. But, at the end of the play, she talks about how she has absorbed 'the ghost of him . . . The christ in him' (ibid.) into the christ in herself. Somehow they must all learn to do this, not only for the ghosts of Christopher and Lily, but for every one of what Marian calls 'our innocent dead' (ibid., p. 208).

As Marian's words – and the title – indicate, *Pentecost* draws heavily on Christian imagery. In place of religious belief Marian offers human compassion, but she presents this in terms of Christian suffering and redemption. The dead Christopher – both ghost and Christ – becomes a redemptive figure for all the city's dead. The final words of the play are a quotation from Chapter Two of *The Acts of the Apostles*, which tells the story of the Pentecostal tongues of fire. '"Therefore did my heart rejoice . . . Thou hast made known to me the ways of life; thou shalt make me full of joy with thy countenance"' (ibid.). The words are spoken in the Bible by the Apostle Peter, who is filled with wonder at the miracle he has witnessed. Parker uses them to express a belief in a possible regeneration, an exorcism of the haunted house that is Belfast. The play, therefore, ends on a note of hope. By means of the Pentecostal allusion, the stories of lost children, and of the unhappy city of Belfast, are recast in a redemptive mode. The characters in the two McPherson plays, which I focus on next, are similarly in quest of redemption. This is achieved to some degree in *The Weir*, but not in *Shining City*, despite the confessional nature of the play and the Christian allusion in its title. Both McPherson and Marina

Carr harness the psychic energy Stewart Parker saw as the source of ghosts and plays. *Shining City* includes the appearance of a terrifying ghost that resists any attempts at exorcism the characters are able to make. Each of the plays evokes the ghostliness of borders and liminality: doorways, for instance, or the edge of water, or the disturbing similarity between dawn and twilight – the two borders of daytime hours. All five plays are steeped in a past that colours and forms the present, but it is a more indefinable, less politically marked, past than that which troubles the present in *Pentecost*. Ghosts in Carr's and McPherson's plays are manifestations of individual or familial guilt, or signs of omission. In place of Parker's overt use of Christian symbolism, Carr draws on Greek tragedies and old legends to create her own distinctive, mythic landscapes; McPherson on ghost stories, including, in *The Weir*, a tale of malevolent fairies who may be a manifestation of the unquiet dead. The rural settings of Carr's plays, and of *The Weir*, bear some resemblance to the remote island where Barrie's Mary Rose disappears, in that they are isolated, haunted worlds. The three Marina Carr plays are set partly in, or close to, homes and these are disturbed and disturbing locations. Anna McMullan writes in *Druids, Dudes and Beauty Queens: The Changing Face of Irish Theatre* that '"Home" in Irish theatre never seems to be a place'. Instead, it is 'a past memory or a future possibility' (p. 72). Carr's plays are haunted by memories. The dead bar the way to the future and they are all-pervasive. The homes in the three plays I explore are all close to water, and, though the protagonists are drawn to water, it turns out to be a source of danger. The ghost stories that are told in *The Weir* destabilise its realistic setting, creating an imagined, spectral halo (of an alternative, haunted, landscape) around what is depicted on stage. The ghost stories tell of uncompleted journeys. A house stands in the path of a fairy road, for example, or a man is afraid to go upstairs in his house because a ghost is blocking his way. The urban, Dublin, setting of *Shining City* is also haunted. It may lack the obvious distortion of the Belfast house in *Pentecost*, but, in subtle ways, it is similarly disfigured by the revenant that claims it as hers.

Seeking absolution

Conor McPherson's award-winning play, *The Weir*, opened at the Ambassadors Theatre (temporarily the home of the Royal Court Theatre Upstairs) in July 1997 to pretty well universal critical and public acclaim. It was still in performance (at the Duke of York's Theatre) almost three years later when the same author's *Dublin Carol* previewed at the Old Vic

Theatre in January 2000, before opening the refurbished Royal Court Theatre the following month. Though superficially simple, *The Weir* is a beautifully crafted piece of storytelling. In a dingy rural bar in the north west of Ireland, two regulars, small garage owner Jack, and Jim, who helps him out with various bits of work, settle down with the publican, Brendan, for an evening's gossip and Guinness drinking. The conversation turns to local businessman Finbar Mack, who has been seen in the company of a young woman from Dublin who has just moved into the area. Finbar comes into the bar, accompanied by Valerie – the young woman – whom he has been introducing to the local sights. This leads to the men showing Valerie some old black and white photographs of the weir and of the view from Brendan's top field, which reputedly contains a fairy fort. It turns out that Valerie has moved into the house that used to belong to old Maura Nealon, and Jack recalls Maura sitting by the fire in the bar and telling a strange story about this house. When Maura was a young girl, Bridie, Maura's mother, used to kid the children that a boyfriend or girlfriend had just arrived to court one of them. She was always saying that there was someone knocking at the door, or coming up the path. One Saturday night there *was* a knocking at the door, but when Bridie opened it, there was no one there. Later, when the others had gone out and only Maura and her mother were there, the knocking began again, but this time it was at the windows, and very low down on the back door. Bridie wouldn't let Maura go to see who was there, and one day, when again only the two of them were in the house, 'a priest came and blessed the doors and the windows' (McPherson, *The Weir*, p. 22). Years later, Maura learned that the house was believed to have been built on a fairy road, 'a row of things . . . From the fort up in Brendan's top field . . . then the old well . . . the abbey further down, and into the cove [with] the little pebbly beach' (ibid.). The fairies must have been on their way to bathe in the cove and they wanted to go though Maura's house to get there. Maura only ever heard the knocking once after this and that was 'in the fifties when the weir was going up. There was a bit of knocking then she said. And fierce load of dead birds all in the hedge . . .' (ibid.).

The play's title relates to the storytelling that goes on in the bar, as well as to the bar's location, because, in a way that is analogous to the power of the foaming waters of the weir, Jack's story releases a potent current of narrative energy. The story of the fairy road is followed by two increasingly perturbing stories about ghosts, then by a harrowing tale from Valerie about her dead daughter, and, finally, by a moving reminiscence about wasted youthful opportunity from Jack. As Dominic Dromgoole puts it in *The Full Room*, McPherson first lulls his audience 'with some chat' and 'a few laughs . . . then gives them a minor fright, then a major one, then a major, major major one'. He then 'changes key brilliantly', and, 'having taken [the audience] out to the edge of where they want to go, he walks them home with the last story, a simple modest, but universal tale of lost love. Then he gently turns out the lights' (Dromgoole, p. 189). The lights are turned out literally immediately after the final words of the play, which are the pay-off of an extended joke. Brendan, Jack and Jim complain, at various points in the play, about the summer invasion of the bar by tourists, whom they call the Germans. As Valerie is preparing to leave at the end of the play, she comments that she won't mind the influx of visitors. After all, she might learn some German. 'I don't know . . . We call them Germans [but] . . . Where are they from. Is it Denmark, or Norway?', Jack asks Brendan. 'Ah I don't know where the fuck they're from', Brendan replies (McPherson, p. 50), and the laughter his words give rise to ameliorates the effect of the darkness when he turns off the light.

McPherson's control is masterly. The main dynamic in *The Weir* is from accumulated terror to cathartic release. Valerie's dreadful story (and the subsequent distress the men feel on her behalf) enables Jack to talk about his memories of missed youthful opportunities. As a young man he lost a girlfriend to another suitor because he failed to appreciate her. On her wedding day, he gave her a cheesy grin as she came down the aisle, to show how little he cared. She looked back at him though as if he were no different from any of the other guests assembled in the church, and then Jack understood both what he had thrown away and the loneliness that stretched in front of him. He left the church and lost himself in a maze of streets, until he stumbled into a little bar. There, the barman treated him with an unsolicited kindness that is still vividly present to him. First, the man cut two slices of bread with careful precision. Then he buttered them, put ham and cheese and a pickled onion between them, and cut the sandwich in half. He put it in front of Jack. ' "Get that down you now," he said', and, though Jack was almost too upset to swallow, he ate the sandwich down to the last crumb 'because someone [he] didn't know had done this for [him]. Such a small thing', and yet a 'huge' one to him at that moment (ibid., pp. 46 and 47). Jack's story of the sandwich draws on Christian imagery, as Stewart Parker does in *Pentecost,* though in a less overt way. The loving creation of the sandwich gives it a sacramental quality, so that it becomes analogous to the host in a Catholic mass. In place of divine grace, however, what Jack remembers is human compassion. What matters is personal kindness. Valerie gains a somewhat similar comfort from the men's pity for her after she tells her story, and Jack's story both underlines this and places it within a wider frame of reference.

Though McPherson brings *The Weir* to a skilful resolution, the balance he achieves between terror and its release is a fine one, and reviews (as well as my own memories of the production) attest to the power of the former as well as the relief of the latter. Surrounding the snug warmth of the bar – the place where the stories are told – McPherson creates two off-stage, imagined landscapes. One is everyday and normal. In this realistic version, Brendan's top field is simply a potential source of income from tourists and old Maura Nealon's place is just a house. The other, shadowy, landscape is created by the ghost stories. In this version the top field is the start of the fairy road, and Maura's house is an obstacle to the fairies' progress. Barriers such as windows and doors are borders between the normal and the supernatural, where psychic energy becomes trapped. Fairies and ghosts haunt these liminal areas, as they do in Jack's story of the fairy road and Finbar's tale about a ghost that blocked a stairway because people were afraid to pass it. The weir forms a part of both the normal and the supernatural landscapes. It generates electricity *and* provides the motive power of the stories the characters tell. McPherson controls the raging narrative torrent of the weir, but only just. The dead birds Maura Nealon saw in the hedges when the weir was created demonstrate its link with the sinister fairy world, and this is always close to manifesting itself.

On the front cover of the edition of *The Weir* published by Nick Hern Books in 1998, there is an image that captures both the ambience of the play's setting and the subject of its most upsetting story. A middle-aged man is holding up a large glass of Guinness in which a small child is swimming. The man could be Jack, and the child, who on further scrutiny seems perhaps to be sinking rather than swimming, could be Valerie's lost, haunted, daughter. Valerie's story of what happened to the little girl is preceded by a story Jim tells about the ghost of a paedophile who wanted to be buried in a child's grave. It is a horrible story that makes Valerie's even more disturbing, if that is possible. Valerie's little daughter was always afraid at night-time. She would see people at the window, or hear them in the attic or coming up the stairs. Most frightening of all was the man she could see standing across the road. The little girl was killed in a swimming accident, and, one morning after she died, Valerie heard the telephone ringing. When she picked it up, at first she could only hear faint voices, as though there was a crossed line. Then Valerie heard her daughter begging her to come and collect her because there was a man outside and he was starting to cross the road. The story is so hauntingly distressing that the solace of the play's ending is only just achievable. In the last chapter, I suggested that the sinister aftertaste Barrie's *Mary Rose* leaves behind could derive from an anxiety that the child Mary Rose never escaped from the island. Valerie's story is worse than that. The terrible thing about it is the mother's total inability to protect her child after its death because the topography of the land of the dead is not navigable by the living.

Valerie's and Jack's need for absolution – his for the callousness of his youth and hers for the failure over which she had no control – is answered to some degree in *The Weir*. In *Shining City* absolution is more elusive. The meaning of the play's title is also elusive, though I think that it is probably an ironic reference to the difficulty of achieving the longed-for state of forgiveness. Some reviewers suggested a connection between the play's title and that of the film *The Shining*, while others, such as Patrick Marmion in the *Daily Mail*, felt that it 'conjure[d] up visions of Heaven' (11.6.04). The latter possibility seems to me more likely – though it is an unobtainable Heaven. The probable reference is, I think, to the Celestial City in Bunyan's *The Pilgrim's Progress*, Part One of which ends with Christian being welcomed by the Shining Ones into the city that shines like the sun. Heaven however is twinned with Hell. As the dreamer who narrates the story awakes from his dream, he sees the Shining Ones 'take Ignorance and bind him hand and foot', and carry him to a door in the side of a hill. In this way the dreamer comes to understand that there is 'a way to Hell, even from the Gates of Heaven'.

Like Christian in *The Pilgrim's Progress*, John in *Shining City* is in quest of salvation – in his case from the ghost of his dead wife, Mari, and from guilt at the way he treated her when she was alive. He had a brief affair with another woman and, on one occasion, he turned on Mari violently. Mari was killed in a horrifying car accident and now John is literally haunted by her. He sees her ghost in liminal places, such as behind the doors in their house. Ian, the ex-priest turned therapist, to whom John has been referred by his doctor, is also haunted by guilt, though he professes not to believe in ghosts. The two men are linked by personal failure, and also by the related roles they play: storyteller and listener, client and therapist, penitent and confessor. John's long confessional monologues are full of hesitations and false starts. Ian's interjections are much shorter, but he frequently tails away into silence. Both characters say 'I know' a lot, but knowledge – certainly self-knowledge – is in short supply. Their lack of completion has something ghostly about it, as do the play's remnants of religious belief. Though faith has gone, the need for absolution lingers. In part, their incompleteness derives from their unfulfilled sexual and family lives. John's relationship with the other woman petered out inconclusively, as did a visit he describes making to a brothel, which he left without having sex. Ian has a child by a young woman, but he gives her little support financially or emotionally. Children are signifiers in the play of lack of commitment, in Ian's case, or lost opportunities, in John's. He and Mari were unable to have children, and this increased the gulf between them. The name Mari seems to be a reference to Mary, the mother of Jesus Christ – thus, by contrast, stressing Mari's barrenness and ghostly malevolence. A reference John makes to Vivien, the other woman, also points to the importance of the lack of children, though in line with the play's general air of elusiveness, the precise significance of their absence is hard to pin down. Vivien 'was a mother', John tells Ian. The layout of the text on the page indicates that this is probably followed by a pause. Then, John adds: 'Whatever that ... means, you know?' (McPherson, *Shining City*, p. 35).

McPherson begins the play with what could easily have developed into an equivalent of the extended joke about the Germans he sets up in *The Weir*. The setting is Ian's office in Dublin. Stage right, there is a door, through which, when it is open, a banister and the top of a flight of stairs can be seen. There is the sound of '*distant church bells*' and of music '*playing softly on [a] stereo*' (ibid., p. 7). Other sounds – a toilet flushing and Ian blowing his nose – establish a sense that this is his personal space, though books on the floor that appear to have been unpacked but not yet put away suggest actions that are only half-finished. This seems to be a temporary resting place, rather than a permanent one. 'Beside the door is a handset for an intercom to the main door to the street on the ground floor' (ibid., p. 5). There is a loud buzzing noise and Ian presses the button on the intercom. 'Are you in? Okay . . . Push the door. Are you in?' he enquires, then, after a pause, 'Hello? No? Okay, okay, hold on' (ibid., p. 7). He goes out of the door and down the stairs, and it is some time before he and John come into view. 'Rarely has a first entrance been so humorously delayed', Kate Bassett commented in the *Independent on Sunday* (13.6.04). The opening sequence is echoed in the final scene, but, in place of the release of laughter at the end of *The Weir*, Conor McPherson concludes *Shining City* with a terrifying apparition that throws into confusion everything that has gone before. In the gathering dusk, Ian watches John go down the stairs to the front door. We hear the door slam, and, then, very faintly, not church bells, but the ice cream van music that was the prelude to John seeing his wife's ghost. 'Did you get out?' Ian calls (ibid., p. 64), and then, unknowingly, goes to what awaits him. Though a few reviewers thought the ending was gimmicky, most – including this spectator – found it spine-chilling. As to what McPherson means by it, the fact that the questions it raises are not answered is presumably deliberate, given the general atmosphere of elusiveness. Does John shift his burden of guilt onto the shoulders of the man whose dual profession – as priest and therapist – is that of healer? Is Ian assailed by his own guilt, or is he perhaps being haunted because he claimed not to believe in ghosts? Perhaps the impermanent nature of the place attracts the same quality in the ghost, or, more disturbingly, perhaps John didn't manage to 'get out' before the front door slammed shut. Maybe he found himself going through the equivalent of the entrance to Hell at the end of *The Pilgrim's Progress*, and he is now trapped on a ghostly staircase that is the shadowy counterpart of the real one he was descending. Whatever the interpretation, through the ability of theatre to create multiple times, what we are confronted with is the terrifying immediacy of a violent death, even though it occurred in the past. Redemption seems a long way off.

Ghosts in *The Weir* and *Shining City* haunt stairs and doors and communication devices (telephones and intercom systems). They rap on walls and windows. Marina Carr's ghosts in *Portia Coughlan* and *By the Bog of Cats*, and the apparition in her slightly earlier play *The Mai*, inhabit the edges of lakes and rivers and the borders of daylight hours. They are easier to interpret than McPherson's ghost in *Shining City*. Why they come back can more easily be defined because they are clearer about what they want. Whereas McPherson evokes the existence of alternative, spectral topographies alongside, or just beneath, 'real' ones, Carr presents worlds in which the living and the dead are equal citizens.

The dark witch called Time

Though they are separate plays, Carr's *The Mai*, *Portia Coughlan* and *By the Bog of Cats* can, I think, legitimately be viewed as a trilogy in that motifs and ideas established in the first play are worked through to a conclusion in the last. In each of the three plays the central figure is a woman who is destroyed by an obsessive desire, and, in each, Carr melds the real, the mythic, the grotesque and the lyrical to create her own distinctive worlds. Her source material derives in part from earlier dramas, and from fairy tales and legends. *Portia Coughlan* owes a small debt to Shakespeare's *The Merchant of Venice* and *By the Bog of Cats* a bigger one to Euripides' *Medea*. In *The Mai*, a daughter narrates a legend that is a mythological version of her parents' story. The eponymous Portia Coughlan relates a local legend which informs her own story, and *By the Bog of Cats* draws on fairy tales and the story of Medea. The strongest links between the plays, however, relate to their depiction of time and of the mother/daughter relationship. Through the story she tells, Millie, in *The Mai*, re-animates a past in which unattainable desires remain locked like insects in amber. Women yearn for absent men, and, though Millie's narrative function sets her apart from the other characters, she, too, is characterised by longing. Portia Coughlan's desire is apparently for her dead twin, Gabriel, but this masks a deeper longing, which is to return to her infant relationship with her mother. And, in *By the Bog of Cats*, the daughter's desire for the return of the lost mother is the central focus of the play.

The story that Millie narrates in *The Mai* is the legend of Owl Lake, *'loch cailleach oíche*, Lake of the Night Hag or Pool of the Dark Witch'. The legend tells of Coillte, the mountain god's daughter, who 'fell in love with Bláth, Lord of all the flowers'. With the swiftness of a young deer, Coillte ran across the mountain and valley and 'over the dark witch's boglands' until she found Bláth lying under a tree, playing his pipes and wearing a crown of forget-me-nots. All through the spring and summer the two were inseparable, but, when the nights grew shorter, Bláth told Coillte that he had to leave her in order to spend the winter with the dark witch. Coillte's heart was broken, and she cried a lake of tears outside the witch's lair. The witch watched and waited for her opportunity, and one night she pushed Coillte into the lake, where she dissolved in her own tears. It is said that, 'when the geese are restless or the swans suddenly take flight, it's because they hear Bláth's pipes among the reeds, still playing for Coillte' (*Marina Carr: Plays One*, p. 147). Millie tells this story at the end of act one. As she finishes it, a ghostly light illuminates her father, Robert, who is holding Mai's body in his arms. The apparition is seen for a few moments, and then it is gone.

The story of the Pool of the Dark Witch prefigures Mai's fate, and, in conjunction with the play's setting – Mai's house overlooking Owl Lake – also some aspects of the protagonists' stories in *Portia Coughlan* and *By the Bog of Cats*. The Mai (as she is often called) has built her home on the shore of Owl Lake as a place to grieve for Robert, who deserted her five years earlier, and to await his return. Robert is a cellist, and therefore a musician, like Bláth. He does come back, and for a time he and The Mai are happy, but then he begins another affair. The Mai's death doesn't occur in the course of the play, but her final exit, to the sound of geese and swans taking flight from the lake, prepares for it, and the ghostly apparition at the end of act one foretells it. While The Mai and Robert are clearly versions of Coillte and Bláth, none of the characters in the play seem to represent the dark witch. Robert's mistress never appears, and she is anyway too insubstantial a figure for such a sinister role. The dark witch's function in the play is indicated in Marina Carr's Introduction to the Faber & Faber edition of the first volume of her plays, where she describes the makeshift theatre she and her friends created in childhood. 'When I was a scut we built a theatre in our shed . . . Our dramas were bloody and brutal . . . still we all lived happily ever after . . . Everyone was capable of redemption except Witches. We had no mercy for Witches, but since the Witch had all the power and all the magic, we could never finally throttle her. . . .' And the name of the Witch? 'Maybe she was Time. Time we didn't understand or fully inhabit . . .' (ibid., pp. ix–x). It isn't really Robert who causes The Mai to kill herself. What destroys her is the limbo-space of desire she inhabits – the stilled, enchanted time of the dark witch where all Mai can do is wait for what she can never have. The Mai's role as the one who waits is prefigured by her ancestry. The hundred-year-old Grandma Fraochlán also waited in her youth, watching by the window of her house for her drowned husband-lover, the nine-fingered fisherman, to return. As a child, The Mai absorbed the old woman's stories, and dreamed of a prince who would come over 'the waves on the wings of an albatross' (ibid, p. 162) to take her to an enchanted land. The place of enchantment has proved to be the house on Owl Lake, beautiful on the outside, but inside the abode of nightmares. The Mai tries to keep them away, but they get in 'anyway with the frost and the draughts and the air bubbles in the radiators' (ibid., p. 158). And, if she escapes from the house, there is only the lake with its premonitory story of the consequences of desire. Portia Coughlan, and Hester Swane in *By the Bog of Cats* are similarly situated between a house and water. They understand more clearly than The Mai the danger the former poses to them, but their response is to claim as their own the watery equivalents of Owl Lake – the Belmont River and the Bog of Cats – that entice them to their deaths.

The dark witch of Time connects Portia and Hester to both The Mai and her daughter, Millie. While The Mai appears as a ghostly apparition, Millie, the play's storyteller, is also a kind of ghost, an anachronistic visitor from the future whose presence conjures up the past. Like her mother, she is consumed with longing, in her case for her lost childhood, which she also fears and hates. Both the story and the storyteller in *The*

Mai are therefore expressive of stasis. Though they are powerful women, Portia and Hester also inhabit limbo-worlds where the future is known, or has already happened. In his Introduction to *Portia Coughlan* in *The Dazzling Dark: New Irish Plays*, Frank McGuinness describes Carr as 'a writer haunted by memories she could not possibly possess, [though] they seem determined to possess her' (p. ix). In *Portia Coughlan*, Carr portrays her protagonist's death in the form of a flash forward. 'Through the disruption of its narrative', McGuinness adds, 'Portia . . . like the ghosts of Japanese theatre, lives, dies, comes back to relive her suffering' (ibid.). Hester Swane is another living ghost, haunted by both past and future. Like Portia, she is haunted also by an actual ghost, that of her brother Joseph. Hester has murdered her brother, while Portia watched her twin, Gabriel, drown in the river. In a Performance Note to the Abbey Theatre production of *By the Bog of Cats*, Frank McGuinness suggested that Emily Brontë was Marina Carr's 'true literary ancestor' (cited in *The Theatre of Marina Carr*, p. 87). Portia's incestuous longing for the dead Gabriel certainly has strong overtones of the relationship between Catherine Earnshaw and Heathcliff in *Wuthering Heights*. Terry Eagleton's description of this relationship in *Heathcliff and the Great Hunger* could, with equal relevance, be applied to that between Portia and Gabriel. The bond between Cathy and Heathcliff, Eagleton writes, is 'a classic case of the Lacanian "imaginary", an utter merging of identities in which the existence of each is wholly dependent on the existence of the other, to the exclusion of the world about them' (Eagleton, p. 18). Eagleton's definition of the way time operates in *Wuthering Heights* is also evocative, both of *Portia Coughlan* and *By the Bog of Cats*: 'Some primordial trauma has taken place . . . so that time . . . would seem to move backwards and forwards simultaneously' (ibid., p. 15). The two plays are set in the Irish Midlands, a region described by Carr in her Afterword to *Portia Coughlan* in *The Dazzling Dark* as 'the crossroads between the worlds' (p. 311). Crossroads evoke journeys, but here the intersections are between the worlds of the living and the dead, with the result that one bleeds into the other and to go forward is the same as to go back. They are, though, vibrant and surprisingly funny worlds. In his Introduction to *The Dazzling Dark*, McGuinness refers to the carnivalesque quality of Hallowe'en or All Souls' Night, which he terms the Irish 'Mardi Gras, a time for wearing masks and remembering the dead, as if by remembering them we resurrect them' (p. ix). Carr's characters are filled with a fierce energy, which cannot be harnessed to changing the future because this is predetermined by their pasts. Instead, it charges the amorphous present with an electric energy that provides a powerful conduit for ghosts.

Portia Coughlan begins with a ghost. A pool of light illuminates Gabriel, singing seductively and hauntingly by the Belmont River. Another pool of light reveals Portia standing in her living room. She wears a nightdress and sweatshirt, and is listening to Gabriel with a 'lost' expression on her face. The pair 'mirror one another's posture and movements in an odd way; unconsciously' (Carr, *Plays One*, p. 193). Raphael, Portia's husband, enters but she is unaware of him. As he begins to speak, lights come up on him and the light on Gabriel fades.

The Shakespearean and biblical references in the characters' names are largely ironic. Like Portia's home in *The Merchant of Venice*, the place where Portia Coughlan lives is called Belmont, but, whereas the Shakespearean Belmont is 'Colchos strond' to which 'many Jasons come in quest' of Portia (the play's golden fleece), Carr's Belmont Valley is 'the dungeon of the fallen world' (ibid., p. 219). Portia Coughlan is wooed, like Shakespeare's Portia, by three suitors, each of whom gives her a gift on her thirtieth birthday. Raphael gives her a flashy diamond bracelet; her lover, Damus Halion, picks a bunch of violets for her; and Fintan Goolan, the barman of the High Chaparral, gives her a free drink. Superficially, Portia Coughlan has freedom of choice between her suitors, and so has the advantage of Portia in *The Merchant of Venice*, who is dependent on her favoured suitor choosing the right casket. In reality, her freedom is non-existent because she is totally in thrall to her fourth suitor, Gabriel.

Gabriel and Raphael are named after angels. Indeed, it was Raphael's name that led Portia to marry him. She thought that, because he had an angel's name, he must somehow be like the dead Gabriel. But Raphael is earthbound, both mentally and physically. An accident lamed him in one foot, and he will never be able to fly like an angel. Gabriel's name is the greatest irony of all, because the biblical Angel Gabriel foretold Christ's nativity, whereas Carr's Gabriel is a harbinger of death. He comes, as ghosts frequently do, to complete unfinished business. Fifteen years earlier, he and Portia made a pact to wade to their deaths into the Belmont River, but Portia turned back and, by the time Gabriel realised this, it was too late for him to follow her. The river pulled him down to his death. As a ghost, he will constantly return until he lures Portia back into the river.

The repetitive pattern of Gabriel's ghostly visitations interrupts the linear narrative in *Portia Coughlan*, and so contributes to its evocation of the static time of the dark witch. The play's temporal structure underlines this. Act one takes place on Portia's thirtieth birthday, and act three on the following day (when Portia is still alive). Act two recalls the ghostly apparition at the end of act one in *The Mai*. Portia's drowned body is hoisted out of the river by means of a pulley. '*She is raised into the air and suspended there, dripping water, moss, algae, frogspawn, water lilies from the river*' (ibid., p. 232). Structurally, *Portia Coughlan* is reminiscent of *Time and the Conways* therefore, but the dislocation of chronology has very different effects in the two plays. Through Kay and Alan, Priestley suggests that human beings are not necessarily diminished by time. Portia's time is dictated by Gabriel. The day following her thirtieth birthday recapitulates the one after her fifteenth, and she completes the action she began then. The fracturing of time in act two is emblematic of this. While the last act of *Time and the Conways* evokes the possibility that past happiness may not be entirely lost to us, act three of *Portia Coughlan* underlines the preordained nature of Portia's death. For Portia, the past is only about loss, not happiness, but it is a loss she has no alternative but to embrace.

The deterministic nature of the play is expressed through its depiction of place as well as of time. As in *The Mai*, a house and a stretch of water are key elements, but Carr adds a third location, the bar of the High Chaparral. Like the characters' names, the name of the bar is ironic, its cod-Americanness underlined by the ridiculous posturing of Fintan Goolan in his cowboy boots. The effect is to emphasise Portia's entrapment through a mockery of the traditional Irish escape route of emigration to the United States. Her so-called 'living room' in the house she shares with Raphael stifles Portia, as do her roles as wife and mother. Portia's rejection of the traditional woman's place and function has been interpreted in positive terms by some commentators on the play. It is difficult, however, to see her identification with the river (which she chooses instead of the home) as anything other than self-destructive. Portia tells her friend Stacia Doyle that she couldn't spend a night away from the Belmont River, but it is the place that claims *her*, not the other way round. Her essential ghostliness is conveyed by her return, over and over again, to the site of past trauma.

Like Owl Lake, the Belmont River has its legend, and, again, the story features a witch. This isn't the dark witch of the bog, however, but a human woman whom locals called a witch because she was different. They impaled her on a stake and left her to die. But Bel, the river god, heard her crying and came down the Belmont Valley for her. In this way, 'the river was born . . . Gabriel used hear the girl when the river was low; said she sounded like a aria from a cave' (ibid., p. 219). Fintan Goolan, to whom

Portia tells the story, links witchcraft with female sexuality. The impaled woman is to him a 'mad hoor of a witch' (ibid.). For Portia however, 'witch' denotes motherhood. She knows her mother, Marianne Scully, is at the door when she hears her 'witchy ring', and she fears her own witchlike tendencies as a mother. She neglects her children because she is afraid that she will harm them if she has too much to do with them. It is initially something of a shock, therefore, to discover that *Portia Coughlan* was commissioned by the National Maternity Hospital in Dublin. 'Suppose some orphanage in ancient Athens had asked Euripides to write a play in its honour, and he had riposted with *Medea*', Benedict Nightingale commented in *The Times* (16.5.96). On closer acquaintance, however, the relevance of the play's commissioning body comes into focus. The 'dark witch' in *Portia Coughlan* is, again, futureless time, at it is in *The Mai*, but now she has a maternal body and a variety of masks. Portia isn't a reincarnation of the murderous witch Medea – she kills herself, not her children. At the heart of *Portia Coughlan* is a story about the daughter's loss of the mother. Marianne is both the wicked witch of fairy tale, and the object of an impossible desire. It is a child's view of things, 'the scuts' view' as Marina Carr terms it. Portia and Gabriel are effectively both frozen in childhood. The 'utter merging of [their] identities' had its source in their mother's womb. Near the end of the play, Portia implicitly links the Belmont River with her mother's womb. 'Times I close me eyes and I feel a rush of water around me and above we hear the thumpin' of me mother's heart . . . and the water swells around our ears, and all the world is Portia and Gabriel packed for ever in a tight hot womb' (ibid., p. 254). All their lives the twins long to return to water. On a childhood visit to the coast, they take a rowing boat, and they are discovered five miles out to sea, still heading away from land. At fifteen, Gabriel drowns, and fifteen years later, in a ghostly doubling of time and event, Portia joins him.

The pronouns Portia uses in her memory of her mother's womb suggest the complexity of her feelings toward Gabriel. 'I' transforms seamlessly into 'we', and yet she claims the beat of her mother's heart as hers alone. Portia's feelings towards Gabriel are an extreme version of Millie's towards the bewitched lake of her childhood. He is both a manifestation of her own being, and a destructive force from which she longs to free herself. When she was fifteen, she slept with Damus Halion in order to try to separate herself from Gabriel. Her brother's response was to wade into the river, and, though Portia had promised to follow him, she remained on the bank. 'One of us was goin', were killin' each other', she tells Marianne. 'Well, we fought it to the death and I won' (ibid., p. 251). It was a pyrrhic victory, though, because it marooned her in a borderland between life and death. This is the reason why house and water are equally destructive, and the High Chaparral bar is unable to provide an escape route. Her powerful energies are consumed by a longing that can be fulfilled only by her death, and so she feels desire and hatred in equal measure. Gabriel has the voice of an angel, but it is as a demon lover that he tempts Portia into the river. Marianne is both the longed-for mother and the feared witch. Portia's unassuageable yearning is fed by her family history, 'the sort of dark, bloody knot that is the basis of many a Greek tragedy' (Sarah Hemming, *Financial Times*, 16.5.96). Portia and Gabriel's incestuous passion has its origin in the fact that their parents are half-brother and sister. The seeds of incest were already present in Marianne's womb. Throughout the play, Portia is at best uncaring towards her mother, but, in the penultimate scene of act three, Marianne gives her a late birthday present, a beautiful dress. Portia was unmoved by the presents the three suitors gave her, but this is a gift – and a giver – she wants. 'Do ya like it?' Marianne asks her, and, in response, she whispers, 'Mother' (ibid., p. 252). It is the only moment in the play when Portia seems to experience normal, human love, and it is directed towards her mother. It isn't enough to prevent her death, however, because Portia is subject to the dark witch's time, and in that realm her death has already happened.

The central theme of both *The Mai* and *Portia Coughlan* is an impossible desire that originates in childhood. The Mai has learned from Grandma Fraochlán's stories that her function in life is to wait for the handsome lover who will hold the key to her future. When she becomes an adult, and Robert leaves her, she waits passively for him to return. In adulthood, her daughter Millie still mentally inhabits the shore of Owl Lake, as she did physically in childhood. Portia and Gabriel's mutual obsession began in the womb. The two characters are mirror images of a hopeless yearning to return to the sense of completeness they knew there. Carr is technically mistaken in making them identical twins, given that one is female and the other male, but in dramatic terms it works both because it adds to the spookiness of their mutual obsession (each is the other's *doppelgänger*), and because it doubles the sense of loss. In both plays, female characters narrate legends that encapsulate key themes and motifs. In *The Mai*, the storyteller frames the action and to some degree remains outside it. Portia Coughlan's narration of the legend of Belmont River emphasises her close connection with the 'witch' and with water. The plays can also be viewed as fairy tales. The Mai and Portia are Cinderella figures who wait to be claimed by an absent husband or a dead lover. These are black fairy tales, though, full of warnings about the dangers the characters are running. The Mai's house is invaded by evil spirits, and she and Robert each dream of the other's death. Robert is motivated to return to Owl Lake by a dream he has in which he sees The Mai lying dead in his cello case. It has become her coffin, and a 'carriage drawn by two black swans' bears it away across 'a dark expanse of water' (ibid., p. 125). The dream perturbs The Mai, but she continues to sit by her window overlooking Owl Lake, waiting for Robert. Portia Coughlan is haunted by her own death, as well as Gabriel's, and by fears of the harm she may do to her children. As in *The Mai*, water and music are linked with death. Gabriel's merman-like voice lures Portia into the maternal waters of the Belmont River, where she drowns.

In *By the Bog of Cats,* Portia's implied longing for the unattainable mother becomes explicit. Carr takes elements of fairy tale and legend, the ghostly stasis of Japanese *Noh* Theatre, carnivalesque All Souls' Night 'masks', 'a dark, bloody [family] knot' and Euripides' *Medea*, and out of them weaves her story. What she creates is a quasi-mythical narrative about a daughter's hopeless desire for the return of the mother who deserted her when she was seven years old. The lost mother is the heart of the play, which is structured around her absence. While Robert and Gabriel, the objects of desire in *The Mai* and *Portia Coughlan*, appear on stage, big Josie Swane does not. Like them, she is connected with water and music. The bog was her place, and she was a creator of songs, a 'song stitcher'. Her absence is therefore doubly significant. She is missing both as the longed-for mother and as the central thread that stitches the story together. Carr builds the play out of contrasts. She takes the certainties of fairy tale and the classical unities of Greek tragedy, and undermines them. In part this is achieved through the play's carnivalesque quality. In an essay entitled 'Carr's '"Cut-throats and Gargiyles": Grotesque and Carnivalesque Elements in *By the Bog of Cats*', Bernadette Bourke traces Carr's interest in the topsy-turvy freedom of carnival to 'her early theatrical endeavours in the family shed'. Here, 'she and her siblings created another world outside the official realm of their everyday lives, a world which adhered to none of the rules' (*The Theatre of Marina Carr*, p. 128). Carr 'possesses a vision', Bourke continues, 'that thrives on the grotesque incongruities and reversals peculiar to carnival' (ibid., p. 129). The pervasively unsettling nature of the play is indicated also by its setting – the Bog of Cats – which is constantly 'shiftin' and changin' and coddin' the eye' (Carr, *Plays One*, p. 267). Given the mother's crucial connection with the bog, its changeableness renders her absence both treacherous and yet potentially remediable therefore. At any moment the bog might form itself into her shape.

By the Bog of Cats begins in the realm of fairy tale, in a bleak, white world of snow and ice. Violin music is heard, and Hester Swane enters, trailing behind her a dead black swan that marks the snow with traces of blood. The colours are reminiscent of the opening of *Snow White*, a fairy story that reverses the roles of desirer and desired in *By the Bog of Cats*. In *Snow White,* the Queen, the would-be mother, longs for a daughter with hair as black as ebony, skin as white as snow and lips as red as . . . the poisoned apple the witch will trick Snow White into eating . . . or as blood. Swans in fairy stories can be women who have been changed into birds, and this transformability links Hester's swan with the bog and with the absent Josie Swane. 'Swane', we learn, 'means swan'. When Hester was born, Josie left her in the black swan's lair for the first three nights of her life, thus designating the bird as both a surrogate mother and an *alter ego* for the child. She prophesied that Hester would 'live as long as [the] black swan, not a day more, not a day less' (ibid., p. 275), and the expectation that the prophecy will be fulfilled adds to the deterministic atmosphere of the play. Hester's fate is sealed by the black swan's death. The ending is known from the beginning. What is not foretold, or expected, however, is the role that little Josie, Hester's daughter, will play in the ending.

Standing watching Hester as she enters is a character called the Ghost Fancier, 'a handsome creature in a dress suit'. The Ghost Fancier, who has come 'ghoulin'' for a woman called Hester Swane, would be at home in a sinister fairy tale or a ghost story, but, like Hester, he also evokes suggestions of Japanese *Noh* Theatre. A *Noh* play typically begins with a conversation between an ancillary figure known as the *waki*, and the protagonist, or *shite* – a living ghost who has returned to the site of a key event in his or her past life. Hester mimics a *shite* in her repeated haunting of the place her mother left thirty-three years earlier, and her essential ghostliness is signalled from the start of the play by the Ghost Fancier marking her out as his prey. In a carnivalesque reversal of expectation, however, the Ghost Fancier misinterprets the time of day. He thinks it is dusk when it's actually only dawn. So, although Hester's final hours are already measured, time is as ambivalent as place. Along with the constantly transforming bog, the similarity between dawn and dusk creates an unstable world where boundaries are blurred.

The play's debt to Greek tragedy provides the clearest temporal framework for its action, which takes place on the wedding day of Caroline Cassidy and Hester's lover, Carthage Kilbride. Like Medea, on whom she is based, Hester is an outsider in her community. She is a traveller (a tinker), while Medea is variously described as a foreigner, an exile or a refugee. She also resembles Medea in that she has witch-like powers (she can see ghosts for example when other people can't), and she has implicated Carthage in a murder, as Medea implicates Jason. Unlike Medea, who escapes the consequences of her actions in a chariot drawn by dragons, Hester dies. Her equivalent of Medea's chariot is a gypsy caravan, but, significantly, it is always stationary. Hester's designation as a traveller is ironic. She wanders the Bog of Cats, where she knows every path and bog-hole, but she always comes back to the place from which she watched her mother walk away from her.

The crucial difference between Medea and Hester is that the former murders her sons as an act of revenge against their father, whereas Hester kills her daughter, at the end of the play, out of love for her. Hester is also unlike Medea in the way she treats her successful rival, Caroline Cassidy. When Medea's husband Jason marries Glauce, daughter of Creon, Medea sends the bride a poisoned gown and coronet, which kills first Glauce, and then Creon as he embraces his dying daughter. Hester describes Caroline as 'only a little china bit of a girl . . . [whom she] could break . . . aisy as a tay cup or a wine glass'. She doesn't hurt her though because she remembers her as she was at Josie's age, 'a scrawky little thing that hung on the scraps of [her] affection' (ibid., p. 337). Hester's refusal to harm Caroline is contrasted with a story she tells in which the roles of poisoner and victim from *Medea* are reallocated. Xavier Cassidy (Caroline's father) is the poisoner: he doses his son's dog with strychnine in the knowledge that the boy will die when he picks up the dog. Xavier's villainy is further underlined by Hester's suggestion that he may have sexually abused his daughter.

The poisoned gown and coronet from *Medea* translate in *By the Bog of Cats* into Caroline's white wedding dress and veil, which are replicated three times, as if in a sequence of distorting mirrors. Seven-year-old Josie wears her First-Communion dress and veil to the act-two wedding reception, because none of her other clothes are grand enough. She resembles a diminutive bride, and also acts as a ghostly after-image of Hester, who was wearing an identical outfit when her mother deserted her. The bride's mother, Mrs Kilbride (note the significance of the name!), is also dressed totally in white. The grotesque inappropriateness of her costume is underlined by a speech she makes at the reception, which ends: 'if Carthage will be as good a son to Caroline as he's been a husband to me then she'll have no complaints' (ibid., p. 311). When Hester arrives at the reception wearing a white bridal dress and veil, her get-up is both a carnivalesque mask that mocks the wedding that has just taken place, and a sign of her determination to hold on to Carthage. The sense of carnivalesque reversal is emphasised by a couple of the wedding guests. One is the priest, whose pyjamas are visible beneath his clothes. When asked to say grace at the reception, he responds instead with a rambling tale about a woman he nearly married. The other is a bizarre character called the Catwoman who eats mice and wears '*a coat of cat fur . . . studded with cats' eyes and cats' paws*' (ibid., p. 271). Bernadette Bourke suggests that she is a grotesque version of the 'blind seer Teiresias' from Greek tragedy (*The Theatre of Marina Carr*, p. 129). She also resembles a fairy-tale character, and, because she can foretell the future, she adds to the sense of fatalism in the play. Hester's attempt at hijacking the wedding fails, and she responds with an act Medea contemplates but doesn't carry out. She burns down the house Carthage gave her – and now wants to reclaim for Caroline. In an additional, wantonly cruel act, she sets fire to the cattle sheds and burns the animals alive.

Act three begins with Hester still in her wedding dress, which is now charred and mud-stained. Behind her, the house and sheds are burning, and, in the flames, her brother Joseph's ghost can be seen watching her, as the Ghost Fancier watched her at the beginning of the play. Joseph, who appears first in act two, is a gentle, lost ghost, unlike the sinister Gabriel. The only thing he wants is to be alive again, but, like Hester's desire for Carthage, and for her mother, what he yearns for is unattainable. He died when Hester cut his throat with a fishing knife. With Carthage's help, she then weighted the body down with a stone, and threw it into a lake. Carthage believed that she did it in order to get her hands on her father's money, but her real motivation was jealousy. When big Josie left Hester, she lived for a time with Joseph and the children's father. She even passed her name on to her son, not her daughter. It is as if Hester's childhood never existed. 'Every day I forget more and more', she tells Joseph's ghost, 'till I'm startin' to think I made her up out of the air' (Carr, *Plays One*, p. 320). Or maybe out of the bog!

Big Josie's abandonment of Hester was the primary traumatic event that fuelled everything that followed. Hester feels passionate sexual desire for Carthage, but it is the fact that his desertion of her mirrors her mother's that impels her to set fire to the house – the place Carthage gave her and then took from her. Carthage's response, which is to brand Hester an unfit mother and insist that little Josie should come to live with himself and Caroline, leads to the child's death. Hester kills Josie because the heartbroken little girl vows to watch for her mother 'all the time 'long the Bog of Cats . . . hopin' and waitin' and prayin' for [her] to return' (ibid., p. 338). In order to put an end to the cycle of fruitless waiting and longing, Hester cuts Josie's throat with the fishing knife she used to kill her brother. 'I'll take ya with me', she promises her daughter first. 'I won't have ya as I was, waitin' a lifetime for somewan to return, because they don't, Josie, they don't' (ibid., p. 339). The character who does return is the Ghost Fancier. It is now dusk and he has already claimed the boundaries of day as his, as he also claimed Hester. The pair dance together with the fishing knife, and, when the dance ends, the knife is plunged into Hester's heart. The final words of the play are: 'Hester – She's cut her heart out – it's lyin' there on top of her chest like some dark feathered bird' (ibid., p. 341).

In its ultimate moments, *By the Bog of Cats* is a fairy tale. Hester's severed heart identifies her as a manifestation of the black swan with whose corpse she entered at the beginning of the play. In its entirety, the play has a mythical dimension. It tells a story that is largely missing from classical myths – though not from fairy tales – of the daughter's longing for the absent mother, and it creates a dramatic narrative of startling originality. To do this it skilfully knits together its various source strands. Carr herself takes on the song-stitching function of the absent Josie. Unfortunately, when the play was staged at Wyndhams Theatre at the end of 2004, few reviewers appreciated its merits. While *Portia Coughlan,* and Derbhle Crotty's performance in the title role, a few years earlier, generally received high praise, *By the Bog of Cats* and Holly Hunter came in for a good deal of adverse criticism. Holly Hunter was particularly taken to task for her inadequate Irish accent, while the play was seen as over melodramatic, its debt to Euripides' *Medea* specious rather than illuminating. Even the normally perceptive John Nathan commented in the *Jewish Chronicle*: 'Here the deed is not born out of rage-driven vengeance, but out of a perverse attempt to protect her daughter' (10.12.04). It is the word 'perverse' that is revealing, because a daughter's neediness is what knits the play's various strands together. Little Josie's death is emblematic of this. As her First-Communion dress foreshadows, she is in part a reincarnation of Hester at the age of seven. 'What have ya done', the Catwoman asks Hester after she has murdered Josie. 'Have ya harmed yourself?'. 'No, not meself and yes meself', Hester replies (ibid., p. 339). Holly Hunter captured the child-like quality of Hester extremely well. She was strong, passionate, vivid, and yet small and lost. Michael Billington complained that it was hard to believe she 'was a creature of the Irish bogs' (*Guardian*, 2.12.04), but she was, in my view, a haunting and potent figure from a macabre fairy tale.

The origin of *By the Bog of Cats*, like that of *The Mai* and *Portia Coughlan*, is in part a dark version of *Cinderella*. 'Cinderella's' mother is dead, and, in her place, is a cruel stepmother, who resembles the wicked witch from *Snow White*. Fairy stories are full of evil stepmothers and witches, whereas mothers are largely absent. As Josie and Hester are dying, each in turn twice whispers the word 'Mam'. Like Portia and Gabriel, Hester and Josie are a composite unit, in their case an amalgam of mother and daughter. Which is which is blurred by the fact that little Josie bears the name of her grandmother, the name Hester coveted as her own. In a sense, the child is the mother and Hester the daughter. Their joint deaths are the only possible escape route from the sinister enchantment of the dark witch's time. The longing for the lost mother can be fulfilled in no other way.

A dark ride across haunted borders

As a coda to the story of the long-lost, desired, mother in *By the Bog of Cats*, I want to turn briefly to a theatrical event that took place in a tent outside Coventry Cathedral at the end of May 2005. The show was called *Carnesky's Ghost Train* and the characters it portrayed were the ghosts of lost daughters. Audience members bought tickets at a booth and then queued for a fifteen-minute ride on what a publicity hand-out described as 'the ghost of an old-fashioned ghost train. One which [had] lost the rest of the fair and become isolated from its community. Like a haunted nomad it [would] make its way from city to city, town to town, and country to country'. Before our journey began, we were instructed by an actress – dressed in the black of mourning – to search for her missing daughter, and for the lost daughters of other mothers.

The ghost-train ride was both disturbing and weirdly beautiful. It was very dark inside the tent, and the space seemed much larger than it had from the outside. There was an eerie sound track, and actresses in isolated booths silently acted out fragments of the vanished daughters' stories. Four sets of images – four skeletal stories – have remained with me especially vividly. In one, a woman carrying a tray of crockery was on the point of entering a tiny, circular house in which a large, expressionless doll with long black hair could be glimpsed. Was the woman a gaoler – a witch guarding Rapunzel – or a mother seeking her child? Was the expressionless doll perhaps a prostitute, and the woman an attendant bringing refreshment for a client? The face of a young woman in one booth was pressed against the bars of a prison, while, in another, a girl repeatedly tried to catch – or perhaps to set free – a fluttering white bird, which then vanished. The story I found most perturbing was of a girl with long blonde hair who struggled to refocus lights in order to stop, or perhaps to alter the course of, our train. Each time she loomed out of the blackness, she seemed on the point of succeeding, and each time she failed. Was she the remnant of a terrible accident? Or an echo of a train headed for a concentration camp? The final time the train passed her, she was in the process of disappearing – being sucked? – into a carpet on which she had been sitting.

In retrospect, I find it difficult to be certain of the sequence of events. I can construct narratives, but they are impositions on free-floating images. I think that the last time I saw the blonde girl she was on the point of vanishing, but perhaps she disappeared, was reconstituted and continued frantically to try to stop the train. Maybe the woman with the tray was always just about to enter the house, or, conceivably, something else happened first. I can't be sure. My memories, like the train and the ghost-daughters, are caught in a loop. And that is in large part the source of the theatrical power of the piece. Its possible meanings shift and reassemble, while its constituent parts remain vivid and arresting. At the end of the ride, the train shuddered to a halt and suddenly all the characters were present, almost close enough to touch. They stared at us unfathomably – or perhaps they simply looked in our direction without seeing us. Then, just as suddenly, and without any apparent change in the lighting, they were gone – leaving no trace except as disorientating fragments of memory.

The sense of uncertainty *Carnesky's Ghost Train* evoked raises questions about our role as spectators. Were we the constructors of meaning? Was there any meaning? Were we simply voyeurs, or had we somehow caused what had happened to the daughters? Once we entered the blackness of the tent and began the recurring loop of the journey, a sense of beginnings and endings vanished. Maybe we too had become *revenant* – that which returns. We had become enthralled by the static time of the dark witch. In *The Mai*, *Portia Coughlan*, and *By the Bog of Cats*, time past disturbs time present and cancels time future. The characters in Conor McPherson's *The Weir* reach some accommodation with the past, but it returns with a terrifying ferocity in *Shining City*. In J. B. Priestley's *An*

Inspector Calls and *Time and the Conways,* the characters are poised between the past and a potential future marked by inadequacy and loss, but they have the present, which they can alter for the better if they choose to do so. In the next chapter, I discuss two related plays that were first performed in the 1990s, Tom Stoppard's *Arcadia* and Michael Frayn's *Copenhagen*, both of which seek a somewhat different relationship between past and present – an affirmation of the 'now', which is perhaps theatre's most essential characteristic.

4

Nunc Instantis: Arcadia and *Copenhagen*

Both *Arcadia* and *Copenhagen* were first performed at the National Theatre, *Arcadia* on 13 April 1993 at the Lyttelton Theatre and *Copenhagen* on 28 May 1998 at the National's studio venue, the Cottesloe. The two plays are also similar in other ways. They each deal with complex scientific and mathematical ideas and, like Priestley's *An Inspector Calls*, they utilise what is essentially a detective-story format. However, while this format is used in *An Inspector Calls* to expose guilt and to highlight the consequences of choices that the characters have made, in *Arcadia* and *Copenhagen* it serves rather as a basis for an exploration of what can – and cannot – be known. Characters in these two plays hunt for clues, through research or into the recesses of memory, but, while a traditional detective story ends with the solution of a mystery, resolution in *Arcadia* and *Copenhagen* derives from a realisation of the co-existence of the then and the now within the simultaneous immediacy and ephemerality of the present moment of theatre. Both then and now in these plays are characterised by precariousness – by the imminence of loss – and this precariousness manifests itself partly in the form of endangered children. What distinguishes the children in this chapter from the lost ghost-daughters in Chapter 3, caught in their temporal loop, or from the grieving children whose remnants haunt Marina Carr's Portia Coughlan and Hester Swane is their authors' different approach to time. In *Arcadia* and *Copenhagen*, along with the need to understand the past, there is an urgent impulse to inhabit the present, despite its dangers and imperfections.

Arcadia is set in a large country house called Sidley Park and in two time periods: 1809–12 and the present day. In 1809, to quote Bristol Old Vic's publicity material for its 2004 production of the play: 'Two handsome young poets, Septimus Hodge and Lord Byron, are regular lovers of the sexually voracious Mrs Chater. Then one weekend her husband finds out.' It is this discovery that motivates the play's most obvious detective story – and its foremost, and most inept, detective, the university don, Bernard Nightingale. Bernard, who is one of the 1990s characters, is in avid pursuit of evidence of a duel that he believes took place at Sidley Park in April 1809. He has found his first important clue, a book of poems entitled *The Couch of Eros* which contains an inscription by the author, Ezra Chater, to Septimus Hodge, dated Sidley Park, Derbyshire, 10 April 1809. Hidden between the pages of the book are three letters, two of which are from Ezra Chater to an unknown recipient whom he challenges to a duel. The third, which is unsigned, reads, 'My husband has sent to town for pistols. Deny what cannot be proven – for Charity's sake –' (Stoppard, p. 41). The likelihood would appear to be that the letters were addressed to Septimus Hodge, but Bernard has discovered (a) that the copy of *The Couch of Eros* was later sold as part of Byron's library, and (b) that there appears to be no trace of Ezra Chater after 1809. His solution is that a duel was fought between Byron and Chater that resulted in Chater's death. This has the further merit of solving a previously inexplicable incident, Byron's sudden departure for Lisbon in July 1809 (admittedly three months after the duel). Bernard has come to Sidley Park to find conclusive evidence that Byron was there in April 1809. If he is successful, he plans to publish his sensational story, to both critical – and, he hopes, popular – acclaim.

The play's other major detective is also a present-day character. This is the author, Hannah Jarvis, who is staying at Sidley Park as the guest of the owner, Lady Croom, for whom she is researching the history of the Sidley Park garden. At the same time, she is carrying out an investigation of her own into the identity of the Sidley Park hermit, a bizarre figure who died in 1834 leaving behind him thousands of pages covered with 'cabalistic proofs that the world was coming to an end' (ibid., p. 36). In the 1809 scenes the garden is in process of being redesigned by Richard Noakes – 'Culpability Noakes' as the current Lady Croom calls him – in line with the new Gothic style. Lady Croom complains that Noakes has replaced 'the familiar pastoral refinement of an Englishman's garden [with] . . . an eruption of gloomy forest and towering crag'. There are now 'ruins where there was never a house', and her 'hyacinth dell [has] become a haunt for hobgoblins' (ibid., p. 16). The hermit is Hannah's lynchpin for a critique of Romanticism she is writing. He lived in a hermitage especially built by Richard Noakes. He 'was *placed* in the landscape exactly as one might place a pottery gnome', she tells Bernard (ibid., p. 36). His use as a 'garden ornament' makes him for Hannah 'A perfect symbol [of the] . . . whole Romantic sham . . . A century of intellectual rigour turned in on itself. A mind in chaos suspected of genius' (ibid.). Hannah is a more skilful detective than Bernard, though she too makes a number of false assumptions. Bernard is wrong on just about every count. It turns out that, not only were the letters addressed to Septimus Hodge, not Byron, but, in addition, no duel ever actually took place. In whodunnit terms it's a red herring. The identity of the Sidley Park hermit *does* matter, however – though why isn't clear until the end of the play.

In addition to Bernard and Hannah, members of the audience are also required to be on the alert for clues. As Michael Coveney commented in the *Observer* (18.4.93), 'Stoppard makes detectives of us all'. On the face of things the audience is better placed to understand what happened in 1809 than the present-day characters. After all, they see events as they unfold. However, Stoppard holds back vital pieces of information until late in the play. *Arcadia* is a 'theatrical whodunnit or rather who didn't' (*Evening Standard*, 14.4.93). Its mysteries are eventually solved in ways that are satisfying in whodunnit terms, but these solutions give rise, in their turn, to more complex questions that can be answered only partially, if at all. The detective-story format finally ties a number of loose ends together, but simultaneously a very different dynamic is working to unravel them.

A number of reviewers considered the detective-story format to be the most successful element in the play. For some, *Arcadia* was both too wordy and too cerebral. In the *Spectator*, for example, Sheridan Morley complained that it 'offers us the terrifying prospect of our most intelligent ... dramatist finally vanishing up his own brilliance' (24.4.93). Like a number of other reviewers, Morley also listed echoes of plays by other dramatists. 'Whole scenes', he wrote, 'start out as *Hay Fever* or *The School for Scandal*, while elsewhere Stoppard seems to be offering us Enid Bagnold on speed or *The Chalk Garden* rewritten by Stephen Hawking' (ibid.). He meant this pejoratively, but *The Chalk Garden* reference seems to me to point to a source of *Arcadia*'s effectiveness. Off-stage characters and the unseen garden play key roles in the action, as they do in Bagnold's play. Neither Byron nor the indefatigable Mrs Chater ever appears. The garden is the site both of Neo-Gothic/Romantic ideals and Mrs Chater's sexual encounters with Septimus Hodge, in the gazebo and the boat house (though Septimus rejects as fantasy rumours of goings-on on the Chinese bridge or in the shrubbery). The garden is also the site of the operations of Noakes' 'heat engine', the Improved Newcomen steam pump, and heat turns out to be of crucial importance.

Not all commentators on the play were put off by what Quentin Letts in his *Daily Mail* review of the 2004 Bristol Old Vic production of the play called 'Sir Tom's faintly un-English intellectualism' (24.9.04). Two in particular were both enthusiastic and informative. One was Roger Highfield in the *Daily Telegraph* of 15 April 1993. As the co-author of a book that explores scientific themes that Stoppard dramatises in *Arcadia*, Highfield's comments offered a valuable insight into the play. The other was Irving Wardle in the *Independent on Sunday*. With regard to the fact that key events happen off stage, while two of the most talked about characters never appear, Wardle wrote: 'In their place, Stoppard develops a dazzlingly elaborate comedy of ideas from literary history, Chaos theory maths, and landscape gardening' (18.4.93). Wardle identified the basic structuring device of the play as being the use of 'binary oppositions – classic versus romantic, Newtonian versus quantum physics, dispassionate inquiry versus the lust for fame'. These oppositions did not all necessarily 'match up'. *Arcadia* 'works rather through affinities and serendipity'. A present-day character 'echoes a line from his Regency counterpart', for example. In a variety of ways, the play's form 'mirrors its ideas' (ibid.). Though Wardle doesn't go on to make this point, the character that best embodies the notion of serendipity is Thomasina Coverly.

Thomasina is one of the Regency characters. In 1809 she is almost fourteen years old, and it is she who speaks the play's opening lines. 'Septimus, what is carnal embrace?' she asks the young man who, in addition to being Byron's friend and Mrs Chater's lover, is her tutor. 'Carnal embrace is the practice of throwing one's arms around a side of beef', he replies jokingly (Stoppard, p. 2). Thomasina's question has serious ramifications, however, partly because hers is the major interrogative voice in the play and partly because of the significance that carnality (a manifestation of 'bodies in heat') assumes. Septimus is a classicist, a believer in a deterministic, Newtonian universe, Thomasina the prodigy whose anachronistic discoveries destabilise the Newtonian order. Shortly after her opening question, Thomasina shares with her tutor the interesting observation she has made that, while it is possible to stir jam into a rice pudding, it is impossible to unstir it. The pudding continues to turn pink regardless. She 'has made an intuitive discovery of the second law of thermodynamics', which would actually be formulated in 1865, partly as a result of 'the invention and development of heat engines, particularly steam engines' (Edwards, 'Science in *Hapgood* and *Arcadia*', *The Cambridge Companion to Tom Stoppard*, p. 180).

In the final scene of the play, Septimus hands Thomasina a copy of a prize-winning essay that contains a contradiction of the ideas of Sir Isaac Newton. After studying it, she exclaims, 'Just as I said! . . . Determinism leaves the road at every corner'. The cause of this, she explains, is probably 'The action of bodies in heat' (Stoppard, p. 111). She links carnality – 'The Chater would overthrow the Newtonian system in a weekend' (ibid., p. 112) – with Mr Noakes' Improved Newcomen steam pump. 'Newton's equations go forwards and backwards, they do not care which way. But the heat equation cares very much, it goes only one way' (i.e. from hotter to colder). One immediate result of this is that 'Mr Noakes's engine cannot give the power to drive Mr Noakes's engine' (ibid., p. 116). The long-term implications are still more disturbing. The universe, Septimus realises, 'must cease and grow cold' (ibid., p. 125).

In addition to the second law of thermodynamics, Thomasina anachronistically discovers Chaos Theory. Roger Highfield noted in the *Daily Telegraph* (15.4.93) that 'Stoppard's starting point is Newton and his classical laws of motion, which are insensitive to the direction of time and seem to leave no room for unpredictability or free will'. Chaos Theory, he continued, has 'shattered' this 'mechanical universe', rescuing 'free will and chance' in the process. The implications of Chaos Theory are explored through one of the present-day characters, Valentine Coverly, a mathematics postgraduate who is engaged in the study of grouse populations on the moors where the Coverly family has shot for hundreds of years. Valentine has discovered the portfolio that belonged to Septimus Hodge, in which there are three items: a maths primer, Thomasina's mathematics lesson book and a diagram, which turns out to be her illustration of heat exchange. The significance of the diagram doesn't become clear until near the end of the play. The primer and the lesson book together contain evidence of 'a truly wonderful method' Thomasina claimed to have discovered 'whereby all the forms of nature must give up their numerical secrets and draw themselves through number alone' (ibid., p. 56). Initially, Valentine believes that Thomasina couldn't have understood the implications of the equations in her lesson book because the mathematical basis for this wouldn't exist for another hundred years or more. His grouse study in fact uses this new form of mathematics, though from the opposite end to Thomasina. She began with an equation, which she transformed into a graph. Valentine has a graph, produced from actual data, and he is trying to find the equation that would produce the graph. The other reason why Thomasina must simply have been 'doodling' in the lesson book, Valentine believes, is that it would have taken several lifetimes for her to complete her calculations working with pencil and paper. The project would only become feasible with the invention of the computer. However, when Valentine extends her equations a few million times on a computer, he discovers 'In an ocean of ashes, islands of order. Patterns making themselves out of nothing' (ibid., p. 101). Thomasina's 'wonderful method' suggests that disorder may eventually resolve itself into order. The world may be doomed, but 'if this is how it started, perhaps it's how the next one will come' (ibid., p. 103). In 'Science in *Hapgood* and *Arcadia*', Paul Edwards writes that Valentine's description of the images on his computer screen 'encapsulates the lure of Chaos Theory in this play: the capacity for nature, and us as part of nature, to recuperate our losses – ultimately, to circumvent time' (*The Cambridge Companion to Tom Stoppard*, p. 176).

Valentine's sources for his research data are the gamebooks that record the number of grouse shot by the Coverly family back to Thomasina's time and beyond. In addition to the role they play in the exploration of Chaos Theory, these books also form part of the detective-story strand of the play. It is from one of the gamebooks that Bernard learns that Byron *was* at Sidley Park in April 1809. The garden books Hannah is studying are another source of evidence of the past. While the dramatic implications of Chaos Theory introduce elements of randomness and apparent disorder, the detective-story strand provides a simpler, seemingly more comprehensible, view of time in which the past defines the shape of the present. These two perceptions of time and causality, the linear and the random, are skilfully interrelated through Stoppard's third representation of time, which is based on symmetry. He achieves this through the affinities he suggests between the Regency period and the present day. In the final scene, when characters from both time periods are on stage together, he emphasises the connections between them through what he describes as 'doubling'. Important objects from the Regency period are on stage in both their original and present-day versions. At one point, Septimus and Hannah both study Thomasina's lesson book; at another, Septimus and Valentine pore over her heat diagram. In both cases, Stoppard describes their actions as being 'doubled by time'. The 'doubling' strand of the play links to the detective-story strand through a replication of the three letters that Bernard discovers in *The Couch of Eros*. Two are letters that Septimus writes (one to Lady Croom, one to Thomasina) on the night before the duel that he believes will take place the following morning. The other is from Byron to Septimus. What it contains is unknown because Septimus burns it without reading it, along

Nunc Instantis: Arcadia *and* Copenhagen   61

with his own letters, when the duel doesn't happen. The three surviving letters therefore refer to an event that never took place, and that Bernard has misunderstood anyway. The three letters that would have enabled the present-day characters to interpret the past correctly have vanished in a puff of smoke. Chance in this instance definitely has the upper hand.

Though the surviving letters are a source of misinformation, the garden books that Hannah is studying *do* contain reliable evidence. It is an entry in one of the garden books, dated 1 October 1810, that proves that Bernard's suppositions about the duel are wrong. In the course of a fruitless trawl through the British Library database for references to Ezra Chater after 1809, Bernard has come across another Chater, 'a botanist who described a dwarf dahlia in Martinique and died there after being bitten by a monkey' (Stoppard, p. 29). What eventually transpires is that the two Chaters – the botanist and the poet – are in fact one. Lady Croom's brother, Captain Brice, another of Mrs Chater's lovers, took the Chaters with him on an expedition to the Indies, employing Ezra Chater as a plant-gatherer. In the course of the expedition, Ezra Chater had his fatal encounter with the monkey, and Captain Brice married his widow. The garden-book entry makes all this clear and provides a gloss on the words in the third letter that Bernard found in *The Couch of Eros*: 'Deny what cannot be proven – for Charity's sake –.' Charity, it turns out, was the writer of the letter, the then Mrs Chater, and Captain Brice named the newly discovered dahlia 'charity', after his bride. When Hannah relays this information to Bernard in the final scene, the plant is on stage, like a vital clue at the denouement of a whodunnit. As Bernard exclaims bitterly, he has been 'Fucked by a dahlia' (ibid., p. 118).

The puzzle of the missing Chater is solved by subtraction. Two Chaters are really one. Another puzzle, the identity of the Sidley Park hermit, is cleared up when a clue is 'doubled'. In Richard Noakes' sketch book, Hannah discovers what she believes is 'The only known likeness of the ... hermit' (ibid., p. 33). At this point members of the audience believe Hannah is mistaken because they have already seen Thomasina draw the picture, which is of Septimus, on Noakes' sketch as a joke. Later, however, a new piece of information suggests that Septimus and the hermit may be one and the same after all. At the start of the play, Septimus is seen using a pet tortoise called Plautus as a paperweight. In scene five, Bernard reads aloud a reference to the hermit that he has found in *The Peaks Traveller and Gazetteer* of 1832. For twenty years this 'lunatic' had been 'without discourse or companion save for a pet tortoise, Plautus by name' (ibid., p. 85). In the final moments of the play, the veracity of the likeness in

Richard Noakes' sketch book is confirmed when Valentine's brother Gus gives Hannah a picture that the audience earlier watched Thomasina draw, entitled 'Septimus holding Plautus'. This second drawing of Septimus completes the detective-story strand of the play. The identity of the hermit has been cleared up. By this point though the detective-story strand has become entangled with Stoppard's investigations of mathematics and the complex nature of time. The question: was Septimus the hermit? is replaced by: why did Septimus become the hermit? Why, in other words, did he spend the rest of his life scribbling page after page of 'cabalistic proofs' that the world was coming to an end? The answer to this question derives from one of the elements Roger Highfield credited Chaos Theory with rescuing from Newtonian determinism – chance.

In scene three of *Arcadia*, the Newtonian classicist, Septimus, and Thomasina, the play's chief espouser of the importance of chance, discuss the great library of Alexandria that was destroyed by fire. Their responses to the destruction are notably different. Thomasina mourns what she sees as an irremediable loss, while Septimus argues that nothing is ever truly lost. 'The missing plays of Sophocles will turn up piece by piece, or be written again in another language' (ibid., pp. 50–1). In some ways *Arcadia* validates Septimus' faith. Valentine's computer demonstrations of the implications of Thomasina's equations hold out the hope that, at least in the very long view, time can be circumvented. Out of the ashes of the old universe a new one may arise. For human beings, however, time is finite, and, for Thomasina, it proves especially brief. '*Et in Arcadia ego!*' (ibid., p. 16), one of the characters remarks, but even in Arcadia death is present. In the final scene of the play, it is 1812 for the Regency characters. This is the night before Thomasina's seventeenth birthday, and we learn that during the night she will die in a fire that will break out in her bedroom. Though she doesn't realise it, Thomasina was right therefore about the irreversibility of loss. Whether or not Septimus' belief that the plays that were burned in Alexandria can be rewritten is correct, it is certain that, once dead, Thomasina cannot be recovered. In fact, throughout the play fire and heat have been equated with loss. Septimus burns the letters that could have provided a true account of the past. The Improved Newcomen steam pump produces less energy than it uses, and the universe is gradually cooling and dying. Though the play ends on the edge of tragedy, however, it ends, too, in the way of comedies, with a dance. This dance, a waltz that Septimus dances with Thomasina, is Hersh Zeifman writes in 'The comedy of Eros: Stoppard in love', 'an act of grace in the face of unspeakable loss' (*The Cambridge Companion to Tom Stoppard*, p. 192).

Nunc Instantis: Arcadia *and* Copenhagen

For the first six of its seven scenes, Arcadia moves symmetrically between two periods of time. In scene seven, times and characters merge. In 1812 it is Thomasina's birthday, in the present a party is in progress in the garden. Both sets of characters are on stage at the same time, and connections between them are emphasised by the 'doubling' of actions, and also by lighting, music and costume. Fireworks at the present-day party seem also to celebrate Thomasina's birthday. The lighting is soft and romantic, an oil lamp on stage, paper lanterns in the garden. The sound of a piano playing off stage in 1812 becomes indistinguishable from the music from the garden party. The contemporary characters are wearing fancy dress from the Regency period, so that sometimes, in half-light, it is difficult to be sure who is who. At one particularly haunting moment, Gus, who is played by the actor who also plays Thomasina's brother Augustus, seems to be his own double, a figure equally present in both times.

Throughout the play, Gus is an odd, silent, occasional presence. Though he never speaks, he understands things that the other characters don't. In addition to the drawing of Septimus with Plautus, he gives Hannah another present, an apple that he has just picked in the garden. As Gus is in love with Hannah, this is presumably in part a reference to the Garden of Eden – though here it is the man who offers the apple, not the woman. In the following scene, Thomasina picks up the apple leaf and begins to 'deduce its equation' (p. 49) in her mathematics lesson book. In addition to her connection with Valentine through Chaos Theory, Thomasina also resembles Gus because both characters transcend their time. Exactly what Gus signifies is never explained. In *Stoppard's Theatre*, John Fleming writes: 'Most of the play's mysteries are solved, but one of the great unanswered mysteries is why doesn't Gus speak? Who is this "natural genius" with psychic-like abilities, but who never utters a word?' When Fleming put this question to the author in the course of an interview, Stoppard replied that Gus represents 'something more mysterious' than 'a mechanistic universe', though just what that is it was impossible to say (Fleming, *Stoppard's Theatre: Finding Order Amid Chaos*, p. 207). While Thomasina signifies chance, both happy and tragic, Gus is an enigma, and at the play's end the random and the unknown mingle with predetermined order through the dance steps of the waltz.

To celebrate the fact that she is almost seventeen, Thomasina persuades Septimus to teach her to waltz. Her words are interspersed with Valentine's explanation of her heat diagram: 'The heat goes into the mix . . . And everything is mixing . . . all the time, irreversibly . . . till there's no time left. That's what time means' (Stoppard, p. 126). Thomasina's solution is that they should dance, and, as she and Septimus begin to waltz together, he kisses her. She responds by saying that she will go to her bedroom and wait for him to join her, but he tells her that this is impossible. So, she puts the candlestick, with the candle that will presumably start the fire in which she will die, on the table. Around it are all the objects that have featured in the play, including the letters and diagrams and the dahlia. Despite their apparently jumbled state, *Arcadia* has shown the order that resides in their apparent disorder. Then, on the eve of her birthday and of her death, Thomasina begins once again to dance with Septimus. She has learned the steps now and she moves easily and gracefully. Gus hands Hannah Thomasina's drawing of Septimus and bows to her *'rather awkwardly'* (ibid., p. 130). They, too, start to dance, though with less fluency. *Arcadia* is a beautiful play and this is a hauntingly lovely moment. On the threshold of the loss of Thomasina's life, and of Septimus' belief in a universe governed by comprehensible laws, the power of theatre holds time captive. It can do this only within 'the momentary standstill of a present withdrawn from duration' – a *'nunc instantis'* – but it is enough.

The last two quotations are taken from the final chapter of Helga Nowotny's *Time: The Modern and Postmodern Experience*. The chapter is entitled 'The Longing for the Moment' and the term *'nunc instantis'* is itself a quotation. Nowotny writes:

> The poetic language of Cacciari, who follows great Hebrew, Christian and Islamic scholasticism, speaks of the *nunc instantis*, the dimension of a temporary interim period, which in its fullness is so temporary, but also so present, that it can hardly be noticed as an instant of time and yet for this very reason is completely transitory – a dimension of total transitoriness, in which the most temporary instant coincides with the moment that remains and that blows open the continuum. (Nowotny, p. 152)

It could be a definition of theatre at its most potent. *Arcadia* finds the longed-for moment. Its mixing of times momentarily suspends time. Michael Frayn's *Copenhagen* likewise seeks, and finds, the inseparability of the present and the transitory, and then the play is over, the moment has gone. As in *Arcadia*, the momentum towards the *nunc instantis* is created by an investigation of the past. Like *Arcadia*, *Copenhagen* is a thriller, a detective story, as a number of reviewers commented after the opening night. In Frayn's play, however, the investigation resembles an exhumation. The three characters are wraiths who breathe life into their 'ghostly limbo' (*Evening Standard*, 29.5.98) through re-enactment of an event in

Nunc Instantis: Arcadia *and* Copenhagen   65

their joint past, the precise nature of which is perhaps impossible to grasp. At the Cottesloe Theatre the playing area was a white circle with three chairs. In the imagined future of this 'frosty Purgatory' (*The Times*, 30.5.98), three spirits from the past probed the ambiguities of what once was, and again is, the present moment.

The event that is the subject of this spectral investigation took place in Copenhagen in 1941. In that year the German Werner Heisenberg travelled to Nazi-occupied Denmark, where he had a meeting with his fellow physicist, Niels Bohr, which has been the subject of speculation ever since. The two men had been friends and colleagues before the war. In the 1920s they revolutionised atomic physics through their work on quantum mechanics and the uncertainty principle. It was Heisenberg who formulated the uncertainty principle and he is the character who best expresses the play's pervasive atmosphere of uncertainty – or 'indeterminability' as Frayn prefers to call it. Like *Arcadia*, *Copenhagen* begins with a question. It is put by the play's third character, Bohr's wife, Margrethe. 'But why?' she asks. 'Why did he come to Copenhagen?' And, when Bohr queries whether it matters now that they're all 'dead and gone', she replies: 'Some questions remain long after their owners have died. Lingering like ghosts' (Frayn, *Copenhagen*, p. 3). Like their 'owners', the questions initially lack solidity, but they gain substance through repetition. Margrethe's 'why?' is the fundamental question, but, in order to attempt to answer it, it is necessary to ask also where? when? what? And even who? What were the characters, especially Heisenberg, like, because from the nature of the participants comes the nature of the meeting. As Heisenberg, Bohr and Margrethe articulate these questions, 'The past becomes the present inside [their] head[s]' (ibid., p. 6). The ghostly questions put on flesh and blood and an act of theatre is created. It is as though at first the shadows of the characters wait in the wings, formulating the ghostly questions through which they are attempting to pinpoint memories. Then, Heisenberg recaptures the sensation of walking up to the Bohrs' front door, 'crunch[ing] over the familiar gravel . . . tug[ging] at the familiar bell-pull' (ibid., p. 12), and, as he imagines Bohr opening the door, he, and the other seen and unseen characters, make their stage entrances. The performance begins.

In a 'Postscript' to the 1998 Methuen edition of the play, Frayn writes that, among other 'forms of indeterminacy', *Copenhagen* 'touch[es] upon . . . the indeterminacy of human memory, or at any rate the indeterminability of the historical record' (ibid., p. 124). Heisenberg initially remembers the meeting taking place in October. In his mind's eye he sees fallen leaves under a street lamp, but in fact it was September, too early for fallen leaves, and the street lamps would not have been lit in wartime. In Bohr's recollection the two of them remained indoors, in his study, though the likelihood is that they went for a walk to escape from hidden microphones. In the past, walking was something they often did together. Both Bohr and Heisenberg recall a trip to Elsinore, where they discussed *Hamlet*, and, 'because uncertainty is one of Shakespeare's themes too' (*Mail on Sunday*, 7.6.98), the *Hamlet* reference adds to the elusiveness of the Copenhagen meeting. As the characters repeatedly recreate the crunch of feet on gravel, the sound of the bell and the opening of the heavy door, the time and place of the meeting become more precise. It was September, they agree, not October. They did go for a walk, but it ended abruptly. What was said, why Heisenberg came to Copenhagen, remains obscure. Did he perhaps want to find out whether Bohr knew anything about the Allied progress on creating an atomic bomb? Did he hope to persuade Bohr to help in the development of a German bomb? The difficulty of knowing is explored in *Copenhagen* through ramifications of the concept of 'uncertainty'. Frayn writes in his 'Postscript' to the play that 'according to the so-called "Copenhagen Interpretation" of quantum mechanics . . . the whole possibility of saying or thinking anything about the world . . . depends upon human observation' (*Copenhagen*, p. 99). Margrethe, the non-scientist, is the first person to grasp the implications of this with regard to understanding what happened at the meeting because her role was that of an observer. Heisenberg doesn't know why he went to Copenhagen because, both at the time, and in all his mental recreations of the event, he is unable to see himself. In one reanimation of his journey to the Bohrs' front door, Heisenberg is overwhelmed by the certainty that he has finally understood his own motivation. The belief lasts only until the imagined door opens and he sees Bohr and Margrethe. The one person he can never observe is himself. His own face and motives remain hidden from him.

Margrethe also speaks of Heisenberg in terms of what is perhaps *Copenhagen*'s central motif – the 'lost child'. 'Look at him', she says, 'He's like a lost child . . . and all he wants is to go home' (ibid., p. 52). Shortly afterwards, as they once again return to the memory of Heisenberg's visit, Bohr repeats her words. As he recaptures the moment of opening the heavy door, he sees again Heisenberg's 'wary schoolboy smile'. It was 'As if a long-lost child had appeared on the doorstep' (ibid., p. 54). To Bohr, Heisenberg is a surrogate son, a replacement – to some degree at least – for the two boys he and Margrethe lost, Harald to a childhood illness, and Christian, the eldest, in a boating accident. The memory of Christian's death by drowning recurs in the play almost as frequently as the memory of Heisenberg's visit, and, while the latter memory is elusive, the former is dreadfully precise. 'Those short moments on the boat, when the tiller slams over in the heavy sea, and Christian is falling . . . Those long moments in the water' (ibid., pp. 29 and 30). The connection that is made between a child and loss in this memory is developed later in the play through references to defeated German soldiers at the end of the war. Though they would have been young adults, Heisenberg remembers them as 'weeping children . . . lost and hungry children, drafted to fight, then abandoned by their commanders' (ibid., p. 93); and the Bohrs link them to their own lost children, and to Heisenberg himself. The two recurring memories – of Heisenberg's visit and Christian's death – are discussed in close proximity to each other, as though the characters are groping towards a connection between them, and eventually that connection is made. The last time that Bohr and Heisenberg re-enact their walk 'Through the blacked-out streets' of the Danish capital, Heisenberg asks the question that causes Bohr to rush away in horror: 'Does one as a physicist have the moral right to work on the practical exploitation of atomic engery?' (ibid., p. 88). He has come, in other words, to ask Bohr, his surrogate father, to give him permission to build an atomic bomb. Then, unexpectedly, Bohr introduces a new element into the scenario, one that he describes as 'a thought-experiment' (ibid.). One of the uncertainties about Heisenberg is whether he had sufficient knowledge of the relevant physics to develop a bomb. If he did, then, as he later claimed, he may have done just enough work on the project to satisfy the Nazis and keep it running, but not enough to succeed in delivering the bomb into Hitler's hands. If he didn't, then presumably he failed out of ignorance. The nub of the question is whether Heisenberg understood 'the amount of fissile material (U235 or plutonium) [that would be] large enough to support an explosive chain reaction' (ibid., p. 113). Did he estimate correctly – or indeed at all? This is the question that Bohr asks in his 'thought-experiment' and, immediately, Heisenberg does the missing calculation and a 'very terrible new world begins to take shape . . .' (ibid., p. 89). Only in the 'thought-experiment' though. In the replay of the meeting, Bohr leaves abruptly, and his question remains unasked and therefore unanswered. Frayn's final, and most persuasive, answer to Margrethe's opening question is therefore that Heisenberg came to Copenhagen to make his 'last and greatest demand' on Bohr's friendship, which was 'To be understood when he couldn't understand himself'.

Bohr's 'last and greatest act of friendship . . . [was] . . . [t]o leave him misunderstood' (ibid.).

It is this 'misunderstanding' that most powerfully links Heisenberg's visit with Christian's death, and, in this way, the image of the 'lost child' is paralleled by images of children who are saved. The connection is made clearly in the final words of the play, but there is a suggestion of it a few minutes previously when Heisenberg returns to a memory he described in act one. Then, he recollected, at the age of seventeen, guarding a 'terrified prisoner' who was 'going to be executed in the morning' (ibid., p. 42), but, near the end of the play, he adds that in the morning he persuaded his fellow soldiers to let the prisoner go. The prisoner's age isn't stated, but Heisenberg's youth at the time suggests that perhaps he, too, may have been very young. The fact that the prisoner was saved doesn't redeem the weeping German soldiers Heisenberg remembers from the Second World War, or Bohr's fellow Jews, or the inhabitants of Hiroshima and Nagaski, who died because, unlike Heisenberg, the Allies succeeded in building an atomic bomb, but it is important nevertheless. At the end of *Copenhagen*, the three ghosts of the past, who have become alive in the theatrical present, look into an imagined abyss where time will cease. Not even the limbo they inhabited when the play began will exist, and there will be 'no more uncertainty, because there's no more knowledge' (ibid., p. 94). Heisenberg has the final speech: 'But in the meanwhile, in this most precious meanwhile, there it is . . . Our children and our children's children. Preserved, just possibly, by that one short moment in Copenhagen' (ibid.). The key words are 'short' and 'precious meanwhile'. The former recalls the 'short moments' in the boat before the 'long moments' of Christian's terrible struggle in the water. His death, and all the deaths that occurred in the war are non-negotiable – they happened – but the 'short moment' in Copenhagen may have prevented countless other deaths. 'Meanwhile' suggests both duration – a time of waiting – and simultaneity, and its effect is to reformulate the concept of limbo with which the play began, changing it from a place to a unit of time. *Copenhagen* starts with a question: 'But why?' The second word is interrogative, the first conjunctive. 'But' joins on to something that went before, and leads on to something new. The 'before' is the ghostly world the wraiths of the characters inhabit before the play begins, the 'new' the theatrical present tense they bring into being. 'Meanwhile' finally reveals this present tense as itself a kind of limbo. It is both immediate – now – and anticipatory – focused towards the future. And it is 'precious' because of the potential for salvation it contains. Different

Nunc Instantis: Arcadia *and* Copenhagen   69

interpretations of the Copenhagen meeting co-exist, at one and the same time, but their indeterminability is the point. Salvation may just possibly reside in an 'event that will never quite be located or defined . . . [in] . . . that final core of uncertainty at the heart of things' (ibid.).

'Spies'

The equation of children with loss, often in the context of a shadowy past or an endangered present and future, is a major theme of many of the plays and novels discussed in this book. Michael Frayn's *Spies*, which won the Whitbread Prize in 2002, was one of a number of excellent novels published that year about lost children. Alice Sebold's *The Lovely Bones* (which is discussed in Chapter 5) is narrated through the voice of a murdered child. William Trevor's *The Story of Lucy Gault*, which tells of the disappearance of eight-year-old Lucy and the consequences that follow, is a stark and haunting evocation of loss, and, in unexpected ways, of redemption. Donna Tartt's *The Little Friend* is about a child who disappears and the sister who attempts to solve the mystery of his disappearance. In *Spies,* a child, Stephen Wheatley, also tries to solve a mystery. Stephen is lost in the sense that his much-older self, who narrates the novel, is trying to understand him, trying to rediscover the child he was when the events in the story occurred. The splitting of the character of Stephen into two selves is reminiscent of *Copenhagen,* because the older self is an observer who struggles with the inherent indeterminacy of memory. He finds himself (rather like the wraiths at the beginning of *Copenhagen*) in a mental limbo, from which he has to return to the past in order to find release into the future. As in *Copenhagen*, the past events that he is trying to understand happened during the Second World War.

The book begins with Stephen's observer self, who is now seventy years old, and, though the reader doesn't learn this until the end, is called Stefan Weitzler. Why he has changed his name – and why this matters – isn't clear until the end of the book. Stefan lives abroad, but he is lured back to the England of his childhood by a scent in the air that disturbs him. It is the third week of June and Stefan is walking past 'well-ordered gardens' in a street in the city that is now his home, when, through the 'sweetness of the lime blossom, for which this city's known' (Frayn, *Spies*, p. 3), he becomes aware of another, 'urgent' smell. It is not so much a scent as a 'reek', and in some indefinable way it is familiar. It returns him mentally to childhood with its complex mixture of fears and intimations of unknown but enticing possibilities. It fills him with a yearning to be elsewhere and at the same time somehow imbues him with a 'homesickness for where' he is (ibid.). He goes back to England in response to this 'shameless summons' (ibid., p. 4), and returns to the suburban Close where he lived as a child. The Close was also the home of his friend Keith. It was here, sixty years ago, that Keith instigated the 'game' that was always more than a game and had implications that became increasingly serious the longer it lasted. The 'game' in *Spies* is the equivalent of the meeting between Bohr and Heisenberg in *Copenhagen*, and, like the meeting, it begins in memory, with sounds. In place of the crunch of Heisenberg's feet on gravel, Stefan remembers the clink of beads against a glass jug of lemon barley. Keith's mother had brought the lemon barley into the garden as refreshment, he recalls. Over the top of the jug was a lace cover that was held in place by four blue glass beads, and, as the breeze stirred the lace, the beads clinked against the side of the jug. Keith's mother left the jug and began to walk back to the house, and, as she did so, Keith spoke the six words that 'changed everything' (ibid., p. 6). ' "My mother", he said . . . "is a German spy" ' (ibid., p. 33).

The Close to which Stefan returns is in some ways the same as he remembers it, in other ways quite different. What he wants to know is whether what he sees as he looks 'at it now' is what Stephen Wheatley, the boy 'with the stick-out ears and the too-short grey flannel school shirt hanging out of the too-long grey flannel school shorts', saw (ibid., p. 12). In an attempt to discover this, he walks up and down the Close and into the surrounding area, and, as he does so, Frayn creates mental 'maps' of the geography of the present and the past for the reader. The 'map' of the present, with its neat grid of streets, is dull and uninspiring, more remote for both Stefan and the reader than the past in which Keith instigated adventures and projects. Then, the Berrill girls, who were 'running wild' because their father was away in the army, lived there, along with 'the pigtailed Geest girls, and the oil-stained Avery boys' (ibid., p. 13), and Mr Gort, who Keith proved was a murderer when he unearthed some bones in his garden. At the end of the Close one turned left into the Avenue, with its postbox and shops, and the manhole cover beneath which Keith and Stephen were sure there was a secret chamber. It is a tribute to the book's mesmerising power that it takes some time for the reader – this reader at any rate – to wonder what is to the right of the Close. So, when Keith's mother disappears on her way to post some letters, even though Keith and Stephen have been keeping her under observation, it is initially baffling. Like the two boys, it can take the reader a while mentally to turn right and follow Keith's mother through the old, narrow, railway tunnel with its dank, slimy walls. When Keith and Stephen eventually explored the tunnel, they discovered what they believed to be the solution of the mystery. Hidden on the railway embankment on the other side of the tunnel, they found the box by means of which Keith's mother communicated with her accomplice, the other 'spy' whom Stephen believes to be indisputably German, unlike Keith's mother who confusingly has no obvious marks of Germanness at all. Beyond the hidden box were the Lanes, with their dirty, tumbledown cottages guarded by fierce dogs, and expressionless children who threw stones. Further on still, were the Barns, ruined farm buildings where the 'German spy' was hiding below ground. The 'map' of the past has initially all the vividness of remembered childhood, but its clarity becomes increasingly obscured as the heroic adventure on which Stephen has embarked becomes clouded by apprehensions of adult emotions that he glimpses and fears. He hunts for clues with Keith, but doesn't understand them when he finds them. He is an observer of other people's actions, but (like Heisenberg) he can't interpret them because he can't see himself. Stefan, the much-older observer, who looks back at the past with knowledge of what is to come, tries to see Stephen clearly. Above all, he wants to know whether Stephen really thought the man hiding in the Barns was a German spy, whether he could really have failed to grasp his true identity, but the closest he can get is that Stephen knew, and didn't know. Both at once.

Despite the uncertainty that is associated with it, the 'map' of the past creates the illusion of multidimensionality. In the mind's eye one can crawl through the privet hedge, or walk nervously through the tunnel into the hostile terrain at the other side. The 'map's' fourth dimension is time, and it is this that is the source of the powerful emotional response it evokes. As in the lime-blossom-laden streets of the novel's opening, it is summer in the wartime Close. It is also the 'Duration', the intermediate, set-apart time of the war. As the story progresses, Stefan is increasingly assailed by memories of this long-ago summer. The reader learns quite early on in the book that the source of the alluring reek that has drawn him back into the past is an almost absurdly ordinary shrub. It is privet, and it was in the middle of an overgrown privet hedge in the garden of a bombed house in the Close that Keith and Stephen made their secret den. Keith found a bathroom tile in the ruins of the house on which he meant to write 'private', but, because he wasn't very good at spelling, it came out as 'PRIVET'. The den with its overpowering smell of privet blossom is the central location of the story, even more than the Barns, or the railway embankment, or the garden where Keith's mother left the jug of lemon barley. It is a place that is sacred to the quest in which Keith and Stephen are involved, and when Barbara Berrill comes there in Keith's absence her visit seems like a desecration. It is also the place where Keith's mother comes to plead with Stephen to help her, and, in this way, it becomes permeated by dangerous, half-understood adult emotions. It is the coarse pungency of the privet blossom that most powerfully evokes the 'map' of the past's fourth dimension of time, and it also adds texture and depth to the 'map' of the present. Stephen Wheatley became Stefan Weitzler because this was his real identity. Though he didn't know this as a child, he is German. His parents came to England at the start of the war because his father was Jewish. So, as Stephen Wheatley hunted for clues to the 'spy's' identity, which he couldn't – or wouldn't – understand when he found them, there really was a German spy in the quiet English Close – himself. Stefan is drawn back to the world of his childhood by a restlessness that is strangely also a longing for home. At the end of the story he names his ambiguous desire by two German words: '*Heimweh* . . . *Fernweh* . . . A longing to be there . . . a longing to be here, even though [he's] here already' (ibid., p. 234). It's time to go, Stefan realises, time to leave the past, which is anyway always just out of reach. Then, as he turns the corner at the end of the street, it is there again in the air, 'a sudden faint breath of something familiar. Something sweet, coarse, and intimately unsettling' (ibid.). The final words of the book are 'Even here, after all. Even now', and they recall, and, in a sense complete, the 'But' that begins *Copenhagen*. 'But' opens up the possibility of *Copenhagen* taking place. It leads to other adjacent, imagined, worlds that might exist in addition to the 'frosty Purgatory' the ghosts of the past inhabit. 'Even' and 'after all' are ambiguous – the familiar 'breath' is unsettling as well as sweet – but they provide a degree of resolution, a scent of hope in the midst of an otherwise unrealisable longing for *Heimweh* and *Fernweh*, for the elsewhere and the here, the past and the now.

5

Stories of lost futures

Michael Frayn's *Copenhagen* was only one of a number of new plays in 1998 in which stories of children played important roles. 'Few theatregoers can have failed to notice the extraordinary preoccupation with children in this season's crop of new plays', Sam Marlowe remarked in his review of Mark Ravenhill's *Handbag* (*What's On*, 23.9.98), which opened at the Lyric Studio on 14 September 1998. His words echoed Michael Billington's comments in the *Guardian* the previous week: 'Babies. They are everywhere this theatrical season. Test-tube babies. Phantom babies. Abducted babies. Even murdered babies' (16.9.98). Subtitled *The Importance of Being Someone,* Ravenhill's *Handbag* was a prequel to Oscar Wilde's *The Importance of Being Earnest*, intercut with a 1990s plot that involved sperm donors and gay parenting. At the Orange Tree in Richmond there was David Lewis' *Sperm Wars*. The world premiere of *The Play About the Baby* by Edward Albee, 'with the infant as symbol of illusion' (ibid.), was staged at the Almeida, while the hit of the Edinburgh Festival that year was Liz Lochhead's *Perfect Days,* a play about a thirty-nine-year-old woman's desire to have a baby. 1998 was also the year in which Macmillan published *Cries Unheard*, Gitta Sereny's book about the damaged childhood of Mary Bell, who, in 1968, at the age of eleven, was convicted of the manslaughter of two small boys. Other damaged childhoods influenced the production of *The Hansel Gretel Machine*, the first part of David Glass' *Lost Child Trilogy*, at the Purcell Room in March 1998. Its 'Expressionist imagery', Jenny Gilbert explained in the *Independent on Sunday* (15.3.98), was 'informed by the drawings and imaginings of real-life traumatised children around the world, which the director spent 12 months researching'. The cast included 'a ghostly omnipresent chorus of "lost children", black-clad performers each wearing a photographic mask of a grinning baby'.

A dark version of another well-known fairy tale, *Little Red Riding Hood*, underlay Bryony Lavery's *Frozen*, first performed on 1 May 1998 at the Birmingham Repertory Theatre. Lavery uses elements of the fairy tale as pegs on which to hang her portrayal of a mother's quest for her lost daughter. Her fictional representation was chillingly echoed two years later when a real little girl, Sarah Payne, was murdered. Like Lavery's Rhona, Sarah Payne was on her way to her grandmother's house when she was abducted. A revival of *Frozen* at the Cottesloe Theatre, on 28 June 2002, was followed a month later by the killing of ten-year-old Jessica Chapman and Holly Wells, and, in a number of ways, these murders, too, recalled Lavery's play. I analyse a selection of journalists' accounts of the three children's deaths in relation to *Frozen*.

Prior to this, I discuss a play, which, like *Frozen*, is about a mother's search for a lost child. This is Shelagh Stephenson's award-winning *The Memory of Water*, which was staged at the Vaudeville Theatre, London, in January 1999. Like Nancy in *Frozen*, Mary in *The Memory of Water* attempts to come to an accommodation with the past, but the most she can achieve is a stoical acceptance of loss – of both her child and her lover. This is not quite Carr's static time of the 'dark witch'. Things have moved on to some extent by the end of *The Memory of Water* (though less so than at the conclusion of *Frozen*). In contrast to *Arcadia* and *Copenhagen*, both of which decipher the past in order more fully to inhabit the present, *Frozen* investigates the past to find a way forward into the future.

The analysis of *Frozen* is followed by a discussion of two further texts about murdered children. The first is a novel, Alice Sebold's *The Lovely Bones*, which was published in 2002, the same year that *Frozen* was revived at the Cottesloe. Rhona never appears in *Frozen*. Others tell her story on her behalf. In *The Lovely Bones*, the narrator is the child-victim, and we see everything that happens through her eyes. The final text is Martin McDonagh's play, *The Pillowman*, which opened at the Cottesloe in November 2003. The protagonist of *The Pillowman* is a writer of gruesome stories about murdered children. The fact that the Cottesloe production of *The Pillowman* took place in the context of Ian Huntley's trial for the Soham murders underlined the importance of questions McDonagh raises (though, I will suggest, does not fully address) in the play with regard to the relationship between stories and life.

A 'winter's tale'

In *The Memory of Water* (first performed on 11 July 1996 at the Hampstead Theatre, London) the past is present on stage in the form of a ghost. Three sisters, Mary, Teresa and Catherine, have returned in mid-winter to their childhood home on the north Yorkshire coast for their mother Vi's funeral. The play begins with a scene between Mary and the dead Vi. Both women are roughly the same age. Though she is a ghost, Vi is sexy and immaculately dressed and made-up. '*She is sitting at a dressing-table... [wearing] a green taffeta cocktail frock circa 1962*' (Stephenson, p. 1). Mary is lying on the bed watching her and their conversation introduces Stephenson's major preoccupations in the play, which are with memory and the instability of the past. Vi accuses Mary of going through the dressing-table drawers, and asks her what she was looking for. Mary denies that she was looking for anything, but almost immediately asks her mother if she remembers 'a green tin box with chrysanthemums on it' (ibid.). Vi draws Mary's attention to a large crack in the wall behind the bed. Has Mary noticed, she wonders, that the sea is fifty yards closer to the house than it used to be? Eventually the house will disappear, Vi adds. 'Nothing left. And all the life that happened here, drowned, sunk. As if it had never been' (ibid.).

Stephenson's evocation of the complex nature of memory is created in part through a Pinteresque contest the sisters engage in over the ownership of memories. Each of the sisters remembers the past differently, and they bicker over what 'really' happened. Catherine, the youngest and scattiest of the sisters, claims memories that the other two say are not hers. Her complaint that she is always excluded, not only in the present but also from the story they create of the past, is justified though because there is a family secret that has always been kept from her. Memories may be difficult to verify, but in this case there is tangible proof of what happened. When Mary was fourteen, she gave birth to a son who was adopted. The birth certificate, the evidence of the child's existence, is in the tin box that Mary is looking for. Finding it would offer her the promise of discovering what happened to the child, and a possible future in which she might have a role to play in his life. She has put her name on a register in case he is trying to find her, and, in the meanwhile, she finds herself glancing covertly at young men on the tube, wondering if one of them could be her son. In an echo of her mother's words, she describes how the sea will one day take the house and everything in it. The birth certificate is the only thing she wants to salvage, the one memento of the past, on which she will construct stories of the future. Tragically, when she finds the tin box it contains evidence of the son's death as well as his birth certificate. He died while he was still a child when a stretch of cliffs near Whitby gave way. The sea took him after all. Vi learned about what had happened and she collected newspaper cuttings of the accident, which she kept in the tin box. The loss even of this 'ghost child' about whose life she had been able to weave imaginary stories is compounded for Mary by the discovery that Mike, her married lover, had a vasectomy without telling her. She had become convinced that she was pregnant, but, it turns out that this child is another 'phantom'. She has a dream about dead babies, and wakes up to find that her period has begun. 'Everything's dead', she tells Vi. 'I can't bear it. I can't hold on to anything' (ibid., p. 84). There seems to be no future and no past. She believes that she can recall a time before she gave birth to her son. She has memories of 'nightlights and a doll's house', but she doesn't know whether this secure, happy, 'half-imagined childhood' (ibid., p. 36) for which she yearns ever actually existed or whether it is an illusion.

While the endangered house and the encroaching sea symbolise the erasure of the past, Vi represents both loss and continuance. In old age Vi suffered from Alzheimer's Disease and she movingly describes the way holes developed in her recall of the past and gradually ate away at her understanding of the present. Her presence on stage, despite her death, confirms, however, the continuity of past and present, and Stephenson's title underlines this. Both Mary and Mike are doctors. One of Mary's patients is a young man who is suffering from amnesia. Fragments of the man's past have begun to come back to him, and, in support of Mary's hopes for his recovery, Mike tells her about research that has been done in a laboratory in France into 'the efficacy of homeopathy'. The researchers removed 'every last trace of the curative element from a water solution', and yet, no matter how much they diluted the solution, it retained 'its beneficial effect'. The conclusion they came to was that water was 'like magnetic tape'. It 'had memory' (ibid.). Vi is the spectral equivalent of this memory trace. Mary cut herself off from her mother, even during Vi's illness. She attempted to concentrate instead on the amnesiac young man whose recovery would offer her a promise of the return of her own lost son. She has wanted to assert her difference from her mother, but Vi points out their similarities: the curve of their cheeks, the way in which they hold their hands. At the end of the play, Mary echoes Mike's words about the French experiment, as a way of explaining Vi's significance for her. Her mother is 'the ghost in the machine'. She 'goes through' her daughters 'like wine through water', proving that 'Nothing ends entirely' (ibid., p. 92).

Unlike the ghosts discussed in Chapter 3, Vi's effect is beneficent. She is a symbol both of loss and of the fact that things carry on. Act one ends with her only appearance with all three of her daughters. Near the end of the act, the sisters dress up in Vi's clothes and Mary tries on the green taffeta dress. They link arms for Frank, Teresa's husband, to take a photograph of them, and, as they freeze into position, there is suddenly a fourth person in this family group. It is Vi, Mary's mirror image, in the green dress, smiling and elegantly holding aloft a cigarette. Memory crystallises in the present. Act two also ends with an evocation of the past. Despite her sophisticated appearance, Vi's married life was unhappy. Her husband was involved in a long-term affair and he barely noticed his wife's presence. The only memories the sisters are able to agree on are of Vi getting them up in the middle of the night when their father was out. She would drink Dubonnet and lemonade and give the girls crisps and ice-cream soda, and they would listen to records of Nat King Cole. 'She must have been lonely', Mary says when they recall this. 'I never thought of that' (ibid., p. 91). The final moments of the play conjure up the girls' memories of these nights. The *'lights dim to gold and blue. The curtains billow into the room and a flurry of snow drifts in. Nat King Cole plays faintly in the distance'* (ibid., p. 93).

Vi's role as a manifestation of the past that we carry within us is placed in the last scene in the context of the bleak impression that is conveyed of Mary's future. Mary has lost the hope of being reunited with her child, and the possibility of having another baby. When she looks out of the window, snow is still falling, obliterating everything. She has always hated the icy darkness of winter, 'the stasis, the waiting for spring' (ibid., p. 92). What will she do now? Mike asks, and her answer, 'Learn to love the cold' (ibid., p. 93), speaks eloquently of resolution and stoicism, but not of hope. She has gained a connection with the past through Vi, but the stories she told herself about the future have turned out to have no substance. In 2000, *The Memory of Water* won the Olivier Award for Best Comedy. It is often a very funny play, but it is a comedy primarily because of the balance Stephenson strikes between pain and ironic humour. It is both a winter's tale of Mary's loss, and a haunting evocation of past desire.

Retelling *Red Riding Hood*

As its title signifies, *Frozen* is also a tale of winter. Externally, it begins and ends in summer, but, emotionally, it charts a journey from an inner wilderness to renewal. It is a play structured around absence. The lost child is its heart, and her disappearance is mirrored by other incidences of loss. Rhona herself is never seen or heard in the play. We learn what happened to her only through the words of Ralph, the paedophile who assaulted and murdered her, but the off-stage, unseen, meeting between the child and her killer is the pivotal event in the play. In *The Trials and Tribulations of Little Red Riding Hood,* Jack Zipes defines the encounter between Red Riding Hood and the wolf as the crucial scene in a 'chain of signification' (Zipes, p. 359), and the encounter between Rhona and Ralph has an equivalent importance in Lavery's play, particularly with relation to Nancy. Until she learns what happened to Rhona, Nancy is in a state of stasis, locked in the emotional arctic wasteland indicated by the play's title. When, at last, Rhona's remains are discovered, the sound 'of great ice floes breaking up' is heard (Lavery, p. 28). Very gradually, as Nancy begins to learn about Rhona's encounter with the 'wolf' who murdered her, a thawing process begins to take place.

In her *Observer* review of 7 July 2002, Susannah Clapp compared Rhona's fate to that of the real-life Sarah Payne: 'A girl, sent, like Red Riding Hood, to visit her grandmother, vanishes', she wrote. Less than a month later, Holly Wells and Jessica Chapman vanished in Soham. There was no grandmother link this time, but a photograph taken probably less than three hours before the girls died suggested a connection with both Sarah Payne and Red Riding Hood, because of the colour of the clothes the girls were wearing. In this photograph, which was used repeatedly in newspapers and television news programmes, the two girls were dressed in identical red Manchester United football shirts. A frequently reproduced photograph of Sarah Payne also showed her dressed in red – a red jumper over a red-and-white checked dress. Jessica Chapman and Holly Wells also resembled Sarah Payne because they disappeared in a place of apparent safety. Gentle, sweet-faced Sarah Payne was crossing a field close to her grandmother's house one summer evening. Holly and Jessica, 'two versions of the perfect middle England everychild, one tomboyish, smart and dark-haired, the other quieter and fair . . . [were] walking through their own quiet town in the middle of the countryside'. These words are taken from a 'Special Report' in the *Observer* newspaper of 21 December 2003, entitled 'The fury that drove Huntley to murder'. The authors, Kamal Ahmed, Mark Townsend and Tony Thompson, who aimed to tell 'the inside story of one of the biggest murder hunts in Britain', cast the story primarily in the form of a whodunnit. Nicci Gerrard, in an article in the Review section of the same edition of the *Observer*, saw it partly as a detective story, and also as a 'horror story', an 'easy tear-jerker' and 'a nasty modern fairy tale'. 'This case', she wrote, 'has been all about stories'. In May 2004, Sara Payne (mother of the murdered Sarah Payne) published her story. Immediately prior to the publication date, Barbara Ellen interviewed Sara Payne for the *Observer* (on 23 May 2004). Before considering Lavery's fictional portrayal of Rhona's lost future, I want to look at what the two articles reveal about the ways in which the story of Holly and Jessica was told, and also at Sara Payne's response to the murder of her daughter.

Whatever narrative style was invoked, whodunnit, fairy-tale, etc., the starting point for the *Observer* articles about Jessica's and Holly's deaths was the same. A tale about absence began with a vivid reminder of presence: the photograph of the girls in their red football shirts, standing under a clock that registered the time as four minutes past five. It was this precise recording of time, repeated in the CCTV footage that captured the girls intermittently as they made their way through the streets of Soham, that rendered their subsequent disappearance so baffling. In Gerrard's words, the girls were shown on CCTV cameras walking 'close together, shoulders touching, arms sometimes linked, giggling. It's 18.28 and 30 seconds; there they are. It's 18.28 and 41 seconds, and they're jerked forward, out of the frame – vanished'. What the various stories attempted to do was to tell what happened next, to reanimate the screen, but in each of the versions it remained stubbornly empty. We now know who killed Holly and Jessica, possibly before 18.46 when Jessica's mobile phone was turned off, and we have some understanding of how they died, but not the details and not why. That remains a blank. 'At the inky heart of the case, in that ghastly little hole in time, the silence remains' (Gerrard).

It was a silence that police and press tried to fill, as did the two most voluble storytellers, Ian Huntley, school caretaker and murderer, and his girlfriend Maxine Carr. These two were storytellers in a dual sense, at once narrators and liars. By his own admission Huntley was the last person who was known to have seen the girls. As he was fond of saying – even at his trial – his was the 'last friendly face' they saw. The glib deceitfulness of this is difficult to take in, almost impossible to comprehend, but then, despite what we now know about Huntley's past and his crime, he remains largely a blank. In a brief 'Commentary' published underneath 'The fury that drove Huntley to murder', Mary Warnock defined Huntley as 'wicked', but added that labelling him in this way didn't help us to understand him. A virtue of the whodunnit version of events was that it gave Huntley an identifiable role. As he 'hung around and introduced himself to the police' and asked 'odd questions about DNA and whether clothes could be incriminating' (Ahmed, etc.), he was the too-obvious suspect, the red herring who deflects attention from the real culprit in a fictional detective story. He and Carr also span their own detailed fabrications of what happened that evening, claiming, for example, that

Carr was upstairs in the bath while Huntley was talking to the girls outside, even though she was actually many miles away in Grimsby. The two became briefly a 'celebrity couple' (Gerrard) on television and it was as a result of this that their stories began to unravel, because people recognised the two of them, and another, and darker, story about Huntley began to emerge. It turned out that he had repeatedly been accused of sexual offences against young girls. However, in a weird replication of the blank screen that replaced the images of Holly and Jessica on the CCTV footage, the accusations had been deleted by the Humberside police force because of a mistaken belief that to retain them would contravene the Data Protection Act. The motif of erasure continued in the frantic cleaning activity that Huntley and Carr indulged in after the murder. Curtains were taken down and washed, bathroom tiles were scrubbed. Huntley cleaned out the car in which he had taken away the girls' bodies and changed the tyres in order to get rid of the evidence of the location of the burial site.

Despite his attempt to destroy the evidence, enough remained to convict Huntley of the girls' murder. At his trial he admitted that Holly and Jessica had died in his house but not his own responsibility for murder. Gerrard described him as 'a fragile, weakly defended man, with few inner resources', but also as someone with 'a prickly sense of his status – he was quick to insist that he was not a caretaker but a site manager, or even a "senior site manager"'. In one extraordinary exchange, he explained how he put on his trainers in place of his 'smart "brushers"' before driving off to dump the girls' bodies, douse them with petrol and set them alight. When asked why, he replied, 'as if there was nothing odd about personal vanity in the middle of brutal double murder, [that] he only wore his "brushers" in the house; he didn't want to get them messy'. It is tempting to see in Huntley's denial of his role as caretaker some faint recognition of the dreadfulness of taking such care of his shoes after he had killed the two children. Tempting, but probably misguided.

In the absence of a means of understanding Huntley as a human being, Nicci Gerrard ofered an interpretation of him in the context of a 'nasty modern fairy tale'. 'Many of the murder cases that have gripped the nation in recent years possess the horror of the strange; the spooky dread of the unknown', she wrote. She went on to instance the toddler, James Bulger, spirited away and killed by two ten-year-old boys; the mutilated murder victims of Fred and Rosemary West buried underneath the floorboards of a 'terraced slaughterhouse'; Sarah Payne 'snatched by a stranger' while she was 'running home across fields'. The murders that we respond to most strongly are the ones that we can frame within recognisable, if disturbing, narratives. Many people have forgotten the name of Sarah Payne's killer, but he lives on in our minds as the 'wicked wolf, the fictive bogeyman'. Ian Huntley's face was everywhere in the aftermath of the murder and during his trial, but it was difficult to equate his young, unremarkable face with the horror of what he had done. In the absence of external marks of depravity, there is a desire to supply them, to place the wolf's mask over the expressionless features as a confirmation of a loss of human identity.

The names that survive in the dreadful tales we tell are significant. So far at least, Jessica Chapman and Holly Wells are as much part of the public consciousness as Ian Huntley. Few people, though, know the names of the victims of Fred and Rosemary West. We still vividly recall the names, Ian Brady and Myra Hindley, but not the names of the children they killed. The fact that we remember Sarah Payne rather than her murderer, Roy Whiting, is in large part due to Sarah's mother, Sara Payne, who not only made repeated pleas on television for her daughter's return, but went on to campaign on behalf of 'Sarah's Law', a register, based on Megan's Law in the United States, which would inform parents if a paedophile was living nearby. In the *Observer* interview, Barbara Ellen asked if the intention behind Sarah's Law was 'an attempt to wrest some good from bad'. She wanted to do something positive, Sara Payne said, and she wanted her daughter to be remembered. 'I don't want her to become a statistic, and people look at her face and think, "Who's that?". As it stands, nobody's forgotten her name or her face.'

Sara Payne's decision to tell her daughter's story, and her own story as a mother, is in stark contrast to the silence of Jessica's and Holly's parents. That it is Sara Payne's story, rather than her husband's or her children's, is clear from the *Observer* interview. 'They all have their own perspective and I'm sure their story would be almost a different story', she said. Through the book, and the various interviews she has given, we know far more about Sara Payne than we do about the Chapmans or the Wells. Some of it is reminiscent of Nancy in *Frozen*, and, though this confirms Lavery's understanding of the mother's trauma, it is also disturbing because one doesn't really want a fictional account to be too accurate a predictor of such a terrible reality. Three aspects of Barbara Ellen's interview with Sara Payne strike me as particularly relevant to *Frozen*. The first is Sara Payne's description of how she would have felt if her daughter's body hadn't been found. She would, she said, have remained 'stuck in time, always half expecting her daughter to walk through the door'. The second is her sense of loss because she never saw Sarah's remains. The police advised her not to do so because the body was badly decayed and had been partly eaten by animals. However, in her book, she writes: 'Although it may have been the right decision at the time, it left me with an awful nagging doubt in the back of my mind that is still there to this day: was it really Sarah?' (Payne/Gekoski, p. 56). It is when Nancy holds her daughter's bones in *Frozen*, and describes them as beautiful, that at least a partial process of healing can begin. The third aspect of the interview that reminds me of *Frozen* is Sara's decision to stare Roy Whiting in the eye at the trial because she wanted him to know that, though he might scare a small child, he didn't scare her. Control of the gaze of course signifies power. The fact that Ian Huntley and Maxine Carr 'never looked at each other' in court, 'not even when he edged past her on his way to the witness box' (Gerrard), adds to our difficulty in interpreting the relationship between them. In *Frozen*, Nancy twice deliberately looks into the eyes of Ralph, the 'wolf' who killed her daughter. Her assertion of control of the gaze is important in the context of Lavery's retelling of the story of Red Riding Hood.

If *Frozen* is read in relation to *Little Red Riding Hood*, it is apparent that Bryony Lavery has made both a crucial change and an important addition to the story. The addition is the mother's encounter with the 'wolf', the change is in the portrayal of the Red Riding Hood figure. In *The Trials and Tribulations of Little Red Riding Hood*, Jack Zipes writes that *Little Red Riding Hood* is 'the most widespread and notorious fairy tale in the Western world, if not in the entire world'. He defines the reason for this as being 'because rape and violence are at the core of the [story's] history' (Zipes, p. xi). Zipes analyses early, oral versions of the tale, which portray the Red Riding Hood character as a resilient young girl who outwits the wolf, and contrasts these stories with the written versions by Perrault and the Grimm Brothers. Perrault, he writes, 'transformed a hopeful oral tale about the initiation of a young girl into a tragic one of violence in which the girl is blamed for her own violation' (ibid., p. 7). Unlike Perrault, the Grimm Brothers provided the story with a happy ending, but made their protagonist naive and helpless, and also disobedient. Little Red Cap, as she is called in the Grimms' version, 'is *instructed* by her mother to behave and walk a *straight* path to her grandmother's cottage'. She 'promises to obey her mother . . . [but] is tempted by the sensuous delights of the forest' (ibid., p. 34). As a result, she falls into the wolf's clutches, from which she has to be rescued 'first by a male hunter or gamekeeper and, second, by a shrewd grandmother' (ibid., p. 33). Lavery retains, and intensifies, the tragic violence of the Perrault version but absolves Rhona from guilt. This is emphasised from the start of the play because Rhona's visit to her grandmother is entirely in conformity with her mother's wishes. Nancy initially meant to send her elder daughter, Ingrid, to the grandmother's house but Ingrid refused to go and Rhona, the obedient younger daughter, went instead. Ingrid therefore takes on the disobedient aspect of Red Riding Hood and, circumstantially, a degree of blame for what happens. If she had gone when her mother asked her to, Rhona would not have been put in danger. Circumstances also conspire to suggest that Nancy is partially culpable. She is the person who sends Rhona on the journey that leads to her death, and she allows her to go despite the fact that Rhona has been trying out some of Ingrid's make-up. Her adult-looking, 'Great black-rimmed eyes' (Lavery, p. 7) could partly explain why Ralph's attention is drawn to her. There is also the gift that Nancy gives to Rhona for her grandmother, not of food, as in *Little Red Riding Hood,* but of secateurs, which the grandmother needs in order to prune some shrubbery. The fact that this substitute gift contributes to Rhona's murder is chillingly evident when Ralph comments that the secateurs 'turn[ed] out useful' (ibid., p. 11). Another character through whom Lavery extends the sense of guilt that is an element of the Perrault and Grimm versions of the Red Riding Hood story is Agnetha Gottmundsdottir, an Icelandic/American academic who is an expert on serial killers. Nancy, Ralph and Agnetha are the only three characters who appear in the play. Rhona, Ingrid and the grandmother are discussed, but never seen. Agnetha's guilt derives from the fact that she slept with a married colleague two days before he was killed in a car accident. At the end of the play, she asks Nancy whether she should tell the colleague's wife. Nancy replies that, instead, Agnetha should accept what she has done and 'Live with it' (ibid., p. 100). Blaming oneself is pointless, but responsibility for past actions is unavoidable.

Frozen retells the story of Little Red Riding Hood through its dissociation of notions of guilt from the Red Riding Hood character, and through its recreation of the 'wolf' and the 'grandmother'. In Lavery's retelling, Nancy at one point becomes a surrogate Red Riding Hood through an encounter with Ralph, the 'wolf', from which she emerges as the more powerful character. In order to become this new, stronger, version of Red Riding Hood, she has first to undertake an inner journey. After Rhona's disappearance, she becomes involved with an organisation called FLAME that attempts to find children who have disappeared. When Rhona's remains are found, she transfers her energies to campaigning, like Sara Payne, for parents to be informed when a dangerous paedophile is living in the area. Meanwhile, Ingrid transforms herself into a version of the 'shrewd grandmother'. She journeys to Tibet, from where she sends parcels of prayer flags to Nancy. On her return from her travels, she finds her mother in the garden, and the prayer flags on the washing line, waving in the wind. For a moment or two, Nancy fails to recognise the 'thin, thin, brown thing head wrapped in a lot of cloth' (ibid., p. 54) that her daughter has become, but the petition signified by the prayer flags is answered through Ingrid's presence. Like the grandmother in the Brothers Grimm version of *Red Riding Hood*, Ingrid is a source of salvation. She persuades Nancy first to look at Rhona's remains and, later, to visit Ralph in his cell and to tell him that she forgives him for what he did. When Nancy sees her child's skull and takes it in her hands, and experiences its beauty and 'resilience', she is '*flooded* with its *joy*' (p. 61). Sound effects are an important element of the play, and the musical notes of birds singing in a summer garden express aurally what is happening inside Nancy.

Nancy's visit to Ralph in his prison cell reimagines, and, at least to some small degree, redeems Rhona's abduction by Ralph. In *The Trials and Tribulations of Little Red Riding Hood,* Jack Zipes analyses illustrations of the encounter between Red Riding Hood and the wolf, which he defines as 'the scene of transgression' (Zipes, p. 359). A key illustration he focuses on is Gustave Doré's 1862 version of the meeting in the wood, which depicts a child-sized Red Riding Hood standing next to a huge wolf. The wolf's head is turned away, but Red Riding Hood seems to be staring directly into his eyes. It is a beautifully created image, but it is also disturbing because of the apparent complicity between the girl and the beast. Zipes interprets it in terms of 'seduction' and 'intimacy' (ibid., p. 357). The unseen, but potent, gaze is erotic, charged with the mutual desire of Red Riding Hood and the wolf. Zipes proceeds to examine other illustrations of Red Riding Hood and the wolf in the Perrault, Grimm and later versions of the story. In some, desire again appears to be mutual. In others, the wolf's gaze seems to devour the girl.

'All the better to eat you with', the wolf famously replies when Red Riding Hood comments on his disturbingly long teeth. Eating in the context of the devouring gaze has strongly sexual connotations, and Rhona's encounter with Ralph in *Frozen* leads to the child's rape and murder. Red Riding Hood also remarks on the size of the wolf's eyes, to which the wolf responds that they enable him to see her more clearly. However, when Nancy meets Ralph in the prison cell, *she* is the character who controls the gaze. She looks intently at him twice. The first time he returns her gaze, but the second time he looks away. Looking is significant throughout the scene. The two characters meet under the watchful eye of a prison guard, and intermittently glance at him, while he monitors them. Nancy has brought some photographs of Rhona with her to show to Ralph, and to try to get him to see the child as a real person who experienced terror and pain during the assault. By means of the photographs, 'Red Riding Hood', the child-victim, is referred to even though she isn't present. Her on-stage representative is Nancy, who plays out, with Ralph, a new version of the off-stage scene of transgression that led to Rhona's rape and death. As in the illustrations of Red Riding Hood's meeting with the wolf that Zipes analyses, the nature of the look is crucial. Lavery writes that, when Ralph tries to look away the second time that Nancy stares at him, 'she holds his gaze' (Lavery, p. 83). When eventually he breaks away from her, she touches his arm, and her gesture and gaze, which are both forgiving and devoid of sexual implication, create an alternative scene in contrast to the earlier one between Ralph and Rhona.

Like Red Riding Hood, therefore, the 'wolf' is re-imagined in *Frozen*. The audience learns details of his abused childhood and this gives him a history. More importantly, his encounter with Nancy leads to a glimmering of understanding on Ralph's part of the pain he caused Rhona – and this allows the wolf mask to slip and the human features behind it to take at least partial form. Like Nancy, Ralph begins an inner journey of transformation, but he experiences remorse in the form of physical anguish and commits suicide rather than bear it any longer. He hangs himself, and his final words as he is dying recall his encounter with Rhona, and place the burden of guilt for the child's death squarely on his shoulders. When he met the little girl, he forced her to look at, and succumb to him by repeating the word 'Hello' over and over until she returned the greeting. Earlier, Nancy had included the word 'Hell' (the first four letters of 'Hello') in her description of sending Rhona to her grandmother's house. Her two daughters had been arguing, she explained, and, when she intervened, Ingrid claimed that Nancy loved Rhona best. In irritation, Nancy retorted that she didn't love any of her family. 'They can all go to hell for all I care', she added (ibid., p. 7). Though her words are not seriously meant, the 'Hell'/'Hello' connection becomes established therefore in relation to both Ralph and Nancy, and this adds to a sense that Nancy is partly to blame for Rhona's disappearance. As Ralph is dying, however, he recapitulates his greeting to Rhona. He chokes out the word 'Hello' three times, but the fourth time he only gets as far as 'Hell. . .' (ibid., p. 96), thus establishing the guilt of the 'Hello'/'Hell' link solely as his, not Nancy's.

His final utterance is 'He...', which could be the beginning of 'Hello', or 'Hell', or even of 'Heaven'.

For a large number of reviewers, Lavery's reimagined 'wolf' was a particular strength of the play in performance. A few found Nancy's forgiveness of Ralph unconvincing, but the more general view was expressed by Madeleine North in the *Independent on Sunday*, who described *Frozen* as 'a brave and vital attempt to tackle [a] subject' usually viewed 'in the context of lynch mobs and throwing away the key' (7.7.02). Though she humanises the wolf and reassigns culpability, Lavery does leave one aspect of her source tale unchanged, and that is Red Riding Hood's status as victim. Most of the seen, and unseen, characters in the play go on emotional journeys. Ralph starts out on an inner journey. Agnetha, the *'psychiatric* explorer' of the 'Arctic frozen sea that is... the criminal brain' (Lavery, pp. 34–5), is an actual as well as an emotional traveller. Unlike Sarah Payne's mother, Nancy holds her daughter's bones, and this is an important signpost on her emotional journey. As well as being a reworking of a 'nasty modern fairy tale', *Frozen* is, as I have stressed, like *The Memory of Water*, a mother's story. The entire action of *The Memory of Water* takes place in wintertime, and, for Mary, even at the end of the play, it is still a long way from an emotional spring. Nancy's story begins and ends in sunshine. When the audience first sees her, she is in her garden after sending Rhona off to her grandmother's with the secateurs. The passage of time in the years after Rhona goes missing is marked by the sounds of clocks, bells and New Year fireworks, and the beginning of Nancy's slow release from a frozen inner world of grief by the noise of ice floes cracking and starting to break up. The last scene takes place at Ralph's funeral, which both Nancy and Agnetha attend, and, in the final moments of the play, the 'sun breaks through' (ibid., p. 101). Rhona's journey to her grandmother's house, however, remains, like Sarah Payne's, forever incomplete. Like the vanished images of Holly Wells and Jessica Chapman, and like Sarah Payne – seen running across a field at one moment, then gone the next – she evokes the irreversibility of loss. The lock-up shed where Rhona's remains are found, along with those of other murdered children, is razed to the ground – as was the house where Ian Huntley killed Jessica and Holly. The erasure of the shed is an important milestone along Nancy's inner journey, but what this fact emphasises is that the journey *is* hers, not Rhona's. Except in the memories of those who loved her, and in photographs, and through her bones, Rhona is 'present' only by her absence.

The Lovely Bones

Absence, photographs, bones and the link between erasure and the site of a child's death all play important roles in a powerful novel that was published in 2002, the same year as the revival of *Frozen*. Alice Sebold's *The Lovely Bones* is in some ways fascinatingly similar to *Frozen*, and in others very different. Both texts tell the story of a murdered girl, but in *The Lovely Bones* the dead girl has a voice. She is the narrator of the novel, which begins with the words: 'My name was Salmon, like the fish; first name, Susie. I was fourteen when I was murdered on December 6, 1973.' In contrast to *Frozen*, therefore, where the child is a passive victim and a signifier of loss, from the beginning of *The Lovely Bones* absence is countered by presence. The relationship that the book goes on to establish between absence and presence provides its central dynamic. Susie tells her story from the vantage point of her heaven. Here, she remembers what happened to her, and also re-members (puts together again) the body that her killer chopped into bits. In her role as narrator she is aided by Ruth, a school friend whom she encounters as her 'soul shriek[s] out of Earth' (Sebold., p. 36), heavenwards, at the moment of her body's dismemberment. The meeting with Susie's ghost haunts Ruth for the rest of her life, but it is a haunting she welcomes. Though she realises this only gradually, it is Ruth's task to seek out the places where women and young girls have been murdered and write down what she senses of their stories in her journal. When she grows up, she moves to New York, where, day after day, she walks around the city, alert for the moment when she will know that she is standing where an act of violence took place. Hands tightening around a neck. A body falling down a flight of steps. A little girl in a dress with an old-fashioned lace collar straying towards the bushes in Central Park.

Ruth, like Susie, makes present what is absent. Susie watches her family on Earth and links the narrative of her death with their continuing stories. Ruth reclaims lost moments and past brutalities – lost because they were unseen and unrecorded. In alleyways and dark corners she becomes a kind of spectral camera, capturing mental snapshots of the dead, which she then recreates verbally in her journal. Ruth's 'photographic' function is a further connection with her murdered friend. Immediately after telling the reader her name and the essential facts of her death, Susie refers to herself in relation to 'newspaper photos of missing girls' (ibid., p. 5). She had also discovered the pleasures of taking photographs during her short time on Earth. In photograph after photograph of her parents and siblings, she practised the skills of perspective and the framing of images that she would need as the eye/I of the story she would tell after her death. In her ghostly visits to Earth, Susie resembles a photographic negative, of which Ruth can at times be seen as the finished print. Ruth, however, inhabits a blurred territory on the edges of life and death and it is often difficult to define which of the two girls most resembles the print, and which the negative. Near the end of the book, in a reversal of their roles in the encounter at the time of Susie's death, Ruth, the ghost-watcher, leaves her body and Susie enters it in order to return briefly to Earth. Susie does this in order to meet up once more with a boy called Ray Singh, whom she fell in love with before she died. At school, both Ruth and Ray were largely isolated from their fellow pupils, Ruth because of her strangeness and Ray because his more exotic background made him seem alien to the other teenagers. Each of them loved Susie, and this unites them in a brief, awkward, physical relationship and an enduring friendship. As adults, they revisit the Pennsylvanian town where they grew up and where Susie died. Though neither of them knows this, Mr Harvey, Susie's murderer, is undertaking a macabre pilgrimage to the sites where he killed his victims, and, when Ruth sees Mr Harvey, she is also able to see the occupants of his car: the bodies of women in 'blood-colored gowns' (ibid., p. 299). The shock causes her to collapse, and her spirit struggles free of her body, leaving it available as a temporary home for Susie.

When she inhabits Ruth's body, Susie feels for one last time the 'marvelous weight' of being earth-bound and therefore human (ibid., p. 301). She makes love with Ray and assuages the yearning that has possessed her since the time she kissed him. She learns, too, the anguish of being in love, 'the helplessness of being alive, the dark bright pity of being human' (ibid., p. 309). When Ruth returns to her body, Susie leaves the Earth for the last time. What she leaves behind her are memories, with Ray and Ruth, and with her beloved and loving family. At the end of the book, before she relinquishes her narrative voice, Susie defines the significance of the absence her death created. Around this absence 'the lovely bones' have grown, 'the connections – sometimes tenuous, sometimes made at great cost, but often magnificent – that happened after [she] was gone'. The 'events that [her] death wrought', the slow, agonising attempts by her family to continue to live, were 'the bones of a body' gradually becoming 'whole' (ibid., p. 320).

Erasure – the dark heart of the book – is finally illuminated by Susie's sister Lindsey and her husband Sam. Absence, in the form of erasure, is linked to Mr Harvey, who kills Susie in a dugout he has made in a field and then buries her body in a sinkhole (an abandoned mine that has collapsed). The strange dugout, which he has transformed into an underground room, complete with a battery-powered lamp, mirror, razor and shaving cream, is part of Mr Harvey's disturbing connection with houses, places that should signify safety but here denote the opposite. His hobby is making doll's houses. He also constructs weird, house-like structures, including a bridal tent, in his garden. After murdering Susie, he takes her body to his home prior to disposing of it, and her blood seeps on to, and stains, his garage floor. When he returns near the end of the book, he sees Lindsey through the upstairs window of her family home, and, as he watches her, the remaining traces of Susie and his other victims leave the house in which he once lived. They move towards Mr Harvey and join the blood-soaked occupants of his car whom Ruth glimpses shortly afterwards. Their departure from Mr Harvey's old home breaks the connection between houses, decay and erasure that he had established, and Ruth is implicitly involved in the link between restoration and birth that Lindsey and Sam forge instead. One night, Lindsey and Sam take refuge from a thunderstorm in a deserted house. It is in a ruinous state and at first seems sinister, but, as the young people explore it, they fall in love with it. It turns out that Ruth's father is the house's owner and he lets them live there in return for renovating it. The importance of their loving restoration of the house is underlined when Lindsey gives birth to a little girl whom they name Abigail Suzanne, or 'Little Susie' as her Aunt Susie in heaven calls her.

At the end of the novel, therefore, on Earth presence replaces absence. Narrator, Susie Salmon, moves to a 'wide wide Heaven', a place of *'comfort'*, but also a place without stories or claims (ibid., p. 325). The final lines of the book relate the discovery of a charm bracelet she was wearing at the time of her death. As the man who found the bracelet fingers the mud-encrusted charms, the 'tiny bike . . . ballet shoe . . . flower basket and . . . thimble', his wife remarks, 'This little girl's grown up by now'. 'Almost. Not quite. I wish you all a long and happy life', Susie adds, before she disappears forever (ibid., p. 328). The story Sebold tells in *The Lovely Bones* takes place in the space of 'Almost. Not quite', the junction between past and future – as Susie and Ruth meet in the intersection of death and life. Like *Frozen*, *The Lovely Bones* is about the need to let go of the dead and the near impossibility of doing so. The fact that the dead child is the storyteller in the novel makes it hard also for the reader to let go at the close of the book.

The Pillowman

From a story narrated in the first person by the victim of a paedophilic killer, I want to turn finally in this chapter to Martin McDonagh's award-winning play *The Pillowman*, which premiered at the Cottesloe Theatre on 13 November 2003 – just over a month before Ian Huntley was convicted of the killing of Holly Wells and Jessica Chapman. At the start of *The Pillowman,* a writer called Katurian is being interrogated about a recent spate of child-murders, the horrible details of which, it transpires, are similar to incidents in his stories. The author of the murders eventually proves to be not Katurian, but his retarded younger brother Michal, who was repeatedly and hideously abused by his parents from the age of seven, though Katurian was kindly treated by them. Michal blames his actions on the influence of his brother's stories, and the play explicitly and implicitly raises a number of questions about the relationship between art and life and the responsibility of the artist. In Paul Taylor's words in the *Independent* (17.11.03): 'Can art (including McDonagh's own) corrupt and cause damage? Is it parasitic on suffering and does its survival count for more than human life?' Though Paul Taylor didn't mention Huntley's trial, the Soham murders clearly gave a topical urgency to these questions, and to Katurian's words when he asks his interrogator, 'Are you trying to say I shouldn't write stories with child-killings in because in the real world there are child-killings?' (McDonagh, p. 26). One thing Katurian's question fails to take into account, however, is the sick humour that is an integral part of most of the stories. In *Frozen,* we are left to guess at the precise details of Rhona's murder; in *The Pillowman,* not only are we provided with all the gruesome facts, but, furthermore, they are presented in the style of a cartoon or a horror comic. For many reviewers the play's style – aptly described by Carole Woddis in her review for the *Herald* of 19 November 2003 as 'Brothers Grimm rehashed by Quentin Tarantino' – appears to have been its greatest strength. The dexterous twists and turns, and the shocking images were sufficient in themselves, even if the points they were making were not entirely clear. A few reviewers considered that the stomach-churning humour sharpened the sense of horror, but others probed beneath the surface style and found a disturbing emptiness. On 14 November, in the *Guardian*, Michael Billington wrote that the 'moral dilemma' of whether Katurian's and his brother's lives should be sacrificed 'to ensure the preservation of his stories . . . never acquires dramatic momentum'. This was partly because the totalitarian state in which the play is set lacks credibility, and partly because Katurian's unswerving belief in the 'sanctity of literature' robs the play of an important source of potential conflict. Paul Taylor went further in the *Independent*, describing McDonagh as 'a dramatist with extraordinary technical talent [but] a disturbingly defective moral sense'.

The tone of *The Pillowman* is undeniably offensive, but, in my view, despite the dizzying and confusing array of theatrical skills, the play has a clear message and it is one that is notably more perturbing than McDonagh's style. This message is stated most clearly through the central story of 'The Pillowman', which begins in the guise of a 'once upon a time' fairy story and develops into a nightmare. The eponymous character is a huge man entirely made of 'fluffy pink pillows' (McDonagh, p. 43), apart from the teeth in his 'smiley mouth' which are 'Little white pillows' (ibid.). The Pillowman has 'to look soft and safe' (ibid., p. 44) because his job is to visit people who are on the verge of committing suicide and take them back to a point in their childhoods before the dreadful things that have made them so unhappy began to happen. He then attempts to persuade the children to kill themselves and so to avoid future suffering, which they will anyway only be able to escape through death. In a twist at the end of the story, the Pillowman meets himself as a little Pillowboy, and, when the Pillowboy realises how unhappy the Pillowman's job makes him, he sets fire to himself. His sacrifice rescues the Pillowman from his horrible task of persuading children to kill themselves, but unfortunately it also resurrects all the dead children, who then have to go on to lead their ghastly lives and die quite alone, without the kindly Pillowman to help them on their way. The Pillowboy's sacrifice was pointless.

Near the end of the play, there is a further twist to the story. When Katurian learns that Michal has killed the children, he smothers his brother with a pillow in order to save him from being executed. Katurian himself *is* executed, but after his death he '*slowly gets to his feet*', takes off the hood he has been made to wear, revealing '*his bloody, bullet-shattered head*', and, '*in lieu of a prayer for his brother*', comes up with 'a footnote' to 'The Pillowman' story (ibid., p. 102). In this version, the Pillowman visits Michal before his parents begin to torture him and suggests that Michal should commit suicide in order to avoid all the horror that is to come. Michal refuses the offer because, if he dies, Katurian will never hear him being tortured and may never write his stories. He decides to 'just keep things the way they are' – because he thinks he's 'going to really like [his] brother's stories' (ibid., p. 103). In this footnote to 'The Pillowman' story, it is not simply a matter, therefore, of whether or not it is acceptable to write about child-killings despite the fact that child-killings occur in the real world. The usual relationship between reality and fiction is overturned, with the result that the former becomes subservient to the latter. Art isn't just 'parasitic' on real suffering, it legitimates it.

It could be argued that Michal's decision is determined by his terrible childhood, but the play as a whole endorses a belief in the pre-eminent importance of stories, and its final moments underline this. After smothering Michal, Katurian claims that *he* killed the children. He does this in the belief that, in return, his interrogators will preserve his stories for posterity. In the play's final speech, Katurian explains that the 'story was going to finish in fashionably downbeat mode' with Michal being abused and Katurian writing the stories, 'only to have them burned from the world by a bulldog of a policeman' (ibid.). What actually happened, however, was that, instead of burning the stories, the policeman sealed them away with Katurian's case file, where they would 'remain unopened for fifty-odd years'. This 'ruined the writer's fashionably downbeat ending, but was . . . somehow . . . more in keeping with the spirit of the thing' (ibid., p. 104). In other words, unlike the Pillowboy's sacrifice, Michal's was far from pointless. By choosing to stay alive and suffer, Michal enabled the creation of Katurian's stories, the preservation of which is the essential point – 'the spirit of the thing'. I find this notion shocking, not because of the value – or lack of it – of the stories, but because the belief that the creation of stories justifies real suffering never seriously seemed to be questioned.

I am aware that this may be an over-literal response. Given the frequent narrative twists and turns that precede it, the ending of *The Pillowman* perhaps contains a measure of irony – a recognition that, though life may be more important than art, the latter tends to survive while individual lives end unnoticed. One has to work pretty hard though to arrive at this, or a satisfactorily equivalent, explanation. The problem, as Michael Billington noted, is the play's lack of either a credible context or a convincing opposition to Katurian's belief in the 'sanctity of literature'. And, without these elements, one is left with a shiny carapace surrounding a moral vacuum.

Like *The Pillowman*, Caryl Churchill's *The Skriker* (the first play to be considered in the next chapter) is centrally concerned with stories and storytelling. In contrast to *The Pillowman*, however, these stories have a clear moral purpose. The majority of the other Churchill plays I address in Chapter 6 resemble *The Skriker* in that they are about children who are damaged in one way or another. Though this damage originated in the past, it has profound consequences for the present, and sometimes also for the future.

6

The Skriker's progeny

In his review of *Far Away* for the *Financial Times* (4 December 2000), Alastair Macaulay described Caryl Churchill as 'the most original playwright in Britain'. Churchill's combination of technical experimentation and acute sensitivity to current social and political concerns has frequently been remarked upon. One innovative aspect of her work that has received little attention, however, is the radical use she makes of two traditional narrative forms that I have explored in earlier chapters, namely the fairy story and the whodunnit. *The Skriker, Far Away* and *A Number*, all of which are discussed in this chapter, rely on the in-built expectations within these forms of an unambiguous resolution of difficulties, which Churchill is then able to subvert. In *The Skriker,* she reconfigures fairy stories in order to create her own dramatic parable about the imminence of ecological disaster. *Far Away* and *A Number* utilise the apparent simplicities of the whodunnit to explore complex notions of culpability. In *A Number,* this results in an investigation into the nature of both parental responsibility and human identity. *Far Away* skilfully manipulates elements of both the whodunnit and the fairy tale to evoke a terrifying vision of a world at war with itself.

Churchill's use of the whodunnit format, at least in *Far Away,* has something in common with Priestley's in *An Inspector Calls* – though Churchill is both more ambitious in scope and pessimistic in her conclusions. Churchill also resembles Priestley in her fascination with the malleability of theatre time. This is particularly evident in the use of time warps in *The Skriker,* and the exploration of the motif of 'return' in *A Number.* 'Return' is also the key feature of *Heart's Desire*, the first part of the 1997 double bill, *Blue Heart.* Both *Blue Heart* plays explore what could be termed 'the disappearing present moment'. 'Return' is both the theme and the mode of action of *Heart's Desire*, and the consequence is that the focus is always on anticipation, never on the 'now'. The loss of the present moment is even more evident in *Blue Kettle*, the second *Blue Heart* play, and, here, it is directly linked to the loss of children. Endangered children feature in many of Churchill's plays. However, the progeny referred to in the title of the chapter are not actual children. They are plays: *Far Away, A Number, Hotel* and *Blue Heart*. I have grouped them together because of the debt each of them owes to Churchill's 1994 play, *The Skriker*.

Time traps

If I were to choose one character to epitomise the major formal and thematic elements of Caryl Churchill's plays, it would be the eponymous protagonist of *The Skriker,* which opened in the Cottesloe auditorium of the National Theatre on 27 January 1994. Brilliantly realised in performance by Kathryn Hunter, the character is simultaneously a storyteller, a shapeshifter and a death portent. Like its author it skilfully manipulates time, and, like her, it experiments with language. The stories it tells are strange, disjointed versions of fairy tales, full of magic time warps and the dangers of eating enchanted food. Dancing in a bluebell wood or eating a plum in an orchard lead to people being tricked into a sinister underworld where fairy time bears no correlation to human time. 'Never eat a fruit or puck luck pluck a flower if you want to get back', the Skriker warns (Churchill, *The Skriker*, p. 3). In one story the Skriker persuades a bridegroom to hold a lighted candle until the flame goes out. The result is that, while time for the bridegroom remains in the present, a hundred years elapse in the world the rest of the bridal party inhabit. When he finds himself once again in *this* world, he eats a piece of bread and, like the bread, he becomes 'crumbs crumbling to dust panic' (ibid., p. 4). Food is the most disturbing element in the Skriker's stories because what should give life represents contamination and danger. In some stories, human beings – and, most alarmingly of all, children – become food. A monstrous creature called Bloody Bones hides in a dark cupboard 'where he sits on piles of bloody [bones] . . . and chews whom he likes. Dollop gollop fullup' (ibid., p. 2). The Skriker gloats about getting hold of a human child: a 'snap crackle poppet to bake and brew' (ibid.). A Dead Child describes how her 'mother killed [her] and put [her] in pies', then her father ate her and her 'brothers and sisters . . . picked [her] bones' (ibid., p. 19). Images of endangered children proliferate in the play. In the human world the Skriker tries repeatedly to get its hands on a child. In the end it succeeds and, through this, Churchill brings together motifs of time warps, contaminated food, endangered children and the damaged human and physical world.

Damage, to human beings and to the planet, has been a preoccupation of Churchill's from the beginning. Her earliest known play, *Downstairs*, which was given a student production at Oxford in 1958, is in some ways an embryonic version of *The Skriker*. Like *The Skriker*, this one-act play is set in both an upper and a lower world, in this case the clean, tidy flat where the Johnson family live, and downstairs, where a character called Catherine lives with her bedridden grandmother and retarded younger brother. The Johnson father and son are fascinated by the unconventional downstairs world, but the mother thinks that the downstairs people are dirty and feckless and she is determined to keep upstairs safe from their influence. The son is in love with Catherine, but his mother goads him to such a pitch of anger and jealousy that he kills her. The play ends with the mother's realisation that now they will never be able to free themselves from 'downstairs'. Its 'dark stain' will infect their lives for ever. In *The Skriker*, downstairs has become the sinister fairy underworld and upstairs the human world, and the connection between them is clear from the beginning of the play. The fairies are a manifestation of human pollution of the planet. 'They poison me in my rivers of blood poisoning', the Skriker complains (ibid., p. 4). Damage is endemic in both worlds. The Skriker itself is representative of damage and, when it enters the human world, it both seeks out and instigates further damage. The first person it latches on to in the human world is a young woman who has killed her baby, and, as the play progresses, violence and ecological disaster multiply. The resulting devastation had a pre-echo in Churchill's 1971 radio play, *Not Not Not Not Not Enough Oxygen* (which was also staged at the Royal Court Theatre in 2002, in conjunction with *A Number*). *Not . . . Enough Oxygen* is set in a London tower block in the year 2010. Outside, the air is thick and acrid with pollution. There are no birds and almost all green places have disappeared. Even opening the windows is dangerous, and Vivian, whose gasping way of speaking is the motivation for the play's title, has to spray oxygen around her room in order to breathe. News of wars and the devastation caused by famines seeps into the room via the television screen. Reviewing the 2002 production in the *Guardian* on 3 October 2002, Michael Billington remarked that Churchill's depiction of 'cosmic chaos' was reminiscent of her 2000 play, *Far Away*. In contrast to *Far Away*, and *The Skriker*, however, damage in *Not . . . Enough Oxygen*, though perturbing, remains relatively distant and muted. In *The Skriker* and *Far Away* it is inescapable.

Just before the Skriker erupts into the human world, at the end of its long opening monologue, it explains its reason for doing so: 'Revengeance is gold mine, sweet', it tells the audience. 'An open grave must be fed up you go like dust in the sunlight of heart . . . Ready or not here we come quick or dead of night night sleep tightarse' (*The Skriker*, p. 5). By laying waste to the human world the Skriker and its fellow fairies return damage to its source. Despite the violent urgency of its desire for revenge, however, this is not the Skriker's only motivation for the destruction it causes. The other is neediness, and it is the two together, a huge and unassuagable longing and an all-encompassing quest for vengeance, that create the endlessly proliferating damage. The Skriker's neediness is aggressive, unpleasant and implacable. The more it is denied, the more powerful it grows. In the various human shapes into which the Skriker transforms itself it insistently demands love. 'Do I smell?' it asks in the guise of a derelict woman. 'It's my coat and my cunt. Give us a hug. Nobody gives us a hug' (ibid., p. 11). In the form of a small child, it demands to be cuddled and hits a young pregnant woman called Lily in the stomach out of jealousy of her baby. It is a horrible child, just as the smelly old woman is offensive, but that doesn't lessen its neediness.

In its need and its violent anger, the Skriker is reminiscent of Angie, the disowned and damaged daughter in what is probably Churchill's best-known play, *Top Girls*. Endangered children appear frequently in Churchill's plays. In the 1972 *Owners,* for example, one baby is the subject of a battle over possession, while another dies in a fire. In *Fen* (1983), Becky is tortured by her stepmother. In *Light Shining in Buckinghamshire* (first performed by Joint Stock Theatre Group in September 1976 at the Traverse Theatre, Edinburgh, and revived by the National Theatre in 1997), one woman kills her new-born baby. Another abandons hers because she is starving and unable to make milk to feed it. A butcher castigates his customers for their greed, linking together children and food in a way that prefigures *The Skriker*. Why do they need so much meat? he asks, and his answer is: 'To make fat. And shit. When it could put a little good flesh on children's bones.' They 'cram [themselves] with . . . children's meat', he adds. They cram themselves with 'dead children' (*Churchill Plays*: *One,* p. 228). It is Angie's neediness, however, that makes her the real forerunner of the Skriker. *Top Girls* is sometimes perceived as a play about the difficulty of being both a mother and having a career, but, though this is part of what Churchill explores, *Top Girls* is essentially a critique of capitalism. The play was first performed in 1982, at the Royal Court Theatre, three years after Margaret Thatcher became Prime Minister, and Marlene specifically states her admiration for Thatcherite policies. She doesn't simply fail Angie as a mother, she fails her also as a fellow member of society. When Marlene tells her sister Joyce, who has brought Angie up as if she were her own, that she has no intention of helping anyone who is 'stupid or lazy or frightened', Joyce immediately relates this to Angie. 'What about Angie?' she asks. 'She's stupid, lazy and frightened' (Churchill, *Top Girls*, p. 42). It is important that Angie is not portrayed in performance as being attractive, or indeed particularly likeable. In his review of the 2001 Oxford Stage and Background revival of *Top Girls*, Jeremy Kingston commended the actress, Pascale Burgess', 'halting tiptoe walk [which] gives the essence of Angie's sweetly simple nature' (*The Times*, 25.9.01), but this is a mistaken view of the character. Angie may be simple, but she isn't sweet, and suggesting that she is masks the depth of her neediness. If she were likeable her situation would be less desperate. She might have more chance of getting a job, or a husband – someone to care for her in a way that she is unlikely to be able to care for herself. Angie is like the Skriker – needy, damaged and filled with desire for revenge. Her speech is frequently violent. She fantasises about killing her mother, for example, by whom she appears to mean Joyce. The difference between Angie and the Skriker is that the latter has power. Angie wants to enact vengeance, but can't. The Skriker is Angie transformed into demonic energy, and, once it begins its revenge, it sets up a chain reaction that is unstoppable.

The third adjective Joyce uses to describe Angie, 'frightened', leads me to *The Skriker*'s other major connection with *Top Girls*, and that is Churchill's use of theatrical time. *Top Girls* famously begins with Marlene's celebration of her promotion to managing director of the 'Top Girls' Employment Agency, in the company of a group of fictional and historical female characters. It ends with a further manipulation of time when the final act is revealed to be chronologically the first. The agent of this revelation is a dress that Angie is first seen wearing in act two. Then, it looks old and it is too small for her. In the final act Marlene gives the, now new, dress to Angie as a present, and, when Angie tries it on, it fits. Her earlier appearance in the dress has in chronological time therefore still to take place. While the dress reassembles time, it is Angie's repetition of the word 'Frightening' at the end of the play that underlines the significance of *Top Girls'* temporal structure. After her rejection of the idea of helping anyone who is lazy, stupid or frightened, Marlene begins to settle down on the sofa, where she will spend the night. She is alone when Angie, who had earlier gone to bed, comes into the room. Angie speaks two words, 'Mum?' twice and 'Frightening' also twice, interspersed with comments from Marlene, who tells her that her mother has gone to bed and asks if she has had a bad dream. Whether or not Angie has realised that Marlene is her biological mother is unclear. In act one, scene three, she tells her friend Kit that she thinks that she is her 'aunt's child' and that her 'mother's really [her] aunt' (*Top Girls*, p. 22), so she may have done. The other possibility is that, in her half-awakened state in the semi-darkness, she isn't quite sure who is in the room. The crucial point, however, is that Angie's use of the word 'Frightening' confirms her as one of the people whom Marlene isn't going to help. At the end of act two, Marlene says in relation to Angie: 'She's a bit thick. She's a bit funny . . . She's not going to make it' (ibid., p. 33). What the audience learns at the end of the play is that Marlene's rejection of Angie is made in the context of her earlier refusal to help anybody who is frightened, including her own daughter. Churchill plays with time in *Top Girls* for a clear purpose therefore. Paradoxically, the effect of her reordering of causality and narrative chronology is to stress linearity and, in this way, to show the culpability of the 'top girl' in relation to one of society's 'failures'.

In *The Skriker* it is Churchill's *alter ego*, the protean shapeshifter, who twists and reassembles time, sometimes elongating it, sometimes compressing it. Its stories of time warps in its opening monologue act as a prologue to the further time warps into which it entices first Josie and then her friend Lily. Both young women find themselves in the Underworld, but, whereas no time at all passes by in the human world while Josie is away, hundreds of years pass in Lily's absence. Lily goes into the Underworld because she thinks that this will stop the Skriker pursuing both her baby and Josie. She leaves her baby behind, secure in the belief that it will be safe, because she expects human time to behave in relation to fairy time as it did for Josie. Unfortunately, she recapitulates the fate of the tricked bridegroom in the Skriker's earlier story. She holds a candle the Skriker offers her and stands stock still while the stage darkens round her. When light returns, the baby has vanished and, in its place, is a deformed girl accompanied by an old woman. The pair are Lily's granddaughter and her great- (or possibly great-great) granddaughter), and, to them, Lily appears to be a ghost, 'a ghastly' (*The Skriker*, p. 51). Like the tricked bridegroom, Lily eats some food from the future time, but pollution has made it lethal, and, like the planet, Lily is 'dustbin' (ibid., p. 52).

Josie's and Lily's journeys into the Underworld together form the central story in a play composed of stories. Just as it transforms its own shape to fit the demands of the moment, so the Skriker remakes the stories it tells. In essence, the story of Josie and Lily is the fairy tale known both as *Diamonds and Toads* and *The Kind and Unkind Girls*. This is made clear before Lily and Josie go into the Underworld through their separate meetings with the derelict woman. In the original story an old woman asks a girl to get water for her from a well and, when the girl complies, she is rewarded with flowers and jewels that fall from her mouth. Another girl refuses to help the old woman and is punished when toads hop out of her mouth. In *The Skriker* the old woman in the fairy tale becomes the derelict woman. Lily helps her and finds gold coins in her mouth. Josie, who realises that the derelict woman is really the Skriker, refuses, and meets the same fate as the unkind girl. However, when first Josie and then Lily go into the Underworld, their apparently opposite roles as the unkind and kind girls are shown to be irrelevant. Despite their apparent differences, both young women are tricked by the Skriker, and both try – ineffectually – to protect others from the danger it presents. Josie does this by doing dreadful things in an attempt to prevent the Skriker from doing something worse. She tries 'to keep the Skriker sated seated besotted with gobbets, tossing it giblets, to stop it from wolfing, stop it engulfing' (ibid., p. 49), but she fails. The Skriker cannot be sated because damage is unstoppable. Lily, the more obvious saviour figure, is also powerless. Something more than kind actions is needed if ecological damage is to be prevented from continuing to the point where humanity is destroyed. Many of the Skriker's stories are about trickery, and the allusion to *The Kind and Unkind Girls* story is itself a trick. Josie and Lily aren't opposites. The results of their actions are the same, and, though Josie killed her child and Lily tried to save hers, both children are destroyed.

The Skriker is in some ways reminiscent of Churchill's 1977 play, *Traps*, in which the six characters exist in a variety of permutations of relationships, but each version has validity only while the characters are on stage. When they exit, they re-enter with the same names but different life histories. The action of *Traps* resembles a Mobius strip (a loop with only one surface) that one of the characters makes in the course of the play. When the characters change to a new set of relationships, they have no knowledge that anything different has occurred. There is only the present 'surface', nothing more. Stories in *The Skriker* are similar to the Mobius-strip-world of *Traps*. Twist the loop any way you will, it has only one surface. But, though Lily's and Josie's attempts to thwart the Skriker fail, through her protagonist, Churchill creates a parable that warns of the fateful consequences of contemporary human actions. The retold story of the tricked bridegroom reveals that it is these actions that have contaminated the future food that destroys Lily, and poisons her descendants. The Skriker, Bloody Bones and the other creatures that seek out human prey are monsters of human manufacture. Along with the present, they are also consuming the future. Time in *The Skriker* warps finally into a near void where soon everything will be destroyed.

As I noted at the end of Chapter 5, through its focus on storytelling *The Skriker* invites comparison with Martin McDonagh's *The Pillowman*. *The Pillowman*, however, is about the importance of saving stories, while *The Skriker* is about the need to save the world before it is too late. Michal in *The Pillowman* resembles the Skriker and Angie because, like them, he is rejected and needy, but, whereas Michal is simply subject matter for his brother's stories, the Skriker – the terrifying reincarnation of Angie – *becomes* the storyteller. Rather than handing over its tale to someone else, it tells it, in its own characteristic language, which articulates both its damaged state and the violent nature of its revenge.

The Skriker's distinctive language divided the critics. Judith Mackrell, for example, in the *Independent* (29.1.94) was of the view that the 'language – skittering between sense and nonsense' was 'partly responsible for the play's brilliantly shifting centre of reality', while Irving Wardle in the *Independent on Sunday* (30.1.94) described the supposedly 'magical language' as 'a flop'. The 'punning sentence mutation' reminded him, not of James Joyce, to whom some reviewers had referred, but of Stanley Unwin. The most entertaining, and perhaps perceptive, review was by John Peter in the *Sunday Times* of 6 February 1994. Apparently taking as his model Brecht's *Messingkauf Dialogues*, Peter cast his review in the form of a conversation between a Reader and a Critic. 'You seem bemused. Not your usual cocksure self', the Reader begins, to which the Critic replies hesitantly: 'Yes. No. The thing is, I'm not sure what I saw in the theatre.' The Critic is baffled by a number of aspects of *The Skriker*. Is it a play, or a poem, for example? Eventually, the Reader asks whether not being sure matters and the Critic concedes that uncertainty may in fact be a help rather than a hindrance. The play is, he decides, 'A piece of inspired, organised confusion', the language of which, seemingly 'invented by Bosch', conjures up 'overlapping worlds'. These worlds are unstable because one 'word undermines' another. Peter's review captures very well the way in which Churchill's language constantly reorientates the audience, stopping us in our tracks so that afterwards we might ask: What have I just seen, and what significance might it have?

Through fragmented, yet powerfully evocative, language, Churchill tells stories in *The Skriker* of an endangered present and a cancelled future. Her depiction of children in *The Skriker* can, as I have noted, be traced back to that of other children in her earlier plays, and also forward to references to children in *Blue Heart, Far Away* and *A Number* – plays which can themselves be seen as dramatic descendants of *The Skriker*. Like *The Skriker*, they are about lost or damaged children. To a greater or lesser degree, they also experiment with language, and sometimes also with time. *Far Away, The Skriker*'s most disturbing progeny, is, like its parent play, a dramatic parable that warns of the imminence of disaster.

Blue Heart and Hotel

Blue Heart consists of two separate one-act plays, *Heart's Desire* and *Blue Kettle*. Though written separately, they were performed in tandem in 1997 by Out of Joint Theatre Company. Like many of Churchill's earlier plays, including *Top Girls* but not *The Skriker*, the production was directed by Max Stafford-Clark. *Heart's Desire* is a kind of theatrical joke. A mother and father are awaiting the arrival from Australia of their daughter (the father's heart's desire) in the company of the girl's aunt. They are engaged in ordinary, domestic activities, putting on a sweater, for example, or laying a table, but 'the action keeps stopping, rewinding and restarting, swerving off down bizarre by-ways and absurdist cul-de-sacs' (*Time Out*, 1.10.97). Without warning, the stage is suddenly invaded by completely unrelated characters. At one point, a noisy horde of children dashes in and then disappears into cupboards. At another, a couple of gunmen burst in and kill everybody. The most extraordinary visitor is a ten-foot-tall bird, described by some reviewers as an emu and by others as an ostrich. It is as though the safe domestic world has been invaded by a theatrical form of a computer virus. The characters unexpectedly make disturbing or nonsensical revelations. The mother announces that she has always hated the father and is leaving, for example, or the father fantasises about eating himself. After each interruption the action reverts to an earlier point in the basic scenario, and the characters behave as if nothing untoward had happened. At some points, the dialogue is played at double speed or in reduced form, but the characters meticulously repeat their earlier intonations and gestures.

Blue Kettle, which was performed after *Heart's Desire*, is a more obviously serious piece, in which a character called Derek pretends to four different mothers that he is the son they gave up for adoption forty years earlier. One of them, Mrs Plant, has the first words of the play. 'I can't speak', she says, in relation to the revelation that Derek has just made to her. As though this inability gradually infects the whole play, the dialogue is invaded by the words 'blue' and 'kettle', which first substitute for other words and then replace language entirely, until, at the end of the play, only the consonants t b k and l are left. Writing in the *Independent* on 25 September 1997, Paul Taylor commented that, far from getting in the way, this 'linguistic tricksiness . . . takes us to the heart of [Churchill's] theme by, as it were, performing it on the level of language: substitution and loss in a play about substitution and loss'. Derek's motivation for pretending to be the women's sons never really becomes clear. He claims at one point to be doing it for money, but never actually makes any money from conning them. There are hints that the affection he receives from the women is a substitute for the missing affection from his mother, who has lost her memory, but this remains on the level of suggestion. For a time Derek becomes for the mothers a substitute for their lost sons, but this ceases to be the case when they learn that he has tricked them. The substitute replaces the vanished original and then that too is lost. *Blue Kettle* is all about loss. Lost children and memories are subsumed into language and then that too disappears.

Disappearance is also the central theme of *Two Nights*, the second part of *Hotel*, which premiered at the Schauspielhaus, Hannover, on 15 April 1997. As it turns out 1997 was a good year for productions of Churchill's work. A revival of *Light Shining in Buckinghamshire* opened at the Cottesloe Theatre after a tour at the end of the previous year. There was a revival of *Cloud Nine* at the Old Vic and a new play, *This is a Chair*, opened at the Duke of York's Theatre in June 1997. *Hotel*, which transferred to the Place Theatre, London, was performed by thirteen singers, two dancers, and three musicians. Caryl Churchill provided the text and Orlando Gough wrote the music. The choreography and direction were by Ian Spink. The designer was Lucy Bevan.

The setting for the first part of *Hotel*, which is entitled *Eight Rooms*, represents eight identical hotel bedrooms superimposed upon one another. Six couples, plus two unattached characters, arrive to spend the night. A fifteenth performer portrays a TV and a ghost. Though they inhabit the same onstage space, sometimes sharing the bed, they don't acknowledge each other's existence. All the dialogue is sung. One couple is silent and the performers who play this couple dance the central protagonists of *Two Nights*, who spend different nights in the same room. The rest of the performers become a chorus who sing fragments from a diary 'written by someone who becomes invisible' (Churchill's Introduction to *Hotel*). These fragments are the only record that remains of bizarre disappearing acts. A magician makes a tower vanish from the bottom upwards, for example. A spell is cast to make someone disappear, while someone else runs away from a party and becomes invisible. The piece ends with a conjunction that connects with nothing: 'held my hand up to the light and' (Churchill, *Two Nights*, p. 26). This lack of connection is symptomatic of both parts of *Hotel*. In *Caryl Churchill*, Elaine Aston describes *Hotel*'s 'aesthetic' as one 'of urban alienation and isolation' (Aston, p. 108). The tone of *Two Nights*, she writes, is dark, 'the music . . . oppressive and sinister', while 'the dancers encode narratives of . . . desolation' (ibid., p. 110). Isolation and desolation also characterise *Blue Kettle*, and, to some degree, *Heart's Desire*. Aston defines *Heart's Desire* as 'a "parody" of the family and reunion motif', but adds that the reunion neither advances the play's action nor leads to 'closure'. Instead, 'it engages in a process of endless deferral' (ibid., p. 114). The whole of *Heart's Desire* is anticipatory. The characters wait – for the arrival of the heart's desire. The weird intrusions interrupt this waiting, but they don't develop in any meaningful way. To quote Aston again, *Heart's Desire* resembles *Traps*, in that it is 'caught in a loop'. However, while *Traps* can be interpreted as reaching a resolution, *Heart's Desire* goes nowhere. It occurs in 'a time of waiting and also of forgetting; an eternal present in which characters cannot make sense of the moment they are in by referring to a past or projecting forward to a future' (ibid.). It is the connection that *Heart's Desire* makes between deferral and this 'eternal present' that seems to me instructive in relation to *Blue Kettle*. I have already likened *Heart's Desire* to a theatrical joke, and this is probably its strongest characteristic. It has a few relatively serious moments, but, essentially, it is a spoof. It takes an important catalyst in western drama, the return of a key character, and empties it of meaning. Susy does eventually arrive, but to no purpose. She comes on stage, is greeted with delight, and then the dialogue reverts to the beginning. The last line is the same as the first, the loop continues.

Though it has perhaps serious implications, *Heart's Desire* is very funny, whereas in *Blue Kettle* the laughter gradually disappears along with everything else. While a major element of dramatic structure is rendered absurd in *Heart's Desire*, *Blue Kettle* questions theatre even more fundamentally. Along with memory (the past), language, and motivation, another vital theatrical ingredient – the present moment (the 'now') – also vanishes. While *Arcadia* and *Copenhagen* seek, and eventually find, the instantaneous moment, the '*nunc instantis*', *Blue Kettle* eradicates it. John

Peter wrote in his review of *Blue Kettle* in the *Sunday Times:* 'Language is a function of time (as you speak, time passes)' (28.9.97). Along with the obliteration of language in *Blue Kettle*, time also vanishes; and the act of theatre, which is so indebted to time, more or less vanishes with it. True, something remains. Mrs Plant's longing for her lost son lingers in the air, but, compared, for example, to the powerful evocation of loss in *Frozen* or *The Memory of Water*, this is a distant grief. Mrs Plant is older than Mary in *The Memory of Water* and Nancy in *Frozen*, and possibly therefore more resigned, but the umbrella title, *Blue Heart*, is well chosen. *Blue Kettle* is, I think, a despairing play even by comparison with *The Skriker*, which after all demonstrates a vigorous belief in the efficacy of dramatic parables. Neither *Blue Kettle* nor *Heart's Desire* shows much evidence of a belief in the power of theatre to contribute to change. They are brittle, uneasy pieces, with, at their centre, the bleakness evoked by the words 'blue heart'.

After the vivid polemic of *The Skriker*, the *Blue Heart* plays convey a sense of getting nowhere, probably that there is nowhere to get. Erasure is not replaced by anything, as it is in *The Memory of Water* or *Frozen*. Storytelling is important in *Frozen* (as it was in the media reportage of the deaths of Holly Wells and Jessica Chapman). In *The Skriker*, though individual stories may be questioned, the parabolic nature of the play affirms the value of storytelling. In *Blue Kettle,* stories are simply fabrications. We don't learn what actually happened to the four mothers' sons, and, as Derek's biological mother is suffering from Alzheimer's Disease, the stories she tells may have no substance in any reality. By contrast, *Far Away*, which was first performed in 2000, demonstrates a re-found belief in the power of stories and, in the main, also of theatre. As she does in *The Skriker*, Churchill questions the validity of some of the stories the characters tell, but the play as a whole powerfully reinforces the importance of stories.

Far Away: adjusting the telescope

Like *The Skriker*, *Far Away,* which opened at the Royal Court Jerwood Theatre Upstairs on 24 November 2000, is a dramatic parable about imminent global disaster. Michael Coveney described it as 'the most astonishing new play of the year . . . about an hour long. And about the end of the world' (*Daily Mail*, 8.12.00). For John Peter in the *Sunday Times* (3.12.00), it was 'terrible', in the 'Yeatsian sense of a terrible beauty . . . a play of Armageddon created by its victims'. For Sam Marlowe in *What's*

On (6.12.00), it was a 'dystopian vision of a world turned against itself ... so filled with horror and disgust that it literally turns the stomach'. Though Churchill's language in *Far Away* at first seems reassuringly normal after *The Skriker* and *Blue Kettle*, this turns out to be a misconception. Yet again, Irving Wardle commented, 'Churchill moves into new territory by inventing new speech habits; in this case, a prosaic acceptance of extreme horror coupled with the old language of middle-class values which lingers on like a twinge in a phantom limb' (*Sunday Telegraph*, 3.12.00).

In addition to its connections with *The Skriker* and *Blue Kettle*, *Far Away* has (as I commented in Chapter 1) noteworthy similarities to Priestley's *An Inspector Calls*. Priestley and Churchill share certain characteristics as dramatists. Both are fascinated by the plasticity of theatre time. Both use theatre to warn about the dangerous consequences of present actions, and, in *An Inspector Calls* and *Far Away*, they do this through an adaptation of the whodunnit format. Priestley's use of the whodunnit is both more straightforward and more hopeful. He includes a detective in his cast list – albeit an other-worldly one – and he builds the action towards a moment of choice that could conceivably alter the future for the better. *Far Away* is more ambiguous. In act one, the audience learns that a crime has been committed, but its precise nature is hard to fathom. In the absence of an Inspector Goole figure, the audience has to try to work out what happened and who is responsible for it. In order to do this, they have not so much to decipher clues as to learn to see things differently.

Like *An Inspector Calls*, *Far Away* was directed by Stephen Daldry and designed by Ian MacNeil, and their staging of *An Inspector Calls* offered a fascinating sidelight on the perspective of events that is gradually established in *Far Away*. When *Far Away* premiered at the Royal Court, *An Inspector Calls* was in performance at the Garrick Theatre, where it had transferred in October 1995. It was still running there on 18 January 2001 when *Far Away* opened at the Albery Theatre in St. Martin's Lane, just a few minutes walk away from the Garrick. Audiences therefore had the opportunity of seeing the two productions in close proximity. A key feature of *An Inspector Calls* was the disparity in size between the set and the actors, so much so that, in her review of *An Inspector Calls* in the *Daily Express*, Maureen Paton described the characters as 'Lilliputians glimpsed through the wrong end of a telescope' (12.9.92). From the beginning of the performance therefore it was clear that the audience was not being invited to see events from the Birling family's perspective. In *Far Away* it is difficult to grasp how we should respond to what we are seeing. Things seem both familiar and strange, and this becomes more perturbing as the play develops. Eventually, 'strangeness' is itself subject to a form of Brechtian estrangement, as a result of which past and present (cause and effect) gradually become correctly aligned. As its title signals, *Far Away* is a play about the distance between the spectator and what is seen. In order to decipher it – to apportion blame for the crime and to grasp the terrible consequences that follow – it is necessary to adjust an imaginary telescope and, in this way, to bring apparently far-away events into focus. What this reveals is our complicity in crimes that are actually taking place under our noses.

On the front cover of the play text of *Far Away* published by Nick Hern Books in 2001 there is an image that brilliantly captures Churchill's distortion of perspective in the play. At first sight it seems to be a picture of a wide expanse of sand, with, in the far distance, a group of tiny figures who are apparently about to walk into the sea. The longer one looks at it, however, the more unsettling it becomes. If the figures are about to go swimming, for example, why are they wearing so many clothes, and why is one of them carrying what might be either a large shopping bag or a suitcase? The more one stares at this figure, the harder it becomes even to be sure that she (if it is a she) is walking away from the viewer. Has she in fact turned back from the others, and is she now coming towards us? Then there is the large beach area, which, on closer inspection, looks as much like water as it does sand. Superimposed on it is a dark, menacing shadow – of whom or what? On top of that is the play's title. Even here something is not quite right because the word 'far' is larger than 'away'. Somewhat like the sand, which could be a darker mirror image of the sea, or the figure that could be moving away from, or (and?) towards the viewer, the disparate sizes of the two words have the effect of somehow reflecting them back on each other. This is odd and perturbing. Like the play, the cover picture slowly and insidiously raises questions that one would prefer not to try to answer.

In performance, the play's disquieting exploration of perspective was hinted at from the moment the audience entered the auditorium by a large, painted front cloth of a pretty country cottage, nestling in green hills. It looked like a picture on the lid of a chocolate box, or, as one looked more closely, like a cloth for a pantomime, and, in the context of a Caryl Churchill play, this seemed peculiar. The colours were too bright, the images too large and obtrusive, the opposite of 'far away'. When the cloth rose, it revealed a stage picture that was initially reassuring. A middle-aged woman sat sewing by the soft light of a lamp, and singing what sounded like a lullaby. The set was minimal, a table and a few chairs, and, around them, simply darkness. The image was beautiful, but almost at once the cocooning darkness became unnerving, its amorphousness suggestive of potential danger. In his essay 'The "Uncanny"' Freud discusses the linguistic connection between '*das Heimliche* [homely] and its opposite, *das Unheimliche*', in order to show the ease with which one term can elide into another. '[S]ome languages in use today', he adds, 'can only render the German expression "an *unheimlich* house" by "a *haunted house*"' (*Pelican Freud Library*, vol. 14, pp. 363 and 4). The house in which act one of *Far Away* is set is simultaneously *heimlich* (homely) and haunted, and the dark secret that haunts it is gradually revealed. In performance, the woman was alone for only a few seconds and then a young girl dressed in a long white nightgown entered. One of Churchill's greatest strengths is her ability simultaneously to orientate and disorientate an audience. The situation here initially seems straightforward, but, increasingly, it begs a number of questions. What is the relationship between the woman and the child, for example? A glance at the cast list reveals the fact that the girl is Joan and the woman her aunt, with the strangely formal name of Harper, but it is some time before their relationship becomes clear from the dialogue. Then there is the house, which Joan appears to find perturbing from the beginning. 'It's always odd in a new place', the aunt reassures her. 'When you've been here a week you'll look back at tonight and it won't seem the same at all' (Churchill, *Far Away*, p. 4). Her words are puzzling: 'won't seem the same' as what? Harper is apparently saying that, though the house seems new and unfamiliar now, it *will* be familiar in a week's time, but the word 'same' unsettles this explanation. It 'won't seem the same'. It won't seem familiar? 'Same' has connotations here that are both *heimlich* and *unheimlich*. Churchill takes the idea of 'strange', in the sense of unfamiliar, and extends it to incorporate suggestions of 'sinister'. This is a sinister house.

In Stephen Daldry's production of *Far Away*, the fact that the audience only ever saw a fragment of the house – a table, a few chairs, a lamp – raised questions about what the rest of it was like. The front cloth had suggested an idealised version of the English countryside, and Churchill's dialogue confirms that the setting is rural. There are no street lamps, for example, and there is a wide variety of birds. It is also somewhere that is hot in the daytime and cold at night, so perhaps it isn't in England. Its location in time is also unclear. The lamp and Joan's old-fashioned nightgown evoke the past, but Harper's talk of selling bottles of water to tourists indicates the present. Joan tries to define the house by the ways in which it is unlike her home. Whereas Harper makes the idea of 'sameness' ambiguous, Joan attempts to clarify difference. The stars are brighter at her aunt's house, for example, and she can climb out of the bedroom window and onto a tree. The tree is important because it was from a perch high up in it that Joan first saw her uncle outside the house in the dark, and began to wonder what he was doing. By recounting what she saw she tries to retain a perspective on it. Harper repeatedly offers anodyne interpretations of the sequence of events, but, each time, Joan refocuses on the violent acts she witnessed. She describes watching her uncle 'bundling someone into a shed' (ibid., p. 8), and, when Harper assures her that it was just a sack and that there was a little party going on in the shed, Joan tells her about the lorry she saw. She got down from the tree and put her ear to the side of the lorry, and she could hear someone crying. Also, there was blood on the ground. She's sure of that because she slipped in it. Harper tries to convince her that the blood came from a dog that had been run over, but Joan recalls looking through the shed window and seeing more blood inside the shed. Her uncle was hitting a man with a metal stick. She saw him hit a child too. Churchill never explains who the uncle is, or the context of his actions. Perhaps it is Nazi Germany, or possibly this is a present-day act of ethnic cleansing. The lack of precision as to place or time makes these, and other, solutions equally possible. So, too, does the strange and sinister storybook quality of act one, for this is a dark and dreadful fairy tale with, at its heart, the corruption of a child. Like the wicked witch in *Hansel and Gretel* (the story upon which David Glass had two years earlier based the first part of his *Lost Child Trilogy*), Harper lures Joan into her 'gingerbread' house. The idyllic, but implausible, cottage on the front cloth prior to the start of the performance signalled the enticing yet disturbing nature of this house. Joan struggles to retain a true memory of what she has seen, but Harper poisons the word truth. 'I'm trusting you with the truth', she tells Joan (ibid., p. 12), and then goes on to explain that the man the uncle hit was a traitor who wanted to harm the other people, while the uncle was engaged in saving them. What Joan has seen is a 'secret', and she must never reveal it, or Harper, the uncle, perhaps Joan herself, will be in danger. By keeping quiet she will be 'part of a big movement ... to make things better' (ibid., p. 14). These vague generalisations, and, above all, the exciting word 'secret' seduce the child into redefining victims as traitors and therefore as legitimate targets of brutality. 'Truth' and 'trust' are corrupted along with the child, with the result that, in the following acts, the characters have no external vantage point, no perspective, from which to judge events.

In act two, as in act one, an apparently normal on-stage world is gradually revealed to be deeply implicated in off-stage horrors. The setting is a hat-making establishment where the now-grown-up Joan and a young man named Todd are engaged in creating exotic headgear for a parade of some kind. In Stephen Daldry's production the small, illuminated area where the action took place was again surrounded by darkness. In this little oasis, Joan and Todd flirted, compared their progress on the hats and grumbled about the management. From their conversation the audience gleaned fragments of information about the location of the hat establishment. Outside it, there were buses and a subway, so it was presumably in a city. The skies were grey, which suggested England. The buses were blue, not red, so it wasn't London – at least not contemporary London. The flats were yellow, which perhaps sounded a little odd. Gradually these oddities became more perturbing. Swimming in the river was dangerous, which could be true of plenty of rivers today, but what were we to make of the news that Joan was 'getting a room in a subway' (ibid., p. 19)? It was Joan's comment, however, that she didn't 'like staying in in the evenings and watching trials' (ibid., p. 20) that was particularly disturbing. Gradually, the setting of act two, like that of act one, revealed itself as both elsewhere and here, and, whereas time in act one was simultaneously past and present, in act two it was both still to come and now. Apart from the occasional remark that hinted at something more alarming, and the outrageous nature of the hats, however, everything seemed fairly normal. There was no preparation for the emergence two thirds of the way through the act of rows of 'ragged, beaten, chained prisoners', who came forward as darkness was replaced by cold fingers of light. They were on their way to be executed, and each one was wearing a bizarre and fantastic hat.

At the end of act two, Joan and Todd start to make new hats in readiness for the next parade. Joan has learned that her earlier hat has been awarded the first prize, and therefore it will be kept in a museum. It's a pity though that more hats can't be saved, she comments. 'It seems so sad to burn them with the bodies' (ibid., p. 25). In the words of John Peter in the *Sunday Times*: 'At this moment your heart stops.' Todd tells Joan that she is wrong to be sad, because the hats are meant to be 'ephemeral'. They're 'like a metaphor for something . . . You make beauty and it disappears'. He 'love[s] that' (ibid.). The obscene irrelevance of the hats initially brings to mind glossy photographs of fashion models posed in poverty-stricken landscapes, but I think the primary reference is to the ephemeral nature of theatre. The *Blue Heart* plays are characterised by an uneasiness about the nature and value of theatre, but the implied criticism in act two of *Far*

Away is more savage. Churchill seems to be suggesting here that the best plays survive, but only as museum-pieces. Worse still, a play – and this includes *Far Away* – may be implicated in the horror it depicts. It is a view diametrically opposed to the belief in the pre-eminent importance of fiction – as opposed to reality – in *The Pillowman*.

In the final act of *Far Away* everything in the world is implicated: 'everything's been recruited' (ibid., p. 37) by one side or another in a global war in which adults, children, animals, objects, the whole of the natural world – everything – are both combatants and victims. There is always an enemy but who that enemy is constantly changes. We learn at one point that the 'cats have come in on the side of the French' (ibid., p. 29), while the 'Mallards . . . commit rape, and they're on the side of the elephants and the Koreans' (ibid., p. 33). Deer are at one moment described as 'terroris[ing] shopping malls', and trampling people with their 'vicious little shining hooves' (ibid., pp. 33 and 34), and then, a few moments later, we are told that their natural goodness has revealed itself and they are now no longer the enemy. For a few reviewers, the absurdity of some of the shifts and juxtapositions weakened the power of the last act, while a number of others either criticised Churchill for stating her case rather than arguing it, or suggested that the play as a whole lacked coherence. In the *Independent* (2.12.00), Rhoda Koenig complained that the characters 'exist only in the moment' and 'nothing knits together the sections of allegory and fantasy'. In the aftermath of 9/11, however, and President Bush's 'axis of evil' speech, Churchill's dystopian vision seems prophetic. Bush's logic was dreadfully simple. Whoever, whatever, was not for him and his vision of America, was against them. In act three of *Far Away* almost nothing exists apart from the fear of attack, and the necessity to kill before one is killed oneself.

Despite the play's intense compression, it *is* coherent. There is a narrative, though large parts of it are inferred, not stated. The starting point is the corruption of the child and of the word 'truth', and the subsequent loss of a moral framework by which to judge events. The violence in the far away darkness of act one comes forward out of the darkness in a new formulation in act two. The audience witnesses it, but the characters are obsessed by the ephemeral beauty of their hats and the corrupt nature of the management (corrupt because of the way they run the hat-making business, not in relation to the executions). In act three, there is no framework of any kind. All sense of proportion has been lost. Joan, who is now married to Todd, has temporarily escaped from the war to Harper's house. When Harper criticises her for endangering them all by her presence, she justifies herself by claiming that she could just as well have been 'on a mission'. On her way to the house she has 'killed two cats and a child under five so it wasn't that different from a mission' (ibid., p. 37). These words are followed by her description of a nightmare journey through a Bosch-like landscape. She was afraid of the weather because it had sided with the Japanese. Rats and girls lay by the sides of the roads, bleeding from their mouths and ears. There were bodies everywhere: 'one killed by coffee or one killed by pins', others by 'heroin, petrol, chainsaws, hairspray, bleach, foxgloves' (ibid.). Everything is a potential killer. The 'Bolivians are working with gravity . . . and there's thousands dead of light in Madagascar'. 'Who's going to mobilise darkness and silence?' she wonders (ibid., pp. 37 and 38), and her words are hauntingly, horribly, beautiful. There is no way of grasping this world. Everything is so close up it is distorted out of all recognition, and the only available response is to lash out in fear. Joan has tried to escape, in order to spend a day with Todd away from the carnage, but there is no place of refuge. Harper destroyed that possibility in act one. When Todd explains that Joan has been trying to get 'to a place of safety', Harper responds by asking, 'Is this a place of safety?'. 'Relatively, yes of course it is', Todd replies. 'Everyone thinks it's just a house' (ibid., p. 29). But there is no relativity. Everything is dangerous and must be destroyed. Harper's house is the place where the contamination that is destroying the whole world began, and now far-way monstrosities have invaded it.

And yet, despite Joan's conjuration of a hellish vision of a world where every thing is divided against every other thing, and finally against itself, there is, I think, at the end of the play a faint note of hope. This is a play filled with stories, and, at the end, Joan tells a story about a river she had to cross in order to reach Harper's house. There were enemies all around her, including an encampment of Chilean soldiers and some black and white cows drinking in the river, but her major fear was of the river itself. Could that be an enemy? She had no means of knowing. Maybe it would help her to swim, or maybe it would drown her. For a long time, she stood on the bank, unsure what to do, and then she began to wade into the river. 'When you've just stepped in', she explains, 'you can't tell what's going to happen. The water laps round your ankles in any case' (ibid., p. 38). These are the last words of a play that begins with a failed attempt to establish truth and a subsequent descent into global violence. In whodunnit terms, the culprit was never brought to justice in act one, and this has meant that he has mutated, becoming more fearsome with each manifestation. Churchill is fond of open endings though, and 'in any case' is clearly one of them. I likened act one to a dark fairy story, and, for me, the final words of the play contain a slight echo of another dramatic fairy story, Shakespeare's *King Lear*. *Far Away* is, I would suggest, a pocket-sized *King Lear*. Both plays begin as a mixture of a fairy tale and a domestic drama. In *King Lear*, Shakespeare stresses that human need is a given, not something that has to be justified. Lear's anguished cry, 'O, reason not the need!' (2.4.259) goes unheard, with the result that 'Humanity must perforce prey on itself' (4.2.49). In *Far Away*, too, humanity turns on, preys upon, itself, and the world it depicts is bleaker even than Shakespeare's. Lear's own need at least teaches him to understand the needs of others, and Cordelia is never corrupted by her sisters' inhumanity. Joan *is* corrupted, as is language, and the world it signifies. *Far Away*, however, perhaps most resembles *King Lear* in its final words. In both plays the endings are tentative. Shakespeare's Edgar says:

> The weight of this sad time we must obey;
> Speak what we feel, not what we ought to say.
> The oldest hath borne most; we that are young
> Shall never see so much nor live so long.

They are surprisingly downbeat lines, given the tumultuous nature of all that has gone before, and there is something oddly comforting about them, perhaps because the onomatopoeic quality of 'long' queries the concept of brevity they convey. *Far Away* ends with 'in any case'. The 's' could be sinister, or soft and caressing, like the water that laps round Joan's ankles. We know, after all, from the fact that she is telling the story, that the river didn't drown her. She crossed it safely. After the horrors that precede it, the story of stepping into the river, with the acceptance this implies of what is to come, contains, I think, a glimmer of hope, though it has to be admitted that it is pretty faint.

A Number: 'King Lear in shorthand'

A Number, which premiered at The Royal Court Jerwood Theatre Downstairs on 23 September 2002, is also open-ended. This is a play for two actors. One of them plays a man in his early sixties called Salter, and the other Salter's sons: the forty-year-old Bernard (B1) and Bernard's two slightly younger clones, B2 and Michael Black. Like *Far Away*, the production was directed by Stephen Daldry and designed by Ian MacNeil. Salter was played by Michael Gambon – the 'great Gambon' as a number of reviewers styled him. The equally brilliant Daniel Craig played the three sons.

Caryl Churchill's plays are generally more concerned with mother/ daughter, than with father/son relationships, the most obvious exception being *Owners,* Churchill's first play to receive a professional stage production (in 1972). In his *Sunday Telegraph* review (29.9.02), Irving Wardle likened *A Number* to Yeats' *Purgatory,* which the Royal Shakespeare Company had staged in 1998 as part of *A Trinity of Plays* by Synge and Yeats. Both plays, he wrote, 'inhabit . . . a zone of disorientated anguish', and, in both, 'a son and father engage in a Dantean dialogue on the mysteries of generation'. In the *Daily Mail* (4.10.02), Michael Coveney compared *A Number* to Terence Rattigan's *The Winslow Boy,* and to Shakespeare's *King Lear.* Despite notable differences between them, both *A Number* and *The Winslow Boy,* he commented, pose the question: 'What would a father do for his son?' *A Number* resembled *King Lear* through the power of its language: 'The density of Salter's memories explodes like the tragic speeches of King Lear, only King Lear in shorthand.' Like *Far Away, A Number* has an enormous, but compressed power. The dialogue, John Peter wrote in the *Sunday Times* (6.10.02), is 'so tightly integrated that a moment's inattention can cost you dear'. It is 'fractured, dissociated from within, like the people who speak it'. In a similar way to Joan in the first act of *Far Away,* B2, and later B1, ask Salter questions, and, like Harper, he initially twists and turns the conversation, leading it down linguistic cul-de-sacs. However, Salter also has questions for which he needs answers, and, in a dislocated, fragmented fashion, the truth gradually emerges: 'Each stage of this 55-minute play advances by unravelling the lies of the previous one', Jonathan Myerson wrote in the *Independent* (1.10.02). Despite the abbreviated dialogue, there is a sense of stumbling forward into ever more complex layers of understanding.

One way in which the form of *A Number* is different from that of *Far Away* is that, fragmented as it is, the narrative of *Far Away* begins at the beginning. Churchill establishes simultaneously the 'once upon a time' of fairy tale and the clues necessary for the solution of a whodunnit. In *A Number,* there is again a mystery that has to be solved, but, rather like one of Ibsen's plays, the action begins at the point where the impact of the past on the present can no longer be contained. In the *Evening Standard* (27.9.02), Nicholas de Jongh, who called *A Number* 'the first true play of the 21st century', described Salter as a 'duplicitous Ibsenish figure with a past'. *A Number* also owes a debt to Pinter's early plays. There is a similar sense of menace, and Churchill's characters, like Pinter's, seem to be cut adrift from their moorings in time and space. Churchill describes the setting simply as 'where Salter lives', and the two men who are seen on stage at the beginning could be almost anywhere and anybody. For Salter, the past is an ominous pressure that threatens to manifest itself in the present unless he is constantly vigilant. For B2, it is a mystery that he is trying to solve. He is motivated by questions. Who is he, and what is his real relationship to his father? Later in the play other questions come to the fore. What is the nature of the relationship between the first son, the 'original', and the clones? How does this relate to a sense of identity? As Susannah Clapp put it in the *Observer* (29.9.02), 'Would you feel less real if you knew you had been cloned? Is there such a thing as a "real me"?'

The Daldry/MacNeil production of the play created a kind of theatrical laboratory in which these questions could be explored. Like Churchill's language, the set was pared down to the bone. The acting area was a raked wooden platform, surrounded by darkness. Two chairs were positioned (one upstage, the other stage left), at the very edge of the acting area. When a character sat on a chair, it seemed as if he might topple backwards and fall silently into the void. There was also a small table with an ashtray, and, at times, smoke hung in the air like the unfinished sentences. On the spare, intensely focused, playing area, the actors' minimal movements and gestures were as precise and finely honed as Churchill's language. As he waited to meet Michael Black, the representative of the clones whose existence he had only recently become aware of, Mchael Gambon adjusted his gold-coloured tie. 'Never has one innocuous action carried such weighty implications', Carole Woddis commented in the *Herald* (2.10.02). Daniel Craig showed the difference between the three sons by minute shifts in his body posture. There was a wonderful *coup de théâtre* when he exited into the upstage darkness as B2, only to reappear immediately as B1. Though this wasn't visible to the audience, there was obviously an off-stage set of steps which allowed the actor to descend and immediately rise again, as though by magic. For a moment it wasn't clear whether this reappearance was a return or a first entrance. Was this the character we had already seen or someone different? Then, the tense, wary quality of Craig's movement confirmed that someone new had entered. Briefly, there had been a sense of the uncanny, a combination of *'das Heimliche'* and *'das Unheimliche'*. In scene one, Salter and B2 discuss the anxiety that is raised by fears of the *doppelgänger:*

> B2:   don't they say you die if you meet yourself?
> Salter: walk round the corner and see yourself you could get a heart attack. Because if that's me over there who am I? (Churchill, *A Number*, p. 9)

For a few heart-stopping seconds after Daniel Craig entered, it seemed as if his *doppelgänger* had appeared, as if a second, identical image had been peeled away from the first.

In the 1997 *Heart's Desire*, Churchill plays with the motif of return, endlessly deferring the moment when the past will become the present. In *A Number*, she uses the theatrical frisson of an unexpected return that proves in fact to be a new entrance in order to investigate the potentiality of the present moment, and, in addition, to raise topical questions regarding individual identity. Oliver Jones began his review of *A Number* in *What's On* (2.10.02) with the words: 'Caryl Churchill can always be relied upon for an acute sensitivity to society's current concerns, and her latest play displays all her customary astuteness.' In 2002, the same year that *A Number* was first performed, two new books on the ethics of genetic engineering were published by Profile Books Ltd: *Redesigning Humans: Choosing our Children's Genes* by Gregory Stock, and Francis Fukuyama's *Our Posthuman Future: Consequences of the Biotechnology Revolution*. Both authors viewed contemporary developments in biotechnology as likely to alter what we perceive to be human nature. Stock defined the significance of the birth of Dolly the sheep (the first mammal to be cloned from an adult cell) as being that 'one of the most intimate aspects of our lives – the passing of life from one generation to the next – might one day change beyond recognition. Suddenly the idea that we could hold ourselves apart and remain who we are and as we are while transforming the world around us seemed untenable' (Stock, pp. 13–14). In *Our Posthuman Future,* Fukuyama identified his aim as being to argue that Aldous Huxley was right in *Brave New World*: 'the most significant threat posed by contemporary biotechnology is the possibility that it will alter human nature and thereby move us into a "posthuman" stage of history' (Fukuyama, p. 7). If what Fukuyama terms 'a stable human "essence"' (ibid., p. 217) can become unstable, what are the likely consequences for individual human identity? This is Churchill's central question in *A Number*. Can there in fact be such a thing as an individual if that individual is a clone?

Though at the time of writing there has been no confirmed case of the birth of a human clone, there have been a number of claims that this has happened. On 29 December 2002, just over a month after *A Number* completed its run at the Royal Court, the *Independent on Sunday* featured two 'cloned baby' claims in its news section. One was by Brigitte Boisselier, a French chemist who was the head of Clonaid, a company affiliated to the Raelian cult; the other by an Italian fertility expert named

Severino Antinori. Though Churchill never uses the word clone in the play, *A Number* assumes the availability of the necessary technology to create a human clone. When B2 probes the secrets of his genesis in scene one, he eventually learns that there was an earlier son, who, Salter tells him, died in a car crash at the age of four. It was because he wanted this perfect son back that Salter had a replica created. 'I am your father', he assures B2, '[I]t was by an artificial the forefront of science but I am genetically' (*A Number*, p. 12). Just before his exit at the end of scene one, however, B2 describes himself as 'a copy . . . not the real one' (ibid., p. 14). His words set the scene for the appearance, a few moments later, of the perturbing *doppelgänger*, who proves to be not the copy but the original, because they highlight Churchill's twinned exploration of identity and the theatrical moment. This moment exists simultaneously both now, and then. The person who enters at the start of scene two in *A Number* is a 'returner' (the actor who was here before), *and* a character whom we are seeing for the first time. Furthermore, it turns out that the new character is actually the source – the origin – of the character we saw first. The thrilling entrance of B1 is a masterstroke that brilliantly evokes both Churchill's central theme and her experimentation with theatrical time.

The following scenes probe further into the past's relationship with the present, and also into the nature of the 'original' and of origins. In scene two, B1, the original son, vents his anger at the father – his originator – who physically abused and then abandoned him. B1 didn't die in the car crash, as Salter claimed. Salter was in a constant state of befuddlement because of drink and drugs, and became an abusive father – the 'dark dark power' B1 terms him (ibid., p. 15). When he came to his senses, he had the child taken into care. He wanted a second chance at fatherhood, and so he had a replica created from B1, not realising that a number of copies would be made. In part, the play is about the relative contributions of nature and nurture to the development of a child. B1 is violent and paranoid, while B2 is well balanced, and in each case this is because of their upbringing. Salter's second chance ends in disaster, because B1 hunts down and murders B2, and then kills himself. Though Salter was a caring father to B2, the dark seeds of his past cruelties come to fruition and destroy his happiness, along with both the original son and the copy. Rather than *King Lear*, *A Number* reminds me in places of Ibsen's *Ghosts*, or of a Greek tragedy. There is a similar sense of inevitability, of hidden guilt coming to light with dreadful consequences.

The tragic elements of *A Number* are framed by the teasing ambiguity of the title and by Michael Black's discovery in the final scene that he is a clone. Throughout the play, Salter views identity in terms of ownership. When he learns that scientists made multiple copies of his first son, he tells B2: 'it's you, part of you, the value' (ibid., p. 6). This value is largely financial for Salter. 'I wonder if we can sue', he speculates (ibid., p. 5). Michael Black has no concept at all of identity as a possession. He's not afraid or angry because he's one of a number, he's fascinated: 'all these very similar people doing things like each other or a bit different' (ibid., p. 49) seem delightful to him. Salter tries to discover Michael's identity by getting him to articulate whatever it is that makes him special. '[T]ell me something about yourself that's really specific to you, something really important', he says (ibid., p. 44), but Michael responds by describing his reactions to other people and to the world around him. Salter is frustrated by this apparent absence of uniqueness, but Michael points out that we have 'ninety-nine per cent the same genes as any other person'. We've even 'got thirty per cent the same as a lettuce' (ibid., p. 50). He loves this information about the lettuce. It makes him feel he belongs. The only clone (apart from B2) that appears in the play is at ease therefore with who he is. 'And you're happy you say are you? you like your life?' Salter asks him, and he replies, 'I do yes, sorry' (ibid.). 'Sorry' is the last word of the play, and, given the sparseness of Churchill's punctuation, the use of a comma before it is clearly important. The pause it indicates adds a comic emphasis to, and a qualification of, Michael's apology. Why apologise for happiness, after all? The play's ending opens up new possibilities. Michael's happiness doesn't erase the childhood abuse of B1, or his and B2's deaths. What it does do is to offer another way of looking at things, an alternative response. The play's title can be interpreted as indicative of anxiety at the idea of seeing people as numbers, but it may also suggest pleasure in the notion of varied possibilities. The word 'sorry' is like a jet of water, balancing coloured balls in the air. Some are dark, some light. This chapter is called 'The Skriker's progeny', and Salter's treatment of B1 when he was a child is worthy of a dreadful tale the Skriker might tell. Michael's story though is in a different key. Like *Blue Kettle*, *A Number* is indebted to Churchill's experimentation with language in *The Skriker*. In *The Skriker,* every phrase, sometimes every word, contains within it the potential for many others and Churchill uses this potentiality to create an unstoppable chain reaction of damage. The minimalist dialogue of *A Number* also generates potentiality because so many of the sentences are incomplete. Much of what is inferred is disturbing, but the ghosts of unfinished thoughts that haunt the little that is said are not all dark. Some are playful, and it is on a playful note that the piece ends. It is striking that a play that explores anxieties about genetic engineering seems finally unfazed by these dangers. Danger in *A Number* arises from a lack of fatherly love – a refusal (as in Mary Shelley's *Frankenstein*) of the creator to take responsibility for what he has made – not from loss of identity.

With the exception of Sarah Kane's *Blasted*, the plays and adaptations of novels discussed in the next three chapters all received productions in London in 2004 or 2005, many of them at the National Theatre. Before moving on to these texts, however, I want to end this chapter with a brief reference to Kazuo Ishiguro's novel *Never Let Me Go*, which was shortlisted for the Man Booker Prize in 2005. There are two reasons for this. The first is that the novel provides a moving counterpart to ideas Caryl Churchill discusses in *A Number;* the second is that it contains a vivid image of a lost child who is also a grieving mother.

Like *A Number*, *Never Let Me Go* owes an implicit debt to *Frankenstein*. In *A Number*, B2 and Michael Black are a composite version of Shelley's Creature, in that they have been artificially created, but it is B1, the rejected, unloved, original child, who inherits the Creature's destructiveness. The Creature's equivalent in *Never Let Me Go* is Kathy H. Kathy has no surname because she is one of a batch of clones. She has been created by scientists to be a living 'donor' – a source of body parts for 'real' people. Like B2 and Michael Black therefore she is a copy, but she displays a truer humanity than any of the more biologically conventional characters in the novel. While Churchill in the final scene of *A Number* separates out parental origin from identity (so that one is not necessarily the source of the other), Ishiguro, like Shelley, links the need to know who one is with the desire to understand where one comes from. Kathy's is the narrative voice in *Never Let Me Go*. It is her story, but for her it lacks a beginning because of her longing to find the 'model' (the mother) from which she was cloned. Kathy also yearns to be a mother herself. While she is still a child, she discovers a tape of a song entitled 'Never Let Me Go', and she dances to it whilst singing very softly, *'Never let me go. Oh, baby, baby. Never let me go . . .'* (Ishiguro, p. 248), and hugging an imaginary baby to her breast. Like all the other clones, Kathy is infertile and the imaginary baby represents the child she can never have. It signifies also the impossibility of her ever being a daughter. She has no past and a future that only consists of pain.

As she dances with her longed-for 'baby', Kathy is simultaneously a grieving mother, a desiring daughter and a lost child. My final three chapters focus almost exclusively on stories of children and parents.

Chapter 7 is about murdered children and avenging mothers, Chapter 8 replaces Kathy's lost daughterhood with two daughters' stories, and Chapter 9 explores the National Theatre's adaptation of Jamila Gavin's *Coram Boy*, with its 'final progression towards long-lost parents "regained"' (Kate Bassett, *Independent on Sunday*, 20.11.05).

7
Blood sacrifice

One of the terrorists had a bit of soul. He let us drink some water. Others didn't. (words of a child survivor in the BBC2 documentary, *Children of Beslan*)

harm hatches harm after harm (*Hecuba*, translated by Frank McGuinness)

The stories of murdered children in this chapter have a topical significance that links them with Rhona's story in Chapter 5, though the contemporary relevance in this case is not to paedophilic killers but to the Iraq war and global terrorism. Anxiety about the aftermath of the invasion of Iraq by American and British forces informed a number of productions in 2004 and 2005. Among the new plays on the topic of Iraq, the most high profile was David Hare's *Stuff Happens*, which opened at the Olivier Theatre in September 2004. The most powerful dramatic anti-war voice, however, was a very old one. It belonged to Euripides, perhaps the greatest anti-war playwright there has ever been. 'Despite being dead for over 2,000 years, Euripides is the man of the moment', Sarah Hemming commented in a review of Kneehigh Theatre's production of *The Bacchae* (*Financial Times*, 9.11.04). Directors turned to his ancient stories for a deeper understanding of present-day brutalities. *Iphigenia at Aulis*, a play about the start of the Trojan War, opened at the Lyttelton Theatre on 22 June 2004, in a production directed by Katie Mitchell. *Hecuba*, another infrequently performed play by *Euripides*, which documents the bloody conclusion of this war, received three productions. One, directed by Jonathan Kent, with Clare Higgins in the title role, opened at the Donmar Warehouse in London on 14 September 2004. An RSC production premiered at the Albery Theatre, London, on 7 April 2005. Originally intended for performance in Stratford-upon-Avon, this production had to be postponed when Vanessa Redgrave, who had been cast as Hecuba, was taken ill. The two productions were still close enough in time for Benedict

Nightingale to begin his review of the Albery Theatre production with the words: 'Chances to compare productions of *Hecuba* come as often as total eclipses or No. 22 buses in the rain, but the Royal Shakespeare Company has provided one' (*The Times*, 9.4.05). A third, touring, production of *Hecuba*, by Foursight Theatre Company, opened at the Arena Theatre, Wolverhampton, on 6 October 2004, less than a month after the premiere at the Donmar Warehouse.

The reason for *Hecuba*'s topicality was spelled out by Naomi Cooke, the director of Foursight Theatre's *Hecuba*. She began her programme note with a reference to the terrorist siege of a school in Beslan (North Ossetia) that took place in September 2004: 'It is the morning after the end of the siege of Beslan . . . It is too early to know how many are dead . . . Hundreds survive, and will begin the impossible process of learning to live with the memory of the trauma.' In his review of the Donmar production in the *Daily Mail* (15.9.04), Quentin Letts commented: 'After the killings in Beslan it is hard to fathom quite how the cast got through rehearsals for this astonishing performance. To have persisted with a play in which a fate-ravaged woman kills children in revenge must have been brutal on the soul'. In the *Observer* (19.9.04), Susannah Clapp referred to both Beslan and 'the shambles of postwar Iraq'. She linked Hecuba's blinding of Polymestor, the father of the children she murders, with related mutilations in *King Lear,* and also in one of the most scandalous plays of the 1990s, Sarah Kane's *Blasted*. I begin this chapter with a comparison of press responses to two productions of *Blasted*, the original production in 1995 and a revival in 2001. While Kane's depiction of mutilation, and the eating of a dead baby was deemed to be gratuitously shocking in the mid-1990s, in 2001 the play was interpreted in the context of the work of a range of other playwrights, including Churchill's *Far Away* and Priestley's *An Inspector Calls*.

Sarah Kane's *Blasted*

Just under five months after the premiere of *The Skriker,* Caryl Churchill's translation of Seneca's *Thyestes* opened at the Royal Court Theatre Upstairs. Seven months later Sarah Kane's *Blasted,* 'The play [that] sparked off the theatrical controversy of the decade' (Charles Spencer, *Daily Telegraph,* 5.4.01), began a brief run at the same theatre, on 12 January 1995. The productions were also linked in two further ways. They had the same director, James Macdonald, and they both included the eating of a child – an act that may have owed a debt in part to the words of the

Butcher in *Light Shining in Buckinghamshire,* and the Dead Child in *The Skriker*. Certainly Atreus' words, as he prepares a banquet out of the nephews he has murdered, for their father, Thyestes, unknowingly to eat – 'I'll . . . cram him / full of his sons' death' – has echoes of the end of the Butcher's speech. The cannibalism in *Blasted* occurs at the end of the play when the blind, starving Ian eats a dead baby. The horrified response of most reviewers to this in 1995, and to an earlier sequence in which Ian is first raped and then has his eyes sucked out and eaten by a soldier, was perhaps hardly surprising. However, Louise Doughty in the *Mail on Sunday* pointed out that, if the play had been by Seneca or Shakespeare rather than 'a 23-year-old woman playwright on [her] first outing', the response would almost certainly have been very different. Doughty made this comment in the 29 January 1995 edition of the paper. In her review the previous Sunday in the same newspaper, she had praised Sarah Kane's 'acute grasp of sexual politics' and her 'sparse . . . stunning' dialogue. She was virtually alone, however. Other reviewers' responses mostly varied from a dismissal of the play as banal and pointless to Jack Tinker's headline in the *Daily Mail*, 'This Disgusting Feast of Filth'.

When James Macdonald directed a revival of *Blasted* at the Royal Court in 2001, reviewers responded very differently. Andrew Smith in the *Observer* (8.4.01) put the changed perspective down primarily to the operations of 'Time', which had 'written two new acts' for the play 'in the form of events in Yugoslavia and . . . Kane's . . . suicide in 1999'. While in 1995 the atrocities in *Blasted* 'seemed unreal', in the interim audiences had become used to reading 'accounts of similar happenings' over their breakfast 'cornflakes'. This time round the critics stressed the play's strengths and placed it within the context of a literary heritage, noting its antecedents, particularly in the plays of Shakespeare and Beckett. The blinding of Gloucester in *King Lear* was referred to, and, in *The Times* (5.4.01), Benedict Nightingale compared *Blasted* with *Endgame*. 'Beckett's vision was metaphysical', he wrote, 'Kane's is moral, social, political and very much of our times'. Kane's play made him think also of Priestley's 'ringing cry' in *An Inspector Calls*: 'if we don't learn responsibility for each other, we'll "be taught that lesson in fire and blood and anguish"'. A number of reviewers noted connections between *Blasted* and Caryl Churchill's recent *Far Away*. John Nathan in the *Jewish Chronicle* commented on the 'air of apocalypse' in both plays, but added that, 'where Churchill describes, Kane shows'. In a sense this is true. *Far Away* is a bleaker play even than *Blasted,* because the destruction it portrays is not simply global. It engulfs the future as well as the present.

Far Away connects with an audience on a more intellectual level than *Blasted,* however. It is a dramatic parable that warns us that we balance on the edge of an abyss, whereas *Blasted* is visceral shock and anguish, shot through with black humour.

Sarah Kane herself understood that this raw immediacy was what the first audiences found so hard to relate to. Aleks Sierz in *In-Yer-Face Theatre* quotes her as saying: 'Personally . . . I think the press outrage was due to the play being experiential rather than speculative . . . What makes [it] . . . experiential is its form . . . In *Blasted,* the form and content attempt to be one. The form is the meaning' (Sierz, p. 98). Reading through the reviews of the 1995 production, it becomes clear that beneath the revulsion there is bewilderment because the play's events appear to lack a recognisable context. *Blasted* begins realistically enough, in a hotel room in Leeds. Two characters enter: a middle-aged hack journalist called Ian and his much younger ex-girlfriend, Cate. From the beginning, Ian's racist and misogynist language creates an atmosphere of menace and impending violence, which becomes actual initially through his sexual abuse of Cate, but, though the dialogue and actions are deeply unpleasant, they are comprehensible at this stage. Halfway through the play, there are indications of a new tone. '*Cate stares out of the window*' and remarks, 'Looks like there's a war on' (Kane, *Complete Plays,* p. 33). Shortly afterwards, there is a knock at the door, and, when Ian opens it, a soldier is standing there holding a sniper's rifle. Perturbing though this is, it doesn't adequately prepare for the astonishing events that follow. '*There is a blinding light, then a huge explosion*' as the hotel is '*blasted by a mortar bomb*' (ibid., p. 39). There is no explanation of what has happened. It is unclear whether the location is still England or whether perhaps we have been transported into the middle of the civil war that was currently raging in central Europe – or even to some unnamed, hellish war zone that conflates both locations. An ugly, but semi-realistic play has suddenly transmogrified into an apocalyptic nightmare.

The sense that *Blasted* consists of two different plays in fact reflects its genesis. Kane was in the process of writing a play about a rape in a hotel room when, during the siege of Srebrenica, she saw an old woman on television crying and begging for help. She thought about abandoning the play she was working on in order to write about what she had seen, but then she came to the realisation that the two were connected. The scene in the hotel room was 'the seed', the carnage in central Europe 'the tree', and the play's form encapsulates this (Sierz, p. 101). At the beginning of the play the audience witness events, later they experience them. Ian is our on-stage representative of this shift of consciousness. Initially, the word 'Blasted' is reminiscent of a headline in a tabloid newspaper. We hear Ian dictating a story over the 'phone to his newspaper about the victim of a serial killer, and his angle on the murder is at once distanced and titillating. Brutality and terror are packaged for his readers' – and the audience's – consumption. When Ian eats the baby, metaphor becomes theatrical reality. For the first audiences in the tiny Theatre Upstairs in 1995, being up close to this must have been a disorientating experience because there was no contextual framework within which to interpret what they were watching.

Kane's description of seeing the old woman on television, and the early critical responses to *Blasted* highlight important questions about the relationship between real violence and its aesthetic representation that McDonagh would later address to some extent in *The Pillowman*. Kane's preoccupation with current political realities, and with the power of form to dictate audience response, bears some similarity to poems Brecht wrote at the onset of the Second World War. 'In Dark Times' warns of the writer's responsibility to speak out: 'they won't say: the times were dark / Rather: why were their poets silent?' (Brecht, *Poems, Part Two*, p. 274). 'Bad Time for Poetry' explores the relationship between subject matter and form. 'In my poetry a rhyme / Would seem to me almost insolent', Brecht wrote. Rhyme, with its enhancement of lyricism, might portray his pleasure in 'the dancing sails on the Sound', or his 'Delight at the apple tree in blossom', but not the 'horror at the house-painter's speeches' that was driving him to his 'desk' (Brecht, *Poems, Part Three*, p. 331). *Blasted* is Kane's response to the contemporary horrors that were driving her to *her* desk. Her equivalent of Brecht's rejection of rhyme was to set up a more or less recognisable situation, only to explode it. Like Churchill, she brings what was far away into close-up, but she begins not with a fairy tale, but with the evasions and lies of media stories.

Kane's stinging criticism of media reportage, and of readers', and audiences', consumption of news stories had a counterpart in an article in the Review section of the *Observer* newspaper on 12 September 2004, about media coverage of the recent terrorist siege in Beslan. The author of the article, Peter Conrad, took TV crews and photographers to task for what he saw as an attempt 'to satisfy our appetite for horror'. In a way that has uncomfortable echoes of *Blasted,* he drew attention to the name given to 'satellite receivers on our roofs'. They 'are called dishes, and they feed us images'. Furthermore, these images are now instantaneous. Whereas once they 'commemorated ... disasters, or the stories told about them, consciously ... [taking] sides and [pointing] morals', today, 'the event is interpreted for us while we're watching it happen, and the interpreters are participants'. Ugly, 'aesthetically irredeemable' truths are framed, narrativised – labelled – as they are in process of happening. Kane, by contrast, attempts to force an audience to experience a representation of extreme violence without a framework of meaning, without interpretation, to meet it head on and to be seared – blasted – by it.

Condemned by geography

Kane's description of the weeping old Srebrenican woman, imploring someone (anyone) to come to her aid finds an echo in James Fenton's poem 'Children in Exile' in which he writes about 'Those whom geography condemns to war'. There seem to be millions of them in our contemporary world. People blown to bits because they happened to be in the wrong place and time. Refugees driven from wrecked homes, who trek helplessly through limbo-like terrains in the hope of finding somewhere safe where they will be allowed to rest. This is why Euripides' Hecuba speaks to us with such a powerful voice. She is a refugee, a seemingly powerless old woman. Once she was a queen, now she is part of the detritus of war.

The first performance date of *Hecuba* was around 424 BC, almost twenty years before that of *Iphigenia at Aulis*, the play that begins the blood-soaked cycle of vengeance that *Hecuba* continues. Iphigenia is sacrificed by her father, Agamemnon, to the goddess Artemis in order to raise a wind that will blow the becalmed Greek fleet to Troy. After Troy's defeat, Hecuba (widow of King Priam) is enslaved by the Greeks, along with her daughters Cassandra and Polyxena and other Trojan women. Polyxena is ritually slain by the Greeks as an offering to their dead hero, Achilles. Hecuba discovers that her youngest son, Polydorus, has been murdered by Polymestor – the man to whom she entrusted him, in order to keep him safe from the Greeks. In revenge, she blinds Polymestor and butchers his children. As in *Iphigenia at Aulis*, a wind rises and the Greeks are able to sail home with their booty. Awaiting Agamemnon is his wife, Clytemnestra, who will murder him in revenge for his taking the life of Iphigenia. Hecuba's vengeance is both her own and a presentiment of what is to come.

Watching a good production of *Hecuba* is a savage experience. The murder of Polymestor's young sons is especially horrible. Even apart from the presence on stage of their dead bodies, there is the father's dreadful description of the way the women kissed and cuddled the little boys, passing them from knee to knee to get them away from him, before killing them. *Hecuba* – somewhat like *Blasted* – is a play in two halves that nevertheless creates a unified whole. In the first part Hecuba suffers the loss of Polyxena and learns of the death of Polydorus. In the second, the anguished mother becomes a killer of children. Euripides shirks none of the horror of this. He shows us with brutal clarity how 'harm hatches harm'. We may recoil from the vengeance Hecuba takes, but we have been led by Euripides to understand why she does it.

On 30 August 2005, BBC2 broadcast a documentary about the siege of the Beslan school and its aftermath that casts a tragic, present-day light on this hatching of harm. On the first day of September 2004, masked men and women wearing bomb belts burst into Beslan's Number One School just as a ceremony to mark the start of the school year was drawing to a close. Children and adults were herded into the school gym, where they were kept under constant threat of death and denied access to food or water. We know what happened partly from the testimony of survivors, and partly because the terrorists videoed the proceedings. In a dreadful travesty of a disaster movie, the video captured images of the hostages sitting with their hands in the air, their faces blank with terror. 'Nothing changed', one child said in the documentary. 'For two days we just sat on the floor and that was it, and nothing else.' He fantasised that a terminator would come and rescue them, or that he could put on an invisibility belt and vanish. When he slept, he dreamed that the walls and ceiling were pressing in on him, and that it was impossible to breathe. For most of the children the hardest thing was having no water to drink, because it was stiflingly hot in the gym. Some children and adults were so desperate that they drank urine. A woman terrorist wanted to give the children some water and the terrorist leader detonated the bombs she wore at her waist, so that she exploded. Perhaps this was the female terrorist who can be seen in the documentary. Her face is veiled, apart from her eyes, but she is clearly young. She is holding a gun, which is pointed towards the ceiling, and she is dressed entirely in black, in contrast to a male terrorist the camera focuses on who wears combat gear. Even his mask – a strange, pudding-basin-shaped object – is made from camouflage material. His eyes, which can be seen through two jagged holes, are, as one child said, 'like glass'.

On the third day there was an explosion. A terrorist's grenade had been hit by a bullet. 'He blew up and his brains hit my face', a child explained. After a further explosion, one little girl said to another, 'All my friends are dead. Can I stay with you?'. Then there was a third explosion, and the child 'was gone'. People 'melted' in the explosions. 'One girl had no legs and she couldn't get up. When the fire reached her, she put her hands in the air and started screaming, "Help me! Help me!"'. In the confusion some of the children and adults managed to escape. One child ran to an outside water tap where children were already drinking but, before she reached it, it was blown up by a grenade, along with the children who had been clustered round it.

Afterwards, when the survivors commemorated their loved ones, water played an important role. One child placed a bottle of water and bar of chocolate by the photograph of his mother who had died in the siege. The chocolate was because she 'loved sweets', the water because 'in the gym she was desperate for water', and it was 'like giving her some now'. On May Day 2005, the survivors decorated the graves of those who had died with pieces of cake, painted eggs, flowers, toys and balloons. One boy placed a cuddly toy and little cars on his friend's grave, and then poured water around his offerings. Everyone loved his dead friend, he said. He was a really kind boy. How these children will cope in years to come it is impossible to say. What was done to them is beyond imagining, even when we see the evidence of it. Many of them spoke of their anger and need for vengeance. 'My greatest desire is to go to Chechnya and kill all those terrorists', one child said. A girl repeatedly drew pictures of terrorists, which she then burnt. 'I do the drawings so I can destroy them and express the anger inside . . .' she explained. 'It's never enough. It's impossible to get enough revenge. All my life I'll have to do this.'

Euripides' mothers and daughters

One particularly memorable aspect of the May Day commemoration in the Beslan documentary was the different ways in which the young and the old expressed their grief. The children and young adults were silent, their faces washed clean by sorrow. The old – mostly women – wailed their despair in a way that seemed centuries old and their faces were so disfigured by anguish that, when they were still, they resembled ritualistic masks of suffering. Most of the old women were dressed in black, like images in television footage of grief-stricken women in so many parts of the world. The programme for the RSC production of *Hecuba* contained a number of pictures of such images, and also a statement about Euripides' time that implicitly connected Beslan to a history of related atrocities. When Euripides wrote *Hecuba* (and years later, just before his death *c.* 406 BC, when he was working on *Iphigenia at Aulis*), Athens was at war with Sparta. Both sides, and their allies, 'treated cities who rebelled against their command with appalling savagery . . . when some mercenaries from Thrace . . . invaded a city in central Greece, they not only slaughtered the women and farm animals, but every single child attending the largest local school' (RSC programme). *Iphigenia at Aulis* depicts the beginning of a different war, but Euripides seemingly views the play's events through the prism of his revulsion at the conflict that had been waged throughout most of his long life. In place of the heroic figures in Homer's *Iliad*, he portrays venal, self-interested, puny men who substitute opportunism and political expediency for integrity. In the Introduction to his translation of *Iphigenia at Aulis* (the version used in the production at the Lyttelton Theatre), Don Taylor commented that 'Euripides does the biggest demolition job on the Homeric heroes before Shakespeare put them to the sword in *Troilus and Cressida*'. '[E]ven Shakespeare', he added, 'doesn't have such obvious contempt for his "heroes" as Euripides does' (Taylor, p. x).

Iphigenia at Aulis and *Hecuba* are both set in the aggressive, male world of an army camp. The Trojan women have become slaves, whereas Clytemnestra and Iphigenia have royal status, but all the female characters are seemingly fixed in marginalised, non-negotiable roles. The two daughters, Iphigenia and Polyxena, are sacrificial victims; the mothers, Clytemnestra and Hecuba, impotent bystanders. But 'harm hatches harm'. Hecuba begins like one of the grieving old women of Beslan and ends as a terrifying avenger. A reworking of the Iphigenia story by Edna O'Brien, which was performed at the Crucible Theatre, Sheffield, in February 2003, spelled out the future revenge that Clytemnestra would take. The wind that rose after Iphigenia's death was accompanied by rain, and, as the lights came slowly up on Clytemnestra, the rain was revealed to be a red shower of blood.

Edna O'Brien made other, more radical, alterations to *Iphigenia at Aulis*, particularly with regard to Iphigenia, whose role she extended in order to emphasise the character's youth and vulnerability. Reviewers' opinions were divided about some of O'Brien's alterations, but the ending was generally deemed to be effective. The scholarly consensus is that the final section of the play that has come down to us is not by Euripides. Don Taylor retained it in his translation in the belief that it worked theatrically, and the Lyttelton production followed suit. The disputed ending, which may have been added after Euripides' death by his son, consists primarily of a long speech by an old man describing Iphigenia's death. In a similar vein to the biblical story of Abraham and Isaac, at the last moment the goddess Artemis substitutes a deer in place of the young girl as a sacrificial victim. Iphigenia is 'saved', however, only in the sense that she is transported to the home of the gods. She doesn't return to earthly life. Clytemnestra roundly denounces the tale as a lie, effectively defining it as yet another example of male cynicism and opportunism.

Other parts of the play, in addition to the ending, have been pronounced inauthentic or, at best, confusing. Don Taylor names Aristotle as 'the first dramatic critic . . . to get it wrong' (ibid., p. vii). Aristotle, he writes, 'uses Iphigenia as an example of an inconsistent character, because she changes her mind – is initially terrified of dying, and then finds herself uttering heroic sacrificial speeches' (ibid., p. xvi). Sudden changes of mind, however, are a key feature of the play. Agamemnon first sends for Iphigenia, and then attempts to countermand the order. When he fails, he vacillates between trying to save his daughter and insisting on her death. Achilles promises to protect Iphigenia, but makes little attempt to do so. Menelaus demands Iphigenia's death at one moment, only to change his mind shortly afterwards. Hattie Morahan, who played Iphigenia in the Lyttleton production, made excellent sense of the young girl's change of heart. High on a mixture of terror and the sexual charge of the army camp, she hyped herself up to become an 'ecstatic martyr prepared to sacrifice all for a violent ideal' (Carole Woddis, *Herald*, 25.6.04). Don Taylor describes Iphigenia 'transforming herself before our eyes into a fascist poster, or a Nazi statue of German womanhood sacrificed for the greater Reich' (Taylor, p. xvi), and some reviewers also interpreted the character in the context of Hitler and Fascism. Others made more contemporary connections. Aleks Sierz compared her 'teenage passion' to that of 'a *Big Brother* fan' (*Tribune*, 25.6.04), and, in the *Observer* (27.6.04), Susannah Clapp linked the 'frightening enthusiasm' with which Iphigenia espouses the role of martyr to 'an age of suicide bombers'.

Visually, the Lyttelton production evoked the Second World War and its aftermath, though reviewers were in no doubt that parallels with the situation in Iraq were being suggested. Hildegard Bechtler's set depicted a military HQ. With its high, drab walls, piles of functional chairs and dusty chandelier, it seemed part municipal building, part requisitioned stately home. Clytemnestra's dress could have been styled by Christian Dior. The men were costumed in white or cream linen suits, while the chorus of women wore 'Vera Lynn-style black evening dresses' (*Independent*, 25.6.04). Described in the programme (and in Taylor's translation) as women of Chalcis, the chorus were tourists who had come to Aulis to eye up the celebrities of the Greek army before the latter set off for Troy. A number of reviewers likened the chorus to members of the Women's Institute, but their edginess suggested something less easily comprehensible. They clutched little handbags, from which they suddenly produced autograph books, or powder compacts. They puffed nervously on cigarettes and, when dance music was emitted from speakers attached to the walls, they began to foxtrot, stiffly, like dolls, holding their arms out to imaginary partners. At some points, overhead strip lights would come on inexplicably, accompanied by loud clunking sounds, and then the chorus would freeze before darting around the stage in agitated little flurries of movement. The chorus epitomised the production's atmosphere of hyperactive unease, 'the oppressive feelings it induce[d] ... of migraine, panic, fever' (*Sunday Times,* 27.6.04), the 'all-encompassing' sense of 'nervous breakdown' (*Observer*, 27.6.04).

There was a constant feeling of trying to grasp something – perhaps who, or what, was in charge. The fact that Agamemnon wasn't in control was indicated by the opening moments of the production. He stumbled in darkness across the stage and bumped into a chair, and his first word – an addition to Taylor's translation – was 'Shit!' Throughout the production the focus was often on what was happening off stage. Important events frequently occur off stage in Greek tragedies, but then someone enters and explains what has happened. Explanations were given, too, in the Lyttelton production of *Iphigenia,* but it was not always clear whether we were being told the truth. The atmosphere was one of uncertainty and dread, though what of, was hard to pin down. In their moments of stillness, the chorus of women seemed to be listening for something – but hoping they wouldn't hear it. The men strutted and blustered. There was no conviction, nothing in which to believe, just a pervasive anxiety because something was about to happen.

When Iphigenia was taken away to die, Clytemnestra's grief and anger were so overwhelming that she had to be physically restrained from following her daughter. In the final moments of the production, a wind of truly awesome power blew open the heavy door stage left, and a torrential downpour drenched Clytemnestra. Whether or not anyone, human or divine, had previously been in charge was now irrelevant. The storm would blow the Greeks to Troy, where they would unleash havoc. Meanwhile a tempest of fury would possess Clytemnestra and transform her into Agamemnon's nemesis.

Three *Hecubas*

It is not her daughter Polyxena's death, harrowing though this is, that releases the maelstrom of vengeance in Hecuba, but the revelation of the murder of the child she believed was safe. Even by comparison with what happened to Polyxena the killing of Polydorus is a shocking act, an example of the furtive atrocities that lurk in the interstices of war. The Ghost of Polydorus opens the play, situating it from the start in an emotional terrain that links the tents of the Trojan women with the land of the dead. He foretells Polyxena's death, and describes his own murder, after which Polymestor threw his body into the sea. Now, his corpse drifts with the tide like a piece of flotsam, while his spirit hovers over the Trojan encampment. He longs for his mother to bury him so that he can find rest. When Hecuba enters shortly afterwards, it is evident that she is temporarily an inhabitant of the shadowy, hybrid world Polydorus has evoked. She has woken from monstrous dreams, which terrify her though she is unable to interpret them. It is only when, after Polyxena's death, she sees the body of Polydorus, that she fully grasps what the dreams portended. In her subsequent vengeance she herself turns into the stuff of nightmare.

The three productions of *Hecuba* all depicted Polydorus in different ways. Foursight Theatre Company used puppets, both for Polydorus and for Polymestor's sons, in order to emphasise the vulnerability of these characters. This was an all-female production. There were seven performers, one of whom played Hecuba, while the remaining six portrayed the chorus and all the other characters. In their role as the chorus, they manipulated the Polydorus puppet, as though it was being buffeted by waves, and, at the same time, spoke the character's opening lines. The central focus of the production was on the omnipresence of war, both geographically and throughout history, especially with regard to its female and child victims. The stage floor depicted an abstract representation of a sea shore, upon which was erected a corrugated iron structure, surrounded by electric fencing, that denoted the women's quarters. There were war-related objects from a variety of historical periods strewn around: gas masks, swords, etc. The costumes for the male characters were on stage from the beginning, and the women put them on in view of the audience, underlining the idea that masculine aggression is something that can be put on and taken off, rather than being inevitable. The ethnic diversity of the cast acted as a reminder of the multiple nationalities of war's victims, particularly through the choral odes, which were sung, *a cappella*, in a mixture of languages: English, Hebrew, Dutch, Mandarin, Patois and Russian.

The chorus of twelve women in the RSC production at the Albery Theatre also sang their lines, but a number of reviewers found the style of the singing too reminiscent of a musical. There were disparaging references to similarities with *Les Miserables, Godspell* and *Evita*. Opinion was divided about the chorus' costumes. Daisy Garnett in the *Sunday Telegraph*, for example, described them as 'droopy' and 'hippyish' (10.4.05), but, in the *Observer* of the same date, Susannah Clapp was impressed by the 'blue and sea-green hijabs [which looked] like a halted surge of Mediterranean waves'. The set also came in for some adverse criticism, but, with its high, curved, stone-coloured walls, it had a monumental grandeur. When the walls opened at the start of the performance to reveal the motionless, marble-white figure of Polydorus, the effect was striking.

The most astonishing opening effect, however, was created at the Donmar Warehouse. In this small theatre the audience was very close to the performance space, the entire downstage area of which was covered with water. The Ghost of Polydorus rose up through this water, as though propelled by a submarine current. It was like a conjuring trick, and it was all the more breathtaking because it was impossible to see how it was done. The actor who played Polydorus was young and frail-looking. His white shirt clung to his body, and water streamed over him like a mobile shroud. Upstage, was a steep, white slope, hard and unyielding by contrast with the water, and, behind that, a high, black wall covered with the names of victims of recent wars, chalked in white. Black, white, and later the red of blood were the chief colours of this production. Hecuba's shapeless black dress was timeless. It seemed equally appropriate for the fifth century BC and present-day Iraq or Beslan, or other troubled parts of the world. The chorus' lines were spoken by one old woman, also dressed in black, with sung contributions from a vocalist suspended high up on a hanging platform. When she was not singing, she chalked additional names on the black memorial wall. The white of Polydorus' costume was echoed by the white shirts Polymestor's sons wore as part of the school uniforms, which, when the production opened in September 2004, were a haunting reminder of the Beslan massacre that had ended a few days previously.

The temporal proximity of the two London productions led reviewers to make detailed comparisons between them, and the consensus was that the Donmar production was by far the most effective. Adverse criticism focused primarily on Vanessa Redgrave's performance, which was considered disappointing in comparison with that of Clare Higgins, who had won the Olivier Award for Best Actress for *her* portrayal of Hecuba. There were dissenting voices, however. In the *Spectator* (23.4.05), Lloyd Evans took up the cudgels on Redgrave's behalf, praising her 'cool, measured and monumental reading [which] develops at an austere pace and succeeds because it faithfully observes the formalities of Athenian stagecraft'. Michael Billington's opinion of the two performers was that Clare Higgins was 'monotonous in grief but outstanding in revenge', while Vanessa Redgrave was 'the precise opposite' (*Guardian*, 8.4.05). The majority of reviewers, however, found Redgrave underpowered. The fact that a great deal had been expected of her didn't help matters. Hecuba was her first role for the RSC since she had played Imogen in *Cymbeline* more than forty years earlier, so her return was much anticipated. In addition, her long-standing commitment to victims of political injustice was expected to add a further dimension to her performance in this topical play.

One of Redgrave's most passionate advocates was Germaine Greer, who identified the problem as being with Tony Harrison's translation, rather than Redgrave's acting. In a perceptive article in the *Times Literary Supplement* (15.4.05), Peter Stothard (who also contributed a commentary on the war between Athens and Sparta to the Lyttelton Theatre programme of *Iphigenia at Aulis*), analysed Harrison's translation in relation to Frank McGuinness' at the Donmar. A crucial difference between the Tony Harrison and McGuinness versions, Stothard explained, was that McGuinness uses 'fewer words'. His text is pared down to the bone, creating a skeleton around which the director, Jonathan Kent, and his actors could build, whereas Laurence Boswell, the director of the RSC production, had 'not so much [to] put flesh on a frame as pummel a fat living thing into shape'. Some reviewers had objected to Harrison's 'twenty-first-century political additions' – 'coalition' for example, and 'terrorist' – but, as Stothard pointed out, current interest in *Hecuba* derived from the contemporary political situation, and, in particular, from the aftermath of the war in Iraq. 'The true problem, as Greer recognized, [was] that Tony Harrison's text is not made (and maybe cannot be made) to deliver its poetic power on stage.'

On the page, the difference between the two texts is very apparent. Both were published by Faber & Faber, McGuinness' in 2004, Tony Harrison's in 2005. (Nick Hern Books also published a translation of *Hecuba*, by Marianne McDonald, in 2005.) McGuinness' lines are much shorter. He tends to use simpler verb tenses, and the language is more direct and easier to speak. McGuinness' powerful 'harm hatches harm after harm' (p. 12) becomes in Tony Harrison's translation 'Zeus grooms me for grief, only grimmer!' (p. 9), which is both difficult to say and less resonant. It misses the sense McGuinness captures of brutality, and its attendant desire for revenge, being passed down through the generations.

Harrison is frequently too complex where McGuinness is straightforward. Compare, for example, Harrison's rendering of Polyxena's words to Oydsseus, 'go easy on a parent understandably distressed' (p. 15), with McGuinness', 'Odysseus, she is my mother./ She has just cause for anger' (p. 21). Harrison is also over-alliterative: 'Two good glugs of blood to glut their thirst' (p. 15), for example, compared with McGuinness', 'The earth can swim with blood' (p. 20). And McGuinness is more immediate and dramatic. He personalises, rather than describes. When Hecuba is talking to Agamemnon about her sense of powerlessness in defeat, the words McGuinness gives her to say are, 'I stink of the smoke of burning Troy' (p. 39). Harrison's equivalent line is, 'I see the smoke-clouds glowering over Troy' (p. 31).

Frank McGuinness' translation of *Hecuba* gave Clare Higgins an effective framework for her performance, but her excellence was her own. Vanessa Redgrave had moments of grandeur, but, at least in the performance I saw, they were not sustained. Almost certainly, as some reviewers realised, the problem was that she had not completely recovered from her illness. Hecuba is a gruelling role, impossible for someone who is not in good health. It's pretty exhausting for an audience! By the end of Clare Higgins' performance I was physically shaking as a result of what I had experienced vicariously. I certainly didn't find her 'monotonous in grief'. From her first entrance, following her 'premonitory nightmare', she was 'in a state of hyperventilating terror' (*Daily Telegraph*, 15.9.04), from which her performance built to ever greater heights. An apparent lull in her developing frenzy, when, at her request, Polymestor brought his two young sons to her, in fact cranked up the escalating horror still further. She played affectionately with the children, and then wrapped one of them up in a blanket and carried him off stage. The other child and Polymestor followed. When she returned, she was clutching the dismembered bodies of the children, which were wrapped in transparent plastic, as though they were butcher's offal. Earlier, the boys had sat by the water and sailed sticks on its surface. Now, their father, whom Hecuba and her women had blinded, stumbled into the water, and Hecuba waded in also, carrying the dreadful parcels, which stained the water red.

At the end of the play, Polymestor prophesies the deaths of Agamemnon and Hecuba. Agamemnon will be murdered by Clytemnestra. Hecuba, who will be transformed into a dog, will climb to the top of a ship's mast, from which she will fall into the sea and drown. The place of her death will be known by sailors as 'The Bitch's Grave' (Harrison), 'The grave of the Drowned Dog' (McGuinness). In the final moments of the Donmar production, as the lights faded, Clare Higgins knelt on all fours and scrabbled in the dirt like a dog trying to dig up a bone – perhaps of one of Hecuba's dead children. Great plays are malleable. They retain their essence, while lending themselves to new generations who interpret them in the light of the urgent problems of their own times. In 2004, *Iphigenia at Aulis*, a play written more than two thousand years ago, became a mirror for our anxieties about escalating conflicts that we were being drawn into against our will. Euripides' debunking of divine and human authority found a counterpart in our own lack of trust in political leaders. The wind that is raised in both *Iphigenia at Aulis* and *Hecuba* by the slaughter of children is a terrible mockery, because it is self-defeating. If Agamemnon had not killed Iphigenia, the Greek fleet would never have reached Troy and the horrors that followed would have been avoided. In *Hecuba,* having won the Trojan War, Agamemnon loses the peace. In 2004 and 2005 the similarity with the aftermath of the war in Iraq was obvious. Hecuba herself offers a different lesson. Euripides is unstinting in his depiction of the justice of her grief and anger, but, when she, in her turn, embraces 'terror', she loses her humanity: 'harm hatches harm after harm' like maggots breeding in a corpse.

8

Daughters' tales

> I have just brushed ten million other worlds, and they knew nothing of it.
> (Philip Pullman, *Northern Lights*)
>
> Time and place do not exist; on an insignificant basis of reality the imagination spins, weaving new patterns . . . (Strindberg's Note to *A Dream Play*, translated by Michael Meyer)

Approximately a quarter of the productions discussed in the preceding pages were staged at one of the National Theatre's three venues, the most recent being *Iphigenia at Aulis*, directed by Katie Mitchell, which played at the Lyttelton Theatre from 22 June to 7 September 2004. The texts that are addressed in this and the final chapter all received productions at the National Theatre in 2005. In my Preface to the book, I wrote that lost children project the possibility of children who are found, and my focus in these two final chapters is primarily on rediscovery and survival. This chapter is about two fictional daughters who were created roughly a hundred years apart. What drew my attention to the connections between them was seeing staged versions of their stories in close spatial and temporal proximity. In February 2005, a version of Strindberg's *A Dream Play*, directed by Katie Mitchell, opened at the Cottesloe Theatre. At the same time, a revival of Nicholas Wright's adaptation of Philip Pullman's *His Dark Materials* trilogy was playing at the Olivier. Watching these two productions in close conjunction, I was struck by a number of similarities between their female protagonists. In both cases the fact that they are daughters is significant. They are also both biblically related figures. *His Dark Materials* is a rewriting of the story of the Garden of Eden, which casts the heroine, Lyra Belacqua, as a new Eve. The two names Strindberg gives *his* protagonist – Indra's Daughter and Agnes – both stress her role as a divine child. As the Daughter of the God Indra, she descends to Earth to find out whether the constant complaints of human beings are justified.

There she becomes Agnes, a name that links her with Jesus Christ: *Agnus Dei*, the Lamb of God. Lyra is also reminiscent of Christ when, in a replay of the Harrowing of Hell, she journeys to the land of the dead to free its inhabitants. A further similarity between Indra's Daughter/Agnes and Lyra is their ability to move fluidly through other worlds. Strindberg presents this in the form of a dream, where, as he writes in his 'Author's Note' to the play, 'everything is possible and probable'. Lyra travels through parallel worlds by means of windows that her friend Will cuts with an enchanted knife.

Only the last of these three connections was evident at the Cottesloe, however, because Katie Mitchell's version of *A Dream Play* omitted Indra's Daughter and treated Agnes as a minor character. The production was described, somewhat disingenuously, on posters and in the programme as 'by August Strindberg, in a new version by Caryl Churchill, with additional material by Katie Mitchell and the company', leading Robert Hanks to comment in the *Independent* (21.2.05): 'It's a moot point whether Katie Mitchell ought to be had up for false advertising . . . it is some minutes before anything recognisable as Strindberg turns up; and then it is given such a different context that it feels like something entirely new.' A contributor to the 'Letters to the Editor' page of the same newspaper (13.4.05) put it more strongly. Though he applauded the ingenuity of the piece and the brilliance of the performers, he lamented the absence of 'Strindberg's mysterious poetry', and speculated as to whether a claim for his money back might qualify 'under the Trade Descriptions Act'.

Katie Mitchell's production was interesting in its own right, but its connection with Strindberg's *A Dream Play* (or even Caryl Churchill's version of it) was tenuous at best. The loss of Indra's Daughter, and, even more importantly, the marginalisation of Agnes, cut out the play's heart. Strindberg's Prologue to the play begins with the voice of Indra calling, 'Where are you, daughter, where?' and ends as the Daughter reaches Earth. The rest of the play explores the nature of this place she now inhabits. Without her, a different kind of play world can be assembled from the remaining elements, but it isn't the one Strindberg created. This matters because *A Dream Play* is not very often performed in this country, and it is not only a very good play but also an important one in the context of the development of Modernism. My aim in this chapter has been to rediscover the Daughter who was lost in Katie Mitchell's production. I do this partly by examining how Strindberg depicts her in his play. In addition, I consider her in the context of related extracts from Strindberg's *Occult Diary*, a selection of his letters, and the exhibition of his paintings and photographs at Tate Modern (which ran concurrently with the Cottesloe production). I also discuss earlier productions of *A Dream Play*, in particular Ingmar Bergman's 1970 production, which treated Indra's Daughter and Agnes as two separate characters. In his Author's Note to *A Dream Play*, Strindberg describes how he sets the audience's imagination spinning in order to lead them into the dream world that characterises his 'flickering tale'. I approach this dream world via the parallel worlds in *His Dark Materials*. Before focusing on Strindberg's Daughter, I concentrate on Pullman's protagonist, whose name is the first and last word in his trilogy.

Dark nights and swirling snow

Pullman is a great storyteller, and, in interviews, he returns frequently to the central importance of narrative. 'The story is the most important thing. The writer's main responsibility is to the story', he said in an interview with Melvyn Bragg on the *South Bank Show* (20.12.04). In response to a question from Melvyn Bragg about the sources of his inspiration for *His Dark Materials,* he talked about ideas coming to him out of images of dark nights and swirling snow, and the imagined sound of striking bells. The words capture a sense of Pullman's particular brand of atmospheric magic, especially in the first book, *Northern Lights*, which tells the story of Lyra's journey from Jordan College, Oxford, to the frozen north in search of her friend Roger who has been kidnapped by the Gobblers. Although Lyra doesn't know it, she is also in quest of her destiny. The title, *His Dark Materials*, is taken from Milton's *Paradise Lost,* which Pullman quotes from at the beginning of *Northern Lights*. The key figure in this retelling of *Genesis* is Lyra, the new Eve.

Paradise Lost and images of snowy nights were not Pullman's only source of inspiration for *His Dark Materials*. He admits to being a 'magpie', picking up shiny bits and pieces wherever he finds them, and weaving them into the fabric of the narrative. 'Apart from Milton, Pullman's books draw heavily on Homer, the Icelandic Sagas, Dante, Blake, Wordsworth, the Shelleys, Wagner, Barrie and Tolkien', Michael Billington remarked in his review of the Olivier production of *His Dark Materials* (*Guardian*, 15.1.04). The list omits Pullman's most obvious source after *Paradise Lost*, which is the Narnia books of C. S. Lewis. Pullman intensely dislikes what he sees as the 'religious propaganda' behind these stories. The *His Dark Materials* books have been criticised in turn as anti-Christian, and, especially, anti-Catholic, but Pullman admits only to their anti-clericalism. The books celebrate love, kindness, tolerance, courage and open-heartedness, he points out – and he respects Jesus as a great storyteller.

Elements of *His Dark Materials* deliberately echo, and rework, the Narnia stories. As Nicholas Tucker explains in *Darkness Visible: Inside the World of Philip Pullman*, both C. S. Lewis and Pullman 'are fascinated by ideas of Northernness, and both create worlds separate from this one where children are put to severe moral tests before finally saving both themselves and everyone else' (Tucker, p. 161). Both authors begin their stories in a similar way. 'The Narnia stories famously start with a child making a voyage to another land that exists at the back of a wardrobe' (ibid., pp. 161–2). In the first chapter of *Northern Lights,* Lyra hides in a wardrobe and overhears a conversation from which all her adventures in other worlds follow. The fact that Lewis' Lucy stumbles into Narnia by accident, whereas Lyra deliberately seeks out a way of beginning her journey, highlights the importance Pullman places on ingenuity and self-reliance. The chief focus of his distaste for the Narnia stories, however, is the final section of *The Last Battle*, in which the children's death in a railway accident is presented as a positive thing because they can now stay in Narnia (Heaven) forever. Pullman also criticised Tolkien in the *South Bank Show* interview. He found 'nothing of human value or interest', he said, in the writings of the Catholic Tolkien for whom 'all questions are settled'. As for Lewis, the 'Ulster Protestant', he 'wrestle[d] with questions', but Pullman considered his answers to be 'profoundly world-hating'. Though Lyra and Will explore other worlds, each finally settles down to grow up in her/his own world. Their re-enaction of the Fall of Adam and Eve enables them to take the first steps towards adult wisdom and responsibility. Pullman rejects a belief in the Kingdom of Heaven, but puts in its place the idea of a republic of Heaven, which is located, not elsewhere, but here in this world – if we work to create it.

Another, more recondite, source for *His Dark Materials* to which Pullman has frequently referred is an essay by Heinrich von Kleist called 'On the Marionette Theatre'. The opening sentence of the essay, 'One evening in the winter of 1801 I met an old friend in a public park' (quoted in *Darkness Visible*, p. 197, translator Idris Parry), stirs pre-echoes of *His Dark Materials*. The winter setting evokes *Northern Lights*, while the park itself is suggestive of the Oxford Botanic Garden that plays an important role at the end of Pullman's trilogy. The most crucial aspect of the essay in relation to *His Dark Materials,* however, is Kleist's exploration of the nature of grace. The friend the narrator meets is a well-known dancer, and the narrator questions him about why he has been attending performances at the marionette theatre. Surely these puppets have nothing to teach him. The friend tells a couple of stories in order to show the narrator that he is wrong. One is about a young man whose unconscious grace vanishes once he becomes aware of it, the other about a bear that can parry the moves of a skilled fencer. For marionettes, grace is instinctive, the friend sums up, but human beings can only attain grace through knowledge. The narrator is baffled at first, but eventually understands that grace, or a 'state of innocence', can be achieved only if we 'eat again of the tree of knowledge' (ibid., p. 207).

Pullman's metaphor for grace is Dust, which can be defined as accumulated human knowledge and experience. Dust is leaking away from Lyra's world, and from Will's (which is also ours), and from all the parallel worlds the two children visit. This loss will continue until Lyra and Will fulfil their destinies as the new Eve and Adam. The villains in the story are the representatives of an authoritarian Christian Church that exhibits the worst features of both Catholicism and Protestantism. They equate Dust with Original Sin and are determined to destroy it. This is the explanation of the story Lyra hears about Roger's capture by the Gobblers. In her world everyone has an external aspect of self, called a daemon, which takes the form of an animal or bird, and corresponds with a soul or spirit. Children's daemons can transform themselves from one shape into another, but during adolescence a daemon's shape gradually becomes fixed. Children are also relatively free of Dust, but they begin to attract it when they become adolescents. The Gobblers, who are really a powerful Church organisation (the General Oblation Board), are taking kidnapped children to a research station in the far north, where they cut away their daemons by means of an operation called intercision. Without their daemons the children no longer attract Dust when they reach puberty. As a result, they become much easier to control.

Children are in grave danger therefore in *His Dark Materials*, and it is Lyra's task to save them. In fulfilment of this task, she travels not only through living worlds, but also, in a re-visioning of the Harrowing of Hell, into the world of the dead. As there is no Christian Kingdom of Heaven in *His Dark Materials*, Lyra leads the dead into a living world, where they become one with the earth and the stars. In order to fulfil her destiny, both as the new Eve and as the Christ substitute who releases the imprisoned dead, Lyra has to define herself as distinct from her parents, as well as from the Church. At the heart of *His Dark Materials* is the story of a great battle between the forces of oppression and freedom, and Lyra's parents are key players in this battle. Her father, the powerful, charismatic Lord Asriel, leads an army against the Authority (Pullman's equivalent of God), while Mrs Coulter (her mother) tries to protect her from the Church which wants to destroy this potential new Eve. In *The Amber Spyglass* (the final book of the trilogy) both parents die in order to save Lyra. However, though they sacrifice themselves for their daughter in the end, Lord Asriel and Mrs Coulter are at best ambivalent figures. Both are capable of great cruelty, and both harm children. After Lyra rescues Roger from the Oblation Board, Lord Asriel severs the boy from his daemon in order to create the great surge of energy he needs to travel to another world in search of the Authority. In the process Roger dies. Mrs Coulter is superficially charming, but her dangerousness is indicated by her daemon, a beautiful but predatory golden monkey. In *Northern Lights*, Mrs Coulter begins by siding with the Church dignitaries. She entices children away from their homes and hands them over to the Oblation Board.

Though she is seduced for a time by her parents' glamour, Lyra's initial belief that she is an orphan protects her from being influenced overmuch by them. She has been brought up in a rough-and-ready way by the masters of Jordan College, believing that her mother and father are dead, and the result is that 'she comes over as someone who has largely invented herself, and who still retains the possibility of reinventing herself once again should the occasion demand' (ibid., p. 107). Both her name and her nickname, Silvertongue, attest to another aspect of her inventiveness, her skill as a storyteller. 'Lyra' refers to her abilities as a liar (a teller of fibs, who is able to fool her enemies and escape from dangerous situations). It also has 'overtones of lyre – the instrument of the gods' (ibid., p. 109). She is simultaneously a weaver of tales and the means by which a new tale will replace a very old one. Like Lyra's name, that of Will, the new Adam, is significant because it expresses his determination and staying power. Will comes from a parallel Oxford, which is in fact the Oxford in our world. Lyra's world is similar in a number of ways to Will's, but there are also anachronistic details such as naphtha lights and zeppelins, and also fantastic creatures like witches and talking bears. Lyra first meets Will in a parallel world called Cittàgazze (city of the magpies) where frightening beings called Spectres are sucking Dust out of adults and turning them into zombies. They leave children alone because they have very little Dust. In Cittàgazze, Will is forced to fight for the subtle knife, which he then uses to cut windows into adjacent worlds.

In his engrossing study of hyperspace theory, *Hyperspace: A Scientific Odyssey through the 10th Dimension*, Michio Kaku notes that 'Gateways between our universe and other dimensions are . . . a favorite literary device' (Kaku, p. 21). He goes on to define a likely source of inspiration for an early alternative world, Lewis Carroll's Wonderland, as being 'the great nineteenth-century German mathematician Georg Bernhard Riemann, who was the first to lay the mathematical foundation of geometries in higher-dimensional space' (ibid., p. 22). 'Wonderland' is also the name of one of Strindberg's paintings that I discuss in relation to *A Dream Play*. The multiple dream worlds in Strindberg's play probably derive in part from what Kaku describes as the 'Interest in higher dimensions [which] reached its peak between 1870 and 1920, when the "fourth dimension" (a spatial dimension, different from what we know as the fourth dimension of time) seized the public imagination and gradually cross-fertilized every branch of the arts. . .' (ibid., pp. 21–2). As Kaku explains, Expressionism (of which Strindberg was an early exponent in the theatre) was 'heavily influenced' by the concept of the fourth dimension. In our time, the cosmologist Stephen Hawking has gone on to explore the possibility of 'an infinite number of self-contained universes . . . and [to] postulate . . . the possibility of tunneling (via wormholes) between them' (ibid., p. 264). The windows in *His Dark Materials* are the equivalent of wormholes, and Lyra and Will use them to journey between parallel worlds.

Near the end of *His Dark Materials,* the now adolescent Lyra and Will fall in love. Pullman gives few details of their sexual encounter, but it is presented in terms that evoke the story of Adam and Eve in the Garden of Eden. Lyra offers Will fruit, which he eats, and, when he kisses her, her mouth tastes of the sweet fruit. Afterwards, Dust stops flowing away because it has 'found a living home again, and these children-no-longer-children, saturated with love [are] the cause of it all' (Pullman, *The Amber Spyglass*, p. 497). The end of the story is initially surprising, given Pullman's emphasis on the importance of freedom and experience. Having just discovered their love for one another, like their teenaged forebears Romeo and Juliet, Will and Lyra have to part   not through death but by returning to their own worlds. The reason for this is that Dust is still being lost through the open windows between the worlds. It is Will's task to close them, and then to break the subtle knife. Lyra and Will each offer to live in the other's world, but they learn that it is impossible to survive for long in a world other than one's own. They promise that every Midsummer's Day they will sit on a bench in the Oxford Botanic Garden, which exists in both their worlds, and think of one another. Pullman writes: 'Will began to close the window, and then it was done, the way was closed,

Lyra was gone' (ibid., p. 539). Lyra and Will must each build the republic of Heaven in their own separate worlds. For them, and for all of us, there is no elsewhere. Except in stories! The republic of Heaven (which 'embodies meaningfulness' and our connections with each other, *South Bank Show* interview) needs its founding story. Lyra's narrative ability has a final significance because it enables her to resolve a paradox. She must fulfil her destiny, but she must not be coerced into doing so. Her ability to create fictional worlds gives her an inventiveness and imaginative freedom that makes this seem possible.

In the translation of *His Dark Materials* from the page to the stage, Lyra retained her role as the protagonist, but her storytelling function was less evident. Originally scheduled for performance in time for Christmas 2003, the two parts into which Pullman's trilogy were restructured didn't open until the New Year 2004 because of technical hitches. With their multilevel sets (created by means of the Olivier's huge drum revolve), wide array of puppets and atmospheric visual and sound effects, these productions were a complex project. Lyra and Will were played by adult actors. Both parts began and ended with the bench in the Botanic Garden, and this created a time-frame for the action. Visually, the productions were immensely inventive. Scenes rose and fell on the drum revolve, enhanced by lighting effects and video projections. There was a particularly wonderful effect of a large rowing boat, complete with sepulchral boatman, that materialised in mid-air out of blackness to take Lyra and Will to the land of the dead. The wraithlike figures of the dead were replicated in a huge, tilted, upstage mirror, creating an image reminiscent of Gustave Doré's illustrations for *Paradise Lost*. The talking bears were created by actors holding masks in front of their bodies. Black-clad actor-puppeteers, as in Japanese Bunraku Theatre, operated the puppets that represented the daemons. These delicate fabrications of gauze and wire, lit from within, were expressive and often very beautiful, notably Mrs Coulter's sinuous golden monkey with its great green eyes, and Lyra's daemon, Pantalaimon, which chiefly took the form of a pine marten 'with a radiant, quizzically-tilted face' (*Observer*, 11.1.04). There was a particularly moving (and economically-created) moment when Lyra had to leave Pantalaimon behind before entering the land of the dead, and take her death with her in his place. This was realised on stage by the actor who manipulated Pantalaimon, and spoke his words, taking off his black hood in order to become this other aspect of Lyra.

In the *South Bank Show* interview, Pullman explained the value of the daemons, and especially Pantalaimon, in the development of the story. Once he had created Pantalaimon, Lyra had someone to talk to, and it became much easier 'to tell a scene'. Pullman also talked about the advantages of telling a story in the third person, which enabled him to move the narrative voice around among his characters. His childhood love of comics, he added, had also fed into his ideas on storytelling, because all the elements of each picture in a comic contributed to the story. There was the caption at the top, and then all the different things that the characters were saying, and thinking. These comments highlight the essentially dramatic way in which Pullman approaches storytelling. On stage, it was the complex layering of visual narrative that is suggested by his response to images in comics that was the strongest element.

Reviewers' responses to the productions varied. Some deplored what they saw as Pullman's anti-Christian message, while others applauded his militant humanism. This was especially the case when the shows were revived in December 2004, following the announcement that the proposed film version of *His Dark Materials* would 'pander to the Christian Right lobby in the US by eliminating all references to the church as the oppressive enemy' (*Observer*, 12.12.04). Many reviewers were impressed by the representation of the land of the dead and of the daemons, but found some of the more spectacular effects too intrusive. Some of the smaller, individual, moments seemed to them more memorable. I would agree with this. I would have preferred a simpler staging that relied more on the exercise of imagination by the audience. This was a show, however, primarily for children, and the enormous Olivier auditorium was packed on the nights that I saw the two productions. A large percentage of the members of the audience were children and it was a great experience to see their eyes fixed on a stage with such rapt enjoyment.

In November 2005, the National Theatre followed up the success of *His Dark Materials* with an adaptation of another children's novel, *Coram Boy*, by Jamila Gavin. This dramatisation of the stories of endangered and lost children, which ends with restitution and redemption, is discussed in Chapter 9. The remainder of this chapter is devoted to Strindberg's *A Dream Play*, and, in particular, to Indra's Daughter/Agnes. In contrast to Lyra Belacqua, Strindberg's protagonist is portrayed as a daughter from the beginning. Even after she descends to Earth, there are references to her role as a divine child – and briefly also to a human father. Lyra begins by believing that she is an orphan, and, though she discovers that her parents are alive, her ability to define who and what she is continues to be of crucial importance. Fundamentally, Lyra is a storyteller, a spinner of tales. *A Dream Play* works at least as much through visual similarities and oppositions as it does through a verbal narrative. What gives the piece its unity is the dreamer, and the Daughter has a strong claim to this key role. The multiple worlds of *A Dream Play* and *His Dark Materials* are expressions of the creative imagination. Both Lyra and the Daughter leave the alternative worlds behind at the close of their stories, but, whereas Pullman presents this as a positive step, Strindberg ends on a more questioning note.

A Dream Play

Strindberg's 'children'

In 1907, the same year that *A Dream Play* received its first-ever performance (at the Swedish Theatre, Stockholm), Strindberg wrote four chamber plays: *Storm, The Burned House, The Ghost Sonata* and *The Pelican*. Thinking about Katie Mitchell's version of A *Dream Play* after watching a performance of it at the Cottesloe, I found myself remembering a speech by the Student, the central character in *The Ghost Sonata*. Like the Daughter in *A Dream Play*, the Student has an other-worldly aspect. He is a 'Sunday child', and therefore has the ability to see things that other people can't see. As the speech makes clear, he is also connected, like the Daughter, with salvation – and its absence. He describes how he was walking down a street when he saw a house beginning to collapse. A wall was about to fall on a child who was passing, and he 'dashed over and picked up' the child. 'The next moment the house collapsed.' The Student was safe, but, in his arms, which he 'thought held the child, was nothing at all' (*Six Plays of Strindberg*, translated by Elizabeth Sprigge, pp. 275–6). Recalling this speech after the Cottesloe production, I was struck by the relevance of this vanished child to Katie Mitchell's version of *A Dream Play*. In the Cottesloe performance a character called Agnes had a peripheral role, sometimes as a secretary, sometimes as an angel, sometimes as a mixture of the two, but, like the vanishing child in *The Ghost Sonata*, Strindberg's Daughter had disappeared.

Before rediscovering her in *A Dream Play*, I want to turn to some of Strindberg's related letters and paintings, and to extracts from his *Occult Diary*. Biographical details can be a distraction from a writer's work, but in Strindberg's case the close link between his life and his plays is generally accepted. This is particularly true of *A Dream Play*, which includes a number of incidents drawn from Strindberg's life. On 2 April

1907 (a couple of weeks before the first night of *A Dream Play*), Strindberg wrote to his German translator, Emil Schering: 'My whole life often seems to me as if it had been staged for me, so that I might both suffer and portray it' (*Strindberg's Letters, Volume Two*, translated by Michael Robinson, p. 737).

Strindberg wrote *A Dream Play* in 1901, the same year in which he married the young Norwegian actress, Harriet Bosse, for whom he created the role of the Daughter. Like Strindberg's two previous marriages, this one was tempestuous, and the difficulties between husband and wife were exacerbated by the fact that Strindberg was almost thirty years older than Harriet. From the start they were apart more than they were together – though they continued to meet, and occasionally to make love, even after their divorce in 1904. In his frequent letters to Harriet, and also in his fascinatingly strange *Occult Diary*, Strindberg often addresses her as 'Child'. There are also many references to their real child, Anne-Marie. When Harriet was three months pregnant, on 4 September 1901, Strindberg wrote a letter, which he addressed 'To my child! (The unborn little one)':

> And you, child of the South and the North, were carried in the light green beech-woods by the blue sea!
> And your beautiful mother rocked you on blue billows in the sea that washes three kingdoms – and in the evenings, when the sun was going down – she sat in the garden and turned her face to the sun to give you light to drink.
> (ibid., p. 684)

Round about the same time, he painted a picture called *A Child's First Cradle*, which is a pictorial counterpart of this letter. In 1894 he had painted *Wonderland*, and in 1901 he returned to, and reworked, key images in this picture. In *Wonderland*, a central area of radiant light (possibly sky or water) is surrounded by dark woodland. The effect is of a cave, but a cave composed of light rather than darkness. (This reversal of expectation creates the suggestion of an alternative or parallel world.) In *The Child's First Cradle* the cave of light is much larger than in *Wonderland*. A setting sun has turned sea and sky to gold, and around them is an oval frame of greenery, like the frame of a mirror. Another 'Wonderland' painting of 1901, *Inferno*, uses a similar structure, but the colours and mood are dark and stormy. Together, *A Child's First Cradle* and *Inferno* capture the paired opposites that Strindberg portrays in *A Dream Play*: light and dark, rising and falling, freedom and imprisonment, beauty and ugliness.

A few days after composing the letter to his unborn child, Strindberg wrote a letter to Harriet about both this child and his other, literary, one, *A Dream Play*. 'I am writing "The Growing Castle"' (an early name for *A Dream Play*), he tells her. 'It is of course about you – Agnes – who will free the Prisoner from the castle . . . May I talk it into being with you?' (ibid., p. 685). The choice of words suggests the verbal gestation and delivery of a baby. A few lines later, a reference to the child Harriet was carrying evokes the idea of theatre. Strindberg describes how he has prepared his home in the hope that Harriet, from whom he was already estranged, will return for the birth. 'I "pretended"', he writes, 'that the little one will be born in the green bed! where the violets on your nightgown are now waiting'. Then the sight of the nightgown overwhelms him with a sense of loss. 'Soon I won't be able to play any more', he continues, 'and then I'll die!' (ibid., pp. 685–6). Strindberg was not given custody of the children from his first two marriages, and his longing for another child was evident from the start of his relationship with Harriet. 'Will you have a little child by me, Fröken Bosse?' he asked her when he proposed. (Bosse's explanatory note, *From an Occult Diary*, p. 34). In Strindberg's mind, Harriet seems to have been simultaneously his child (in correspondence he addressed her also as Indra's Daughter, Agnes, and the Easter girl – another role he created for her), and both a literal mother and a maternal muse.

Harriet gave birth to Anne-Marie on 25 March 1902. Strindberg's references to the daughter he frequently calls Lillan (a Swedish pet name for a little girl) show his great affection for the child. Anne-Marie sometimes lived with Strindberg when Harriet's career took her away from Stockholm. He records details of their life together: the child's distress when she was missing her mother, or was stung by a mosquito, for example, or the way in which she took his hand when they were staying by the sea and guided him 'over the stones' (*Letters*, p. 710). There is a brief entry in the *Occult Diary* that I find oddly moving. 'Lillan came to see me', Strindberg wrote on 5 May 1904, when the little girl would have been two: 'lost a button from her coat'. It is the simple ordinariness in association with loss that is notable here in contrast to Strindberg's anguish when Harriet left him. A few months before he died, he wrote to Anne-Marie: 'Good day little child; dreamt of you last night; it was summer . . .' (*Letters*, p. 826). This was in winter, on 17 February 1912. (A late photograph of Strindberg shows him walking down a snow-bound, deserted street, coat collar turned up to protect his neck, hands in his pockets. He looks ill and haggard and in the desolation of the image there is an echo of Munch's painting, *On Karl Johan Street*). On 19 April 1912, Strindberg wrote to Anne-Marie probably for the last time:

> My dear little daughter,
> Thank you for your red flowers! But you mustn't try to see me. There are so many medicine bottles, doctors and things here that it is no fun.
> Rejoice in your youth, among the young, and do not grieve for an old man, whose only wish is to depart.
> Father (ibid., p. 828)

'Fun' is hardly the most obvious thing one associates with Strindberg, and I find it particularly poignant that he wanted to protect the child from its absence. He died of stomach cancer the following month, on 14 May.

For a number of years prior to this he was in great pain, to the degree that he was possessed by it. The *Occult Diary*, which Strindberg began writing in February 1896 at the height of his 'Inferno' crisis when he was close to madness, is a record of possession – by Strindberg's demons, by his need to create, and, in the later years, by Harriet and by his illness. There are repeated references to smell and taste. He himself smells of celery and incense, Harriet is in his mouth like violets or roses. In letters, he writes as if Harriet were physically present: 'Dear Child, You are storming and pressing upon me today' (13 March 1906, *Letters*, p. 727), or as if she were part of him: 'At times I have you inside my coat, and I am you –' (8 December 1905, ibid., p. 725). Increasingly, Strindberg believed that he and Harriet were in touch telepathically and that she sought him repeatedly in 'love and eros'. These, presumably masturbatory, fantasies became more frequent in the final pages of the diary, and, increasingly, they were entwined with the physical pain he was suffering. On 18 May 1908, for instance, he wrote in the *Occult Diary:* 'I woke at 1.30 to find H-t stretching my Epigastrium [pit of the stomach] . . . she stormed me in eros'; and, on 12 June, 'H-t gave me shooting pains all night. The pain in my ventricle [obsolete word for stomach] was excruciating but I did not fall, even though I knew I should be free of it if I embraced her (in my thoughts)' (pp. 138 and 150). Sometimes the violence of his pain was so great that he thought Harriet was dying, sometimes that she was murdering him.

Harriet remarried in May 1908, and shortly afterwards Strindberg stopped writing the diary. Clearly the close proximity of the two events suggests that the first may have motivated the second. However, a letter Strindberg wrote to his publisher on 24 June 1908, in which he stated his belief that he had stomach cancer, may point to a need to end the diary and face up to reality. Three days earlier, he had written in the diary 'A terrible night! Was tortured for five hours! Dreamt of H-t, modest, beautiful, like she was the time she knotted my cravat and afterwards kissed my lips as if I were her child' (p. 156). This dream of being Harriet's child, being cared for and comforted by her, may relate to Strindberg's desire, in his illness, for the mother he had lost in childhood. There may also be an echo of the request he made to Harriet in 1901 to talk *A Dream Play* into being with her. If so, what she would be talking into being with him this time would be an awareness of the illness that was killing him. This knowledge would be their final 'child'.

Of all his literary children, *A Dream Play* was Strindberg's favourite. When it opened at the Swedish Theatre on 17 April 1907, with Harriet as the Daughter, Strindberg was at home (as he generally was during premieres of his plays). At eight o'clock that evening, he wrote a letter to Emil Schering in which he described *A Dream Play* as 'my best loved Play, the child of my greatest pain' (*Letters*, p. 738). The equation of love and pain recalls the similar connection between life and suffering that Strindberg made in his letter to Schering on 2 April. The word 'child' suggests not only the play, but also Harriet and the role of the Daughter that she was playing while Strindberg was writing his letter.

Falling into Wonderland

The exhibition of Strindberg's paintings and photographs that ran concurrently at Tate Modern with Katie Mitchell's production of *A Dream Play* included a number of photographic self-portraits. In an article published in the *Sunday Times* the day before previews of *A Dream Play* began, theatre director Dominic Dromgoole drew attention to the way that 'Strindberg glares wildly at you' from photographs, but, he added, 'In the effort of the glare, there is something fragile'. Strindberg, he wrote, had 'a particular insight into the fragility of the human figure lost in the great broil of everything', and he defined the 'best paintings' in the exhibition as those in which 'small figures . . . [maintain] . . . a frail existence between turbulent skies and seething seas'. The plays, too, Dromgoole added, 'most exquisitely *Easter* [which he was currently directing] portray his characters' lonely dazzle under the stars'. These final words seem to me wonderfully apt in the way they capture both the sense of isolation in Strindberg's work, and his continuous (usually anguished and possibly hopeless) quest for meaning in human existence. Strindberg lived, almost always, close to the edge of despair, and yet again, almost always, he experienced, and expressed the 'dazzle under the stars'. To my mind, *A Dream Play* is his loveliest play. My favourite paintings in the exhibition weren't the obviously dramatic ones. They were studies of deserted beaches that Strindberg painted in 1892, often on cardboard or zinc. In each one, in the bottom left or right-hand corner, there is a small flower – a weed really (a thistle, a purple loosestrife) or, in one instance, a fly-cap toadstool. They are tiny, solitary elements in luminous expanses of sea and sky. One of these pictures in particular, a small, almost white, painting entitled *Beach, Summer Night,* seemed to me especially beautiful, but they were all simultaneously serene and irradiated with longing. It is a strange, haunting combination that, in conjunction with the 'Wonderland' paintings, reminds me of *A Dream Play*.

The 'Wonderland' paintings evoke the related otherness of a parallel world. I have already referred to Michio Kaku's comments in *Hyperspace* on Lewis Carroll's Wonderland as an early parallel world. In her book on Strindberg's plays for the *Macmillan Modern Dramatists* series, Margery Morgan writes: 'The opening of *A Dream Play* is Alice in Wonderland stuff, absurd in the popular sense of the word. Against a backcloth painted with gigantic hollyhocks, surrounding a castle with a gilded dome crowned by a chrysanthemum in bud, a daughter asks her father how much growth the building has made in a year' (Morgan, pp. 122–3). Another of Kaku's analogies for a parallel world is also helpful in thinking about the beginning of *A Dream Play*. In his 2005 book entitled *Parallel Worlds*, Kaku advises his reader to:

> Imagine the stage of life consisting of multistory stages, one on top of the next. On each stage, the actors read their lines and wander around the set, thinking that their stage is the only one, oblivious of the possibilities of alternate realities. However, if one day they accidentally fall into a trapdoor, they find themselves thrust into an entirely new stage, with new laws, new rules, and a new script. (p. 112)

This is similar to what happens to Indra's Daughter at the end of the Prologue. Having fallen into the 'trapdoor', she becomes Agnes, and her father – at least for the time being – is a character called the Glazier. The world she has entered resembles a dream. 'Everything can happen, everything is possible and probable. Time and place do not exist; on an insignificant basis of reality the imagination spins, weaving new patterns . . . The characters split, double, multiply, evaporate, condense, disperse, assemble' ('Author's Note' to *A Dream Play*, Meyer, *Strindberg Plays*, p. 553). Ruling over all these disparate elements, and providing coherence, is the consciousness of the dreamer.

In *The Writer in Extremis: Expressionism in Twentieth-Century German Literature,* Walter H. Sokel explains that, in *A Dream Play,* Strindberg imitates 'the form and pattern of dreams, not their actual subject matter'. Strindberg's intention, he adds, in *A Dream Play,* is 'to reproduce a universe in which the empirical laws of causality and relationship are suspended and only a single purpose rules'. This is what makes the play an important early example of Expressionism. 'The Expressionist dramatist, like the dreamer, concentrates entirely on the purpose of expressing an inner world'. The stage environment is a 'projection' of the protagonist's 'inner self'. Moreover, 'the Expressionist character is not a fixed individual personality, but the crystallization of psychic forces, [which modify] the scene surrounding him' (Sokel, p. 38).

Sokel's words describe the effect of an expressionist performance, of course, not how this is to be achieved by the director or designer. Victor Castegren, the director of the original production in 1907, 'planned to use magic lantern slides' in order to create the effect of dematerialisation that Strindberg hoped for. Unfortunately, 'the German apparatus gave trouble in rehearsal, and they had to resort to ordinary decor' (Meyer's introduction to Bergman's adaptation of *A Dream Play,* p. xiii). The resulting lengthy scene changes worked against the play's hypnotic, dreamlike quality. Four years earlier, Strindberg had tried to interest the theatre director Hjalmar Selander in a simpler production of *A Dream Play,* using a mixture of 'projected back-cloths' and 'a few ordinary back-drops' that could be flown out during blackouts (*Letters,* p. 702), but nothing came of this.

In the twentieth century, two famous Swedish directors, Olof Molander and Ingmar Bergman, explored a variety of solutions for staging *A Dream Play*. In Stockholm in 1935, Molander used well-known Swedish locations to underline its autobiographical nature. Twelve years later, in a production in Malmö, he emphasised both its autobiographical content and Strindberg's reliance on Christian imagery, by means of a cross over an altar in the final scene, inscribed with the words on Strindberg's grave: *Ave o crux spes unica* (Hail, o cross, our only hope). A few months later, Molander directed *A Dream Play* again, this time in Gothenberg. In the final scene, 'a large, simple wooden cross' with a background of ruins echoed the devastation of the Second World War. The Daughter's constant refrain in the play, '"Human beings are to be pitied", acquired a topical connotation' (Ingvar Holm, 'Theories and Practice in Staging *A Dream Play*', *Strindberg's Dramaturgy,* p. 253).

Ingmar Bergman's best-known production of the play is probably that of 1970 in the small studio auditorium of Stockholm's Royal Theatre, for which he used his own abbreviated adaptation of the text. This played for approximately an hour and three quarters, without an interval. There was no attempt to follow Strindberg's stage directions. A table, a few screens and wooden chairs constituted the entire set. The colours were chiefly black, white and grey. This was particularly effective when the action moved from Foulstrand to the opposite location, Fairhaven. Foulstrand was portrayed almost entirely in black, while, in Fairhaven, everything apart from the Poet's costume was white. Bergman's minimalist approach capitalised on the fact that most people dream in black and white, though actually *A Dream Play* is very colourful. There is the gilded roof of the Growing Castle, for example, and an abundance of flowers – roses, sunflowers, the chrysanthemum, an enormous blue monk's hood and gigantic white, purple, pink and yellow hollyhocks. In 1909, when Strindberg wrote to members of the Intimate Theatre about a proposed new production of the play, he was still emphasising the importance of colour. Colourful costumes from a variety of periods, he suggested, might create a dreamlike effect. He would, however, have approved of the visual simplicity of Bergman's approach, which gave primacy to the words. In May 1908, he wrote to August Falck (founder of the Intimate Theatre) in support of a simple approach to the staging of his plays: 'the spoken word is all!' (*Letters*, p. 783).

The dreamer

A key decision that faces a director of *A Dream Play* is the identity of the dreamer. In his 'Author's Note' Strindberg wrote that 'one consciousness rules over [all the characters] . . . that of the dreamer; for him there are no secrets, no illogicalities . . . He neither acquits nor condemns, but merely relates . . .'. Strindberg seems to be referring to himself here as the dreamer, given that he is the one from whom nothing about the dream is hidden. Directors, however, have sometimes designated one or more of the characters as the dreamer. 'Molander's 1935 production of *A Dream Play* . . . identified the three principal male characters [the Officer, the Lawyer and the Poet] with aspects of Strindberg' (Morgan p. 168), effectively creating a composite dreamer. Ingmar Bergman, in his 1970 adaptation, made the Poet the controlling consciousness of the play. In 2005, Katie Mitchell gave the role of the dreamer to an updated version of the Officer.

The Officer, to whom Strindberg gave some of his own childhood memories and his feelings towards Harriet Bosse, is the most obviously autobiographical character. In the first scene he is a prisoner in the Growing Castle, until he is rescued by the Daughter. I have already quoted Strindberg's letter to Harriet Bosse where he styled himself as the prisoner in the castle and Harriet as his hoped-for rescuer. The Growing Castle was inspired by the 'new cavalry barracks with its gilded onion-shaped dome ("the most beautiful building in Stockholm", [Strindberg] called it in an essay), which he could see from his windows in Karlavägen', (Meyer, introduction to Bergman's *Dream Play*, p. xii). The Officer waits near the stage door for his beloved, a singer called Victoria, and, as he waits, time speeds up so that night follows day, and winter follows summer, in bewildering succession. When he first arrives, he is a young man clasping a fresh bunch of roses, but he rapidly ages, growing old and infirm, while his roses wither. In a dreamlike way this replays incidents in Strindberg's life. In his youth, he waited backstage at the Royal Theatre in Stockholm for his first wife, Siri von Essen. Many years later, he waited at the same theatre, for Harriet. In *A Dream Play,* time telescopes as a whole life is defined by waiting.

The Lawyer epitomises suffering, which is portrayed expressionistically through physical distortion. 'His face reflects extreme suffering; it is chalk-white and lined, with purple shadows.' It mirrors the 'crime and vice which his profession forces him to experience vicariously' (Meyer, *Strindberg Plays*, p. 578). The Lawyer and the Daughter marry, and their relationship is unhappy in ways that echo Strindberg's experience of married life. The Poet resembles Strindberg in his attempt to transcend suffering through writing. Apart from the Daughter, he is probably the character with the strongest claim to be the dreamer. Towards the end of the play, when the Daughter tells the Poet that she has dreamed all that has happened, he replies that he 'wrote' it . The Poet (Strindberg's surrogate), and the Daughter would seem therefore to be co-creators of the dream. He is the origin of it. She experiences it.

The Daughter is the character who provides a stable reference point throughout the rapid montage of scenes. Strindberg added the Prologue to the play shortly before the first production. He made the Daughter the child of Indra partly because he was reading about Indian religions at the time, and partly because he felt that Harriet's particular style of beauty suggested that she could be of eastern origin. ('You are from Java', he used to tell her.) The religious references in the Prologue seem dated today, and it is sometimes omitted in performance. If the Prologue is performed, there is a strong suggestion that Indra's Daughter is the controlling consciousness, while Agnes is her human counterpart who struggles to comprehend the dream. References to Indra's Daughter in the main body of the play could possibly indicate Agnes' half-memories of her divine origin. In addition, they add layers of ambiguity. The deeper the Daughter, and the audience, sink into the dream, the less certain it is who is dreaming it. A further function of the Prologue is to establish from the outset the importance of oppositions in the play. The Daughter's words, 'I'm falling', with which the Prologue ends, are immediately juxtaposed with her comment to the Glazier (whom she now calls 'father'), at the beginning of the next scene: 'The castle is still rising from the earth' (ibid., p. 564). If the Prologue is omitted, the audience is plunged immediately into the dream, which they must try to make sense of.

The Prologue provides a clear beginning for what Strindberg called 'this flickering tale', but, even without it, the play is not as difficult as is sometimes suggested. There is a narrative, though, given the play's reliance on juxtapositions, repetitions and key themes, it might be helpful to think of its form more in terms of music. Provisional titles that Strindberg used at various stages of *A Dream Play's* composition point to some of its major themes: 'Prisoners', 'The Corridor Play', 'Setting up House' and 'The Growing Castle'. The action moves from the Growing Castle, via the Officer's childhood home, to the theatre corridor where he waits for Victoria. Here, the Daughter meets the Stage Doorkeeper (another representative of suffering) and offers to wear her shawl, which is weighted down with human sorrow. Locations and characters then proliferate and dissolve in more complex ways, but the central oppositions of sinking/rising and imprisonment/freedom provide coherence. The Daughter's donning of the shawl leads to her sinking deeper into the hardship of human existence. She finds herself imprisoned within an unhappy marriage, and her nightmarish sense of suffocation – of being literally unable to breathe – is expressed by means of a character called Kirstin who pastes over every crack in the window joints, ostensibly to prevent heat from escaping. She is rescued by the Officer, whom *she* earlier rescued from the castle, and together they visit the contrasted locations of Foulstrand and Fairhaven. She meets her final companion, the Poet, whose connection with the Lawyer is underlined by two related scenes in Fingal's Cave, the first between the Daughter and the Lawyer, the second between the Daughter and the Poet. Margery Morgan suggests that 'Fingal's Cave (the grotto . . . which opens on to the sea) . . . corresponds to [the] series of "wonderland" pictures' (Morgan, p. 128). In this peripheral location, on the borders of land and water, the Poet and the Daughter discuss the meaning of reality and dreams, and of poetry, which is a 'waking' dream. Finally, having learned the anguish of being human, the Daughter enters the Growing Castle, which is now on fire – to reascend to her father. By the light of the fire human faces can be seen, 'enquiring, grieving, despairing'. The bud on the roof of the castle, 'bursts open into a giant chrysanthemum' (Meyer, *Strindberg Plays,* p. 632). Despair and fertility – Strindberg continues his use of contrasts until the end.

In his final production of *A Dream Play,* Olof Molander omitted the Prologue. Bergman retained a shortened form of it in 1970, but transposed it to immediately before the scene in the theatre corridor. In their invaluable description of the production in *Ingmar Bergman: A Life in the Theater,* Lise-Lone Marker and Frederick J. Marker quote the response of *Svenska Dagbladet* to Bergman's treatment of the God Indra. 'The entire Indra phenomenon is transformed by Ingmar Bergman into the supreme theatrical gesture' (Marker and Marker, p. 114). This was a secularised, consciously theatrical interpretation of the play. It began with the entrance of the entire company, including extras and the prompter. The Poet sat at a table centre stage, 'with his back to the audience . . . Slowly the characters circled' in front of him. Then, 'After fifteen seconds, in the midst of a step, the rotating circle of dream figures suddenly froze in position' (ibid., pp. 107 and 109) and, quietly, the Poet read out the lines which, in Strindberg's original text, the Daughter speaks in Fingal's Cave in the hope that Indra will hear them.

> The earth is not clean.
> Life is not good.
> Men are not evil.
> Nor are they good.
> They live as they can,
> One day at a time. (ibid., 109)

Some of the actors then left the stage, while others took seats around its periphery. The actors who would play Agnes and the Glazier 'sat silently in a corner, eating. In a whisper, like a prompter feeding an actor his cue, the Poet spoke again – "Agnes, the castle is still rising from the earth"' (ibid., pp. 109–10). It was only on hearing these words, which she speaks in the original, that Agnes began the scene.

In Bergman's version, the Poet, a composite writer/director figure, was the controlling consciousness. This was his dream. Indra's Daughter and Agnes were two separate characters, played by different actresses. The former wore 'a long white robe with a mantle attached to it', the latter 'a simple pale blue or gray [*sic*] dress with a white collar' (Egil Törnqvist, 'Staging *A Dream Play*', *Strindberg's Dramaturgy*, p. 283). Indra and his Daughter were 'remote presences from a... world of fantasy that existed, perhaps, only in the Poet's vivid imagination' (Marker and Marker, p. 113). Agnes was always earthbound, subject to human pain and sorrow. At the end of the performance, the actors silently left the stage:

> The spotlight on the Poet's table was extinguished. The final image was certainly no symbolic depiction of a flowering castle of redemption and deliverance, but simply a glimpse of Agnes, the woman who had taken upon herself all of mankind's suffering in her heavy gray [*sic*] shawl, still seated alone on the empty stage, her hand pressed convulsively to her face in speechless anxiety. (ibid., p. 119)

Bergman's adapation of *A Dream Play* could have taken its cue from Strindberg's statement in his letter of 2 April 1907 to Emil Schering: 'My whole life often seems to me as if it had been staged for me, so that I might both suffer and portray it.' In this version of Strindberg's *Dream Play*, life, suffering and theatre were inextricably mixed, and the poet, Strindberg's representative, was simultaneously author, actor and audience.

Katie Mitchell's 2005 adaptation of *A Dream Play*

In her 'Director's Note' for the Cottesloe programme, Katie Mitchell described the company's exploration, in rehearsals, of ways of staging their own dreams. They also discussed Freud's and Jung's writings on dreams, and 'investigated the reasons for dreaming given by neuroscience, psychology and religion. One overriding fact emerged: there is always one dreamer in whose consciousness the action of the dream occurs'. There were three possible candidates for the role of dreamer, they decided: Agnes, the Officer and the Poet. They chose the second option because they felt that he was the character who was most obviously connected with Strindberg. The setting was transformed to the 1950s, and the Officer became a stockbroker called Alfred.

Caryl Churchill's version of Strindberg's play, which the company used as a starting point, omits the Prologue, and the production followed suit, substituting in its place a sequence in which Alfred fell asleep at his office desk and began to dream. The set consisted of symmetrically arranged desks in front of a line of partially-glazed rear doors. In contrast to the formality of the setting, accompanying sound effects of a ticking clock, loud typing noises and unintelligible telephone conversations evoked a sense of distortion. Everyone left to go home apart from Alfred, who continued working for a while and then fell asleep. His secretary, Agnes, who had now sprouted angel's wings, appeared upstage of the rear doors and tapped on the glass as if she was asking to be let in. When Alfred tried to escape from her, four replica angels appeared and surrounded him, drawing him into the dream. '[O]n an insignificant basis of reality the imagination spins', Strindberg wrote in his 'Author's Note'. Here, the physical reality of the desks and the back wall provided this basis. They seemed to be constantly in motion. The back wall advanced threateningly downstage, and then retreated to re-establish a peripheral view of narrow corridors that vanished into off-stage darkness. The desks went through a variety of metamorphoses, including, in a particularly effective transformation, into a sea of pitching and tossing waves. The result was dreamlike but unified, because all the images were constructed out of the same basic materials.

Mitchell's portrayal of Alfred's inner world through a constantly changing environment was in line with the expressionist nature of *A Dream Play*. Her decision to focus on the equivalent of the Officer yielded only limited returns, however. Strindberg's characters multiply, disperse and reassemble, as he explained in his 'Author's Note'. Even the Daughter is a double character. That is why it is so difficult to decide which, if any one, of the characters is the dreamer. Maybe together they form a composite dreamer, or perhaps the dreamer is the audience whose dream has spawned them all. The Officer is anyway a more limited choice as dreamer than the Poet. He has obvious autobiographical links with Strindberg, but it is through the Poet and the Daughter that Strindberg most clearly articulates the central theme of the play, which is the meaning of suffering. Bergman downplayed Strindberg's religious frame of reference, and substituted instead a conscious theatricality. If there was any meaning, it resided in human creativity. Bergman's dreamer was the author of the other characters' actions, as well as their words, but he had no power beyond the framework of the dream. When the play ended, the characters, apart from Agnes, 'wander[ed] back into the darkness'. The 'vision' had 'vanished' (Marker and Marker, p. 118). Agnes and her heavy shawl of suffering were all that remained.

Katie Mitchell's *Dream Play* lacked an equivalent depth. Alfred was well portrayed by the actor, Angus Wright, but one, rather mundane, character couldn't compare with the resonance Strindberg achieves in the play. In place of the Officer's beloved Victoria, Katie Mitchell gave Alfred a ballerina wife, and this justified the inclusion of a recurring motif of a male, cross-dressed *corps de ballet* from *Giselle*. It was entertaining, but it never accrued the layers of meaning that Bergman derived from his manipulation of theatricality. There were some very effective visual sequences. At one point, for example, Alfred's dead mother washed her long, golden hair in a bowl of water, and then replayed her actions in reverse order in a way that effectively evoked a sense of the reordering of time. There were two memorable images connected with children, and with loss. In one, a wardrobe door opened to reveal dolls (dead children?) hanging inside. In the other, a trapdoor was lifted, and beneath the stage floor there was a sliver of light and the sound of a child crying. Otherwise, the production seemed to me to be skilful, but not particularly moving or meaningful, especially by comparison with Strindberg's play. As Robert Hanks commented in the *Independent*, this version was 'no longer a play that takes the form of a dream, but a play about the mechanics of dreaming'. Michael Billington's summing up was particularly apposite. 'A Virgilian portrait of human sadness has been diluted into a private fantasy', he wrote. He had felt closer to Strindberg looking at the paintings in the Tate Modern exhibition than he had 'watching Mitchell's capriciously inventive production' (*Guardian*, 16.2.05).

'This flickering tale'

To me, the dolls hanging in the wardrobe and the crying child underneath the stage floor in Katie Mitchell's *Dream Play* seemed like remnants, ghosts of Strindberg's linked preoccupation with loss and the word 'child'. In 1901, when he was writing *A Dream Play*, and six years later when he added the Prologue, he was filled with yearning for his little daughter, and for Harriet, the 'Child' for whom he created the Daughter who experiences loss and suffering in *A Dream Play*. Strindberg wrote in his 'Author's Note' that 'an undertone of melancholy and of pity for all mortal beings accompanies this flickering tale' (Meyer, *Strindberg's Plays*, p. 553), and the Daughter also embodies a sense of compassion. The Swedish words for 'flickering tale', *vinglande berättelsen*, literally mean a tale that weaves in and out, but 'flickering tale' captures Strindberg's fascination with 'magic lanterns [and] their . . . capacity to provide seemingly disconnected yet suggestively relevant images' (ibid., p. 548); and also his description of *A Dream Play* as 'a dream picture'. 'The world . . . is really only a dream picture. (Consequently my *Dream*

Play is a picture of life), a phantom . . .', he wrote in his diary on 18 November 1901 (*From an Occult Diary,* p. 55*).*

When the Officer ages, as he waits near the stage door for his Victoria, the stage picture literally flickers. Strindberg's directions read, '*The stage is spasmodically illuminated as by a lighthouse*'. The Officer's words keep time with the changing light: 'Light and darkness – light and darkness?' he queries. The Daughter picks up his rhythm: 'Day and night. Day and night. A merciful Providence wishes to shorten your waiting; so the days flee the pursuing nights' (*Strindberg Plays*, p. 575). The flicker of light and darkness is just one of the ways in which Strindberg experiments with time in *A Dream Play*. Here, it speeds up, but the repetitions, the recurring motifs and the use of opposites (the juxtaposition of the scene in Foulstrand with the one in Fairhaven, for example) all contribute to the illusion Strindberg creates that time is malleable; that it can elongate, or apparently vanish. Similarly, space is apparently negated by one scene merging out of, and into, another. As Helga Nowotny writes in *Time: The Modern and Postmodern Experience*, 'the period between 1880 and 1918 laid the foundations for the drastic changes people experienced in the sense of space and time'. She instances the importance of inventions such as the telegraph, the radio and the telephone in diminishing spatial distances. The cinematograph, she adds, created 'totally new ways of seeing' when it 'succeeded not just in making pictures move but in slowing down and speeding up the captured movements at will' (Nowotny, p. 19). *A Dream Play* was in the vanguard of experimentation that explored these new ways of seeing in a theatrical context. Its seamless transformations from one location to another can be described as filmic. Alternatively, in Margery Morgan's words, 'Strindberg dissolves logic and narrative plot into an approximation to symphonic form' (Morgan, pp. 124–5).

And yet, there is a story, and the Daughter is at the heart of it. It is her tale. She sinks into the dream, taking the audience with her. Through the Growing Castle, she enters the dream's multiple, and parallel, worlds. Like Lyra in *His Dark Materials*, she is present in all these worlds, and, like Lyra's, her journey has an important goal. Lyra is the new Eve, the Daughter a reimagined Christ. Pullman destroys the Authority, and, in place of *Genesis*, creates a founding story for his proposed republic of Heaven. The Daughter leaves her author, her father, in order to learn about human existence. Her first earthly father, the Glazier, is a peripheral figure. He is the character who succeeds in opening a door that is believed to hide the meaning of life, but he fails to understand what he finds behind it. Later, she meets an alternative 'father', the Poet, who is an earthly author as Indra was a heavenly one. This time the relationship between daughter and 'father' is a more equal one. She dreamed the dream. He wrote it. He composes a petition about human suffering. She speaks it. At the end of the play, she prepares to return to her heavenly father, in order to make the petition to him directly. Unlike Christ, she plans to ascend not from the grave, but through fire. She enters the burning castle, but Strindberg is ambivalent about whether human suffering is redeemed. The chrysanthemum bud on top of the castle bursts into flower, but the castle illuminates the grieving, despairing faces of human beings who have found no answer to their pain.

Like *His Dark Materials*, *A Dream Play* creates an alternative story in place of its biblical source. Pullman's story is positive and hopeful despite its definition of the limits that human beings are subject to. Indeed, its seeds of hope arise out of an acceptance of these limitations. It extols the inspirational value of the imagination, while insisting that, in the give and take of actual life, there is no elsewhere. Strindberg's lifelong search was for meaning in human existence. He lived at a time when many intelligent people questioned the received 'truths' of religion, and these questions underlie *A Dream Play*. Strindberg articulates his philosophical quest, however, within a structure derived from his reading of Indian religions, and from the Christian story of Christ as co-sufferer with, and redeemer of, mankind. In order to understand the nature of human existence, the Daughter travels, like Pullman's Lyra, through parallel worlds. Strindberg forms these worlds out of both the creative potentialities of the expressionist fourth dimension, and the multiple possibilities that exist within the theatrical present moment, the *nunc instantis*. In *A Dream Play*, 'on an insignificant basis of reality the imagination spins' to create the 'flickering tale'.

9

Coram Boy: a final story

> in a valley near Hebden Bridge in Yorkshire, Crying Wood was named after the children who died working in the nearby mills and were buried there (from the National Theatre Programme of *Coram Boy*)
>
> They come by night as well as by day,
> To take your little child away.
>
> Everything is time. (*Coram Boy*)

Virtually all the plays and novels I have discussed are strongly reliant on narrative. Sometimes the way in which the story is told can restructure time, as it does in *Dangerous Corner* and *An Inspector Calls,* where a moment is recreated in order to investigate both the events that led up to it and its likely future consequences. Tales about ghosts also bring the past into the present because time is no longer subject to linear progression. It can move backwards, or leap forwards, or apparently stop altogether. Some stories recreate the past in order for the characters to find release from it, or, alternatively, to deepen their perception of the present. Some of the stories are whodunnits, others fairy tales, or parables, or individual memoirs of loss. Whose story it is is important. In *The Memory of Water, Frozen* and *Hecuba* it is primarily the mother's; in *By the Bog of Cats, The Lovely Bones, His Dark Materials* and *A Dream Play* it is the daughter's. In *The Skriker,* the story-telling protagonist is foregrounded because it is an embodiment of the story that is being told. Many of the stories reflect present-day anxieties, and reviewers interpret performances from the perspective of current narratives. Stephen Daldry's production of *An Inspector Calls* was initially perceived as a riposte to an uncaring, Thatcherite attitude to society's have-nots, but its collapsing house took on a new meaning after 9/11. In 2004 and 2005, productions of Euripides' plays were read in the context of fears of global terrorism, and the murdered children of Beslan haunted the productions of *Hecuba*. The fictional child victim of a serial killer in *Frozen* became enmeshed with the murder of real little girls after the Soham tragedy.

With a few exceptions, all the lost children in this book are girls: Carol in *Time and the Conways;* Mary Rose; Little Josie, and abandoned seven-year-old Hester in *By the Bog of Cats*; the dead child who is afraid of the man across the street in *The Weir;* Thomasina in *Arcadia*; Rhona in *Frozen*; the storyteller in *The Lovely Bones*; Lily's deformed descendant in *The Skriker;* Joan (whose childhood is corrupted in *Far Away*); Euripides' Polyxena and Iphigenia. Only Lyra is a survivor, and her reclamation of the tainted name 'Eve' is bracing in the context of all these dead or damaged girls. My reclamation of the Daughter in *A Dream Play* – Strindberg's moving attempt to find meaning in suffering – is also meant as a counterweight to their loss. I began my search for her in relation to the Student's speech about the collapsing house and the vanished child in *The Ghost Sonata*. His description of the house is reminiscent also of the collapsing house with which I began Chapter 1. In Stephen Daldry's production of *An Inspector Calls*, the house was reassembled, however, and, when it was opened up for the audience to see inside it, there, in the middle, was the little boy who had earlier been playing in the bomb craters and the rain. He was a survivor, like Lyra.

I wanted to end the book with an emphasis on survival, because, though theatre takes place within the present moment, and is adept at recreating the past, it is orientated towards the future. The 'now' is always on the threshold of becoming the 'new'. For this reason, there is almost always a degree of hope at the end of a performance. Even Churchill's *Far Away* contains the seeds of a possible regeneration. Helen Edmundson's adaptation of *Coram Boy*, which opened at the Olivier Theatre as I was close to finishing the book, was an unexpected bonus. I hadn't read Jamila Gavin's Whitbread-Children's-Book-Award-winning novel, and was unaware of its relevance. In *Coram Boy,* Gavin weaves together a number of stories about endangered children. The book's villain is Otis Gardiner, 'the Coram man', who, for money, takes away orphaned, abandoned, or illegitimate children. His nickname derives from the Coram Hospital, which was founded in 1741 by Captain Thomas Coram to care for unwanted children. In her Foreword to the book, Gavin explains that, in the eighteenth century, there was talk of '"the Coram man"... who collected abandoned children, ostensibly to deliver them to the newly founded Coram Hospital', though in fact the Hospital 'never employed such a man' (p. vii). Otis Gardiner sells the older children he collects to mill owners or to the navy. If the babies don't die quickly, he murders them. He forces his simple-minded son, Meshak, to help him to bury the bodies in woods and ditches and by deserted hedgerows. Meshak is haunted by the dead babies. He sees their faces in trees and brambles, or staring up at him from the depths of a pond where his father made him hide some of the babies. One autumn night he is terrified by the sight of 'little ... white naked bodies of babies', in the boughs of a crab apple tree. He hears 'a choir of sobbing voices' and the sounds seem to come from deep inside the tree, as if the tree itself were singing and wailing (p. 178).

Despite this equation of singing with ghostliness, music is a source of healing in *Coram Boy*. The book is divided into two parts, the first set in 1741, the second in 1750. In the first part, which is about separation and loss, the adolescent Alexander Ashbrook is told by his father that he must give up all hope of the music career he has set his heart on. Instead, Alexander renounces his right to the family estate and leaves home. Before he goes, he and a young girl called Melissa consummate their love. When Melissa gives birth to a son nine months later, her mother tells her that the baby is stillborn, and hands it over to Otis Gardiner. Meshak rescues the child and takes it to the Coram Hospital. Part Two focuses on this child (Aaron) and his friend Toby, whose slave mother gave birth to him on a voyage to England from her native Africa. Like his father, Aaron is musically gifted, and it is through Aaron's performances with the Coram choir that he and Alexander are eventually reunited with their family. Toby finds a surrogate mother in Melissa. At the end of the book therefore loss is succeeded by restitution. Gavin, however, never downplays the distressing nature of the fate of the children who are not redeemed for her young readers. 'I still find myself grieving for those who were not so lucky as the Coram boy', she writes in her Foreword, and the ghostly cries of murdered babies haunt the pages of the book. As well as the children who are sold to mill owners, there are others who meet even worse fates. Though he is believed to have been hanged for his crimes, Otis Gardiner survives into the second half of the book, where, under the assumed name of Philip Gaddarn, he is part of a secret ring of traffickers who sell children into slavery (including sexual slavery) overseas.

These children had disturbing equivalents in the 1990s and early 2000s. According to a programme note for the Olivier production of *Coram Boy*, '[s]ome 1.2 million children around the globe are trafficked every year, some into forced marriage, others into exploitative labour and domestic service, and others into prostitution'. Aaron and Toby are almost shipped abroad by Philip Gaddarn, and their imprisonment (along with other children) in a secret chamber under his house has echoes of the dreadful revelations that emerged from the trial of Marc Dutroux in Belgium in 2004. Dutroux was accused of sex crimes against children, who were imprisoned and reapeatedly raped. Two eight-year-old girls were left to starve to death in a pit Dutroux dug underneath his home. One girl who survived, Sabine Dardenne, was rescued after eighty days in Dutroux's cellar. She had marked her diary with crosses or stars, in order to differentiate between days on which Dutroux merely visited her, and days when he abused her. This was in 1996, when she was twelve. In 2004 she insisted on testifying against him, in order to prove to him that he had not destroyed her.

In the National Theatre production of *Coram Boy* the great height above the Olivier stage was used to create a sense of soaring release and freedom, while trapdoors in the stage floor served as burial sites for the murdered babies. The set was majestic yet uncluttered, its diamond-shaped wooden floor lending itself to both indoor and outdoor scenes. High above the stage was an organ, and towering wooden posts around the stage suggested both organ pipes and the 'crying woods' in which the babies were buried. As Susannah Clapp wrote in the *Observer* (20.11.05), 'music [notably, Handel's *Messiah*] fuels the plot', and, in addition to the live organ, there were onstage musicians and a choir. The nightmarish 'choir of sobbing voices' Meshak hears coming from the crab apple tree, with its fruit of dead babies, was evoked by the heartrending sobbing of mothers as their babies were placed beneath the trapdoors. The babies were represented by doll puppets, and one was still 'alive' when it was buried. This mother and child were downstage centre, and the tiny puppet shuddered as it sobbed. After it was buried, the mother took over the sound of its crying, extending the notes of grief so that loss seemed irredeemable. Near the end of the first act, however, death was countered by the possibility of resurrection. Tiny skeletons were unearthed to the accompaniment of the choir singing 'O Death where is thy sting? O grave thy victory?'. It was a prelude to the joyful rendition by the whole company at the end of the performance of the Hallelujah Chorus.

The movement from division and loss to healing and redemption in the second half of the performance was achieved through the power of the music, and through imagery suggestive of Shakespeare's late, magical plays of grieving separation and regeneration. In these plays, children are reunited with their parents by means of tokens that have been left with them at birth. Characters are lost at sea and almost drowned. Some, like Hermione in *The Winter's Tale*, are presumed dead, but return to life. In the production of *Coram Boy,* the haunted trees of the 'crying woods' were transformed into branches, from which were suspended the tokens left by mothers of babies who were accepted by the Coram Hospital. A photograph in the programme movingly recorded a selection of actual tokens that were left behind there: a key, a ring, a necklace, half a coin, a silver locket inscribed with initials, a medallion, a padlock, an elegant silver fish. According to the programme, 'Of the 2,523 children seeking places between January 1750 and December 1755, only 783 were admitted'. There was no information about whether any of the children were redeemed by means of the tokens. In the production, though Toby's necklace token could not reunite him with his far-away mother, he found a maternal substitute in Melissa. In place of a token, Aaron had Meshak, who had brought him to the Hospital, and, in the stage version, it was Meshak who gave Aaron the chance to be restored to his parents. When Aaron, Toby and Meshak were forced on to a slave ship by Philip Gaddarn, all three ended up in the water, but Meshak managed to push the boys up to the surface. Their struggle to survive was represented behind a huge transparent plastic sheet that covered the entire front of the stage. Aaron and Toby were in flying harnesses that enabled them to sink as if they were near to drowning, and then somersault up to freedom. *Coram Boy* is a tale of rebirth and return. Aaron and Toby survive their watery grave and make their way to Aaron's, and Alexander's, family home. Gavin writes in the book that, when Alexander saw his son and his son's friend, his 'heart stopped beating. Everything ceased; even the birds in their flight seemed suddenly suspended. The children of the crying woods faded away' (Gavin, p. 367). Charles Spencer, who described the production as 'gripping, terrifying, beautiful', defied 'anyone to watch its final scene without being moved to tears' (*Daily Telegraph*, 16.11.05). I certainly wept, and so did the people sitting around me. Later, I recalled the children who did not survive, but, in the final moments of the performance, loss was replaced by joy. The past was redeemed within the present, which was irradiated by hope of a happier future.

Bibliography

Primary texts

Barrie, J. M., *Mary Rose*, in *Peter Pan and Other Plays*, edited by Peter Hollindale, Oxford, 1995.
Carr, Marina, *By the Bog of Cats, Portia Coughlan* and *The Mai*, in *Plays One*, London, 1999.
Churchill, Caryl, *A Number*, London, 2002.
—— *Top Girls*, London, 1982.
—— *Light Shining in Buckinghamshire*, in *Plays One*, London/New York, 1985.
—— *Traps*, in *Plays One*, London/New York, 1985.
—— *Not . . . Enough Oxygen*, in *Shorts*, London, 1990.
—— *The Skriker*, London, 1994.
—— *Blue Heart*, London, 1997.
—— *Hotel*, London, 1997.
—— *Thyestes*, in *Plays Three*, London, 1998.
—— *Far Away*, London, 2001.
Euripides, *Hecuba*, translated by Frank McGuinness, London, 2004.
—— *Iphigenia at Aulis*, translated by Don Taylor, London, 2004.
—— *Hecuba*, translated by Tony Harrison, London, 2005.
Frayn, Michael, *Copenhagen*, London, 1998.
—— *Spies*, London, 2002.
Gavin, Jamila, *Coram Boy*, London, 2000.
Kane, Sarah, *Blasted*, in *Complete Plays*, London, 2001.
Lavery, Bryony, *Frozen*, London, 2002.
McDonagh, Martin, *The Pillowman*, London, 2003.
McGuinness, Frank, ed., *The Dazzling Dark: New Irish Plays*, London, 1996.
McPherson, Conor, *The Weir*, London, 1998.
—— *Shining City*, London, 2004.
Parker, Stewart, *Three Plays for Ireland: Northern Star, Heavenly Bodies, Pentecost*, London, 1989.
Priestley, J, B. *I Have Been Here Before*, London/New York, 1937.
—— *An Inspector Calls*, London/New York, 1948.

—— *The Plays of J.B. Priestley, Vol. One*, London/Melbourne, 1948.
Pullman, Philip, *Northern Lights*, London/New York, 1998.
—— *The Amber Spyglass*, London/New York, 2001.
—— interview with Melvyn Bragg, *South Bank Show*, 20.12.04.
Sebold, Alice, *The Lovely Bones*, London, 2003.
Stephenson, Shelagh, *The Memory of Water* and *Five Kinds of Silence*, London, 1997.
Stoppard, Tom, *Arcadia*, London, 1993.
Strindberg, August, *The Ghost Sonata*, in *Six Plays of Strindberg*, translated by Elizabeth Sprigge, New York, 1955.
—— *From an Occult Diary: Marriage with Harriet Bosse*, edited by Torsten Eklund, translated by Mary Sandbach, London, 1965.
—— *A Dream Play, an Interpretation by Ingmar Bergman*, translated by Michael Meyer, London, 1973.
—— *A Dream Play*, in *Strindberg: The Plays, Vol. Two*, translated by Michael Meyer, London, 1975.
—— *Strindberg's Letters, Vol. Two, 1892–1912*, edited by Michael Robinson, London, 1992.

Secondary texts

Aretxaga, Begõna, *Shattering Silence: Women, Nationalism, and Political Subjectivity in Northern Ireland*, Princeton, 1997.
Aston, Elaine, *Caryl Churchill*, Tavistock, 1997.
Bourke, Bernadette, 'Carr's "Cut-throats and Gargiyles": Grotesque and Carnivalesque Elements, in *By the Bog of Cats'*, in *The Theatre of Marina Carr: 'Before Rules Was Made'*, edited by Cathy Leenay and Anna McMullan, Dublin, 2003, 128–44.
Brecht, Bertolt, *Poems, Part Two, 1929–1938* and *Part Three, 1938–1956*, edited by John Willett and Ralph Manheim, London, 1976.
Buse, Peter and Stott, Andrew, eds, *Ghosts: Deconstruction, Psychoanalysis, History*, Basingstoke, 1999.
Children of Beslan (BBC 2 documentary, broadcast 30.8.05).
Cook, Judith, *Priestley*, Bloomsbury, 1997.
Dromgoole, Dominic, *The Full Room: An A-Z of Contemporary Playwriting*, London, 2000.
Eagleton, Terry, *Heathcliff and the Great Hunger: Studies in Irish Culture*, London, 1995.
Edwards, Paul, 'Science in *Hapgood* and *Arcadia'*, in *The Cambridge Companion to Tom Stoppard*, edited by Katherine E. Kelly, Cambridge, 2001, 171–84.
Evans, Gareth Lloyd, *J.B. Priestley – The Dramatist*, London, 1964.
Fleming, John, *Stoppard's Theatre: Finding Order Amid Chaos*, Austin, 2001.
Freud, Sigmund, 'The "Uncanny"', in *The Pelican Freud Library, Vol. 14: Art and Literature*, edited by Albert Dickson, Harmondsworth, 1985, 339–76.

Fukuyama, Francis, *Our Posthuman Future: Consequences of the Biotechnology Revolution*, London, 2002.
Garber, Marjorie B., *Shakespeare's Ghost Writers: Literature as Uncanny Causality*, New York/London, 1987.
Holm, Ingvar, 'Theories and Practice in Staging *A Dream Play*', in *Strindberg's Dramaturgy*, edited by Göran Stockenström, Stockholm, 1988, 245–55.
Hughes, David, *J.B. Priestley: An Informal Study of His Work*, London, 1958.
Ishiguro, Kazuo, *Never Let Me Go*, London, 2005.
Kaku, Michio, *Hyperspace: A Scientific Odyssey through the 10th Dimension*, Oxford, 1994.
Kaku, Michio, *Parallel Worlds: The Science of Alternative Universes and Our Future in the Cosmos*, London/New York, 2005.
Llewellyn-Jones, Margaret, *Contemporary Irish Drama and Cultural Identity*, Bristol, 2002.
McMullan, Anna, 'Unhomely Stages: Women Taking (a) Place in Irish Theatre', in *Druids, Dudes and Beauty Queens: The Changing Face of Irish Theatre*, edited by Dermot Bolger, Dublin, 2001, 72–90.
Marker, Frederick J. and Lise-Lone, *Ingmar Bergman: A Life in the Theater (Directors in Perspective)*, Cambridge, 1992.
Morgan, Margery, *August Strindberg (Macmillan Modern Dramatists)*, Basingstoke, 1985.
Murray, Christopher, *Twentieth-Century Irish Drama: Mirror up to Nation*, Manchester, 1997.
Nowotny, Helga, *Time: The Modern and Postmodern Experience*, translated by Neville Plaice, Cambridge, 1994.
Payne, Sara, with Anna Gekoski, *Sara Payne; A Mother's Story*, London/Sydney, Auckland, 2004.
Sierz, Aleks, *In-Yer-Face Theatre: British Drama Today*, London, 2001.
Stock, Gregory, *Redesigning Humans: Choosing our Children's Genes*, London, 2002.
Törnqvist, Egil, 'Staging *A Dream Play*', in *Strindberg's Dramaturgy*, edited by Göran Stockenström, Stockholm, 1988, 256–90.
Tucker, Nicholas, *Darkness Visible: Inside the World of Philip Pullman*, Cambridge, 2003.
Zeifman, Hersh, 'The Comedy of Eros: Stoppard in Love', in *The Cambridge Companion to Tom Stoppard*, edited by Katherine E. Kelly, Cambridge, 2001, 185–200.
Zipes, Jack, ed., *The Trials and Tribulations of Little Red Riding Hood*, New York/London, 1993.

Index

Note: page numbers in **bold** refer to main entries.

Abbey Theatre (Dublin) 42
Adams, Sarah 26
Agate, James 10
Ahmed, Kamal 78, 79
Albery Theatre 105, 120, 121, 131
Aldwych Theatre 1, 18
Ambassadors Theatre 33
Arena Theatre (Wolverhampton) 121
Aretxaga, Begoña 31, 32
Aston, Elaine 103

Baddeley, Angela 25
Barrie, James
   Mary Rose 5, 9, **23–7**, 28, 37
   Peter Pan 5
Bassett, Kate 38, 119
Bechtler, Hildegard 129
Beckett, Samuel 122
Bergman, Ingmar 151
   adaptation of *A Dream Play* 7, 138, 152, 155, 156, 158
Beslan massacre 2, 121, 124, 126, 127, 128, 132, 161
   Children of Beslan 120, 126, 127
Bevan, Lucy 102
Bible, The 32
   Genesis 138, 159
Billington, Michael 52, 73, 90, 92, 95, 133, 138, 158
Birmingham Repertory Theatre 74
Bosse, Harriet 146, 147, 148, 153, 158

Boswell, Laurence 133
Bourke, Bernadette 47, 50
Bragg, Melvyn 138
Brecht, Bertolt 100, 124
Brontë, Emily 42
Brown, Ivor 10, 19, 21, 25, 26
Bunraku Theatre 143
Bunyan, John 37, 39
Buse, P. 28, 30

Carnesky's *Ghost Train* 6, 29, **52–3**
Carr, Marina
   By the Bog of Cats 5, 29, 30, 39, 40, 41, 42, **47–52**, 53, 161, 162
   Mai, The 5, 29, 39, **40–2**, 44, 46, 47, 52, 53
   Portia Coughlan 5, 29, 30, 39, 40, 42, **43–6**, 47, 51, 52, 53
Carr, Maxine 79, 80, 82
Carroll, Lewis 142, 150
Castegren, Victor 151
Cavendish, Dominic 22
Chaillet, Ned 19
Chapman, Jessica 2, 74, 78, 79, 80, 81, 86, 90, 104
Churchill, Caryl 3, 137, 156
   Blue Heart 5, 93, 94, 101, 104, 109
      Blue Kettle 94, 101, 102 103, 104, 105, 117
      Heart's Desire 5, 93, 101, 103, 104, 115

Index

Cloud Nine 102
Downstairs 95
Far Away 4, 6, 93, 94, 95, 101, **104–12**, 113, 121, 122, 123, 162
Fen 96
Hotel 102
  Eight Rooms 102
  Two Nights 102, 103
Light Shining in Buckinghamshire 96, 102, 122
Not.... Enough Oxygen 95
Number, A 4, 93, 94, 195, 101, **112–18**
Owners 96, 113
Skriker, The 6, 92, 93, **94–101**, 104, 105, 117, 121, 122, 161, 162
This is a Chair 102
Thyestes 121
Top Girls **96–8**, 101
Traps 99, 103
Clapp, Susannah 78, 121, 129, 132, 164
Compton, Fay 25
Conrad, Peter 124
Cook, Judith 10, 12, 13, 23
Cooke, Naomi 121
Coveney, Michael 57, 104, 113
Craig, Daniel 112, 114, 115
Crotty, Derbhle 51
Crucible Theatre (Sheffield) 128

Daldry, Stephen 105, 107, 112, 114
  production of *An Inspector Calls* 1, 3, 4, 9, **14–17**, 21, 29, 162
Donmar Warehouse 120, 121, 132, 133
doppelgänger 46, 114, 115, 116
Doré, Gustave 84, 143
Doughty, Louise 122
Dromgoole, Dominic 149
  The Full Room 35
Duchess Theatre 18, 22, 28
Duke of York's Theatre 5, 33, 102
Dunne, J.W. 18

Eagleton, Terry 42
Edmundson, Helen 162

Edwards, Paul 58, 60
Ellen, Barbara 78, 81
Euripides
  Hecuba 2, 6, 7, 120, 121, 125, 126, 127, 128, **130–5**, 161
  Iphigenia at Aulis 6, 7, 120, 125, 127, **128–30**, 133, 135, 136
  Medea 40, 45, 47, 48, 49, 51
Evans, Gareth Lloyd 12, 13, 22
Evans, Lloyd 132

fairy stories 6, 45, 48, 51, 52, 93
fairy tales 30, 39, 40, 46, 47, 78, 80, 86, 99, 108, 112, 124, 161
  Cinderella 46, 52
  Hansel and Gretel 108
  Little Red Riding Hood 6, 74, 78, 82, 83, 84, 85, 86
  Snow White 48, 52
Falck, August 152
Farrow, Mia 25
Fenton, James 125
Field Day Theatre Company 29
Finding Neverland 5
Fleming, John 63
Foursight Theatre Company 121, 131
Frayn, Michael
  Copenhagen 4, 6, 54, 55, **64–9**, 72, 73, 74, 102
  Spies 6, **69–72**
Freud, Sigmund 107
Fukuyama, Francis 115

Gambon, Michael 112, 114
Garber, Marjorie 30
Garnett, Daisy 132
Gavin, Jamila
  Coram Boy 7, 8, 119, 144, 161, **162–5**
Gerrard, Nicci 78, 79, 80, 82
ghosts 5, 6, 24, **28–54**, 65, 68, 75, 87, 98, 161
ghost child 76
ghost-daughters 6, 53, 55
Ghost Fancier 48, 50, 51
ghost in the machine 76

ghost stories 33, 36
Gilbert, Jenny 73
Glass, David
  The Lost Child Trilogy 73, 108
Gough, Orlando 102
Greenwich Theatre 19
Greer, Germaine 133
Guildhall (Derry) 29

Hampstead Theatre 74
Hanks, Robert 15, 137, 158
Hare, David 120
Harrison, Tony 133, 134
Hart-Davis, Rupert 21
Haymarket Theatre 24, 25
Hemming, Sarah 46, 120
Higgins, Clare 120, 132, 133, 134, 135
Highfield, Roger 58, 59, 62
Hollindale, Peter 24, 25, 26
Holm, Ingvar 151
Hughes, David 10, 12, 18
Hunter, Holly 5, 51
Hunter, Kathryn 94
Huntley, Ian 79, 80, 81, 82, 86, 90

Ibsen, Henrik 113, 116
Ishiguro, Kazuo
  Never Let Me Go 118

Joint Stock Theatre Group 96
Jones, Oliver 2, 115
Jongh, Nicholas de 15, 26, 113

Kaku, Michio
  Hyperspace 141–2, 150
  Parallel Worlds 150
Kamerny Theatre (Moscow) 12
Kane, Sarah
  Blasted **121–5**, 126
Kent, Jonathan 120
Kingston, Jeremy 1, 20, 97
Koenig, Rhoda 12, 110

Lavery, Bryony
  Frozen 2, 6, 74, 77, 81, **82–6**, 87, 90, 104, 161, 162
Lawson, Wilfred 18

Leningrad Theatre Company 12
Letts, Quentin 58, 121
Lewis, C.S. 138, 139
Llewellyn-Jones, Margaret 29
lost children 2, 7, 21, 24, 26, 28, 29, 30, 66–9, 73, 74,102, 118, 136, 144, 162
lost daughters 52
lost sons 76, 102
Lyric Studio 29
Lyric Theatre 10

McCaughrean, Geraldine 5
Macaulay, Alastair 93
McDonagh, Martin
  The Pillowman 74, **90–2**, 100, 110, 124
Macdonald, James 121, 122
McGuinness, Frank 42, 120, 133, 134
Mackrell, Judith 100
MacNeil, Ian 4, 14, 17, 105, 112, 114
McPherson, Conor
  Dublin Carol 33
  Shining City 5, 29, 32, 33, **37–9**, 53
  Weir, The 5, 29, 32, **33–7**, 38, 39, 53, 162
Manchester Opera House 12
Manchester Royal Exchange 3, 18, 19, 20
Marker, Frederick J. and Lise-Lone 155, 156, 157
Marlowe, Sam 73, 104
Marmion, Patrick 37
Meyer, Michael 25, 136, 150, 151, 153, 155, 158
Milton, John 138, 143
Mitchell, Katie 7, 120, 136, 137, 145, 149, 152, 156, 157, 158
Molander, Olof 151, 152, 155
Morahan, Hattie 129
Morgan, Margery 150, 152, 154, 159
Morley, Sheridan 57
Murray, Christopher 29
Myerson, Jonathan 113

Nathan, John 51, 122
National Theatre 1, 2, 6, 7, 17, 55, 94, 96, 118, 136, 144
　Cottesloe 7, 55, 65, 74, 90, 94, 102, 136, 137, 138, 145, 156
　Lyttelton 17, 55, 120, 128, 129, 130, 136
　Olivier 1, 7, 8, 17, 120, 136, 138, 144, 162, 163, 164
New Theatre 12, 14
Nightingale, Benedict 45, 121, 122
Noh Theatre 47, 48
North, Madeleine 86
Nottingham Playhouse 5
Nowotny, Helga 64, 159

O'Brien, Edna 128
Old Vic Theatre 33, 102
Ouspensky, P.D. 18
Out of Joint Theatre Company 101

Parker, Stewart
　Heavenly Bodies 31
　Northern Star 31
　Pentecost 5, 6, 29, 30, **31–3**, 35
Paton, Maureen 15, 105
Payne, Sara 78, 79, 81, 82, 83
Payne, Sarah 2, 74, 78, 80, 81, 82, 86
Peacock Theatre (Dublin) 29
Peter, John 100, 104, 109, 113
Pinter, Harold 26, 113
Playhouse Theatre 1, 18
Priestley, J.B. 3, 105
　Dangerous Corner 3, 4, 8, 9, **10–12**, 13, 14, 18, 28, 161
　Eden End 3, 4, 5, 9, **22–3**, 24, 28
　I Have Been Here Before 18
　Inspector Calls, An 3, 4, 8, 9, **12–14**, 16, 21, 28, 29, 54, 55, 93, 105, 121, 122, 161, 162
　Time and the Conways 3, 4, 9, **18–22**, 23, 28, 44, 54, 162
Pullman, Philip
　His Dark Materials 7, 136, **138–44**, 145, 159, 160, 161
　Amber Spyglass, The 141, 142

Northern Lights 136, 138, 139, 141, 143, 144
South Bank Show interview 138, 139, 143, 144

Redgrave, Vanessa 2, 120, 132, 133, 134
Richardson, Ralph 22
Robson, Flora 11
Royal Court Theatre 7, 29, 34, 95, 96, 105, 112, 115
Royal Court Theatre Upstairs 33, 104, 121, 124
Royal Shakespeare Company 113, 120, 121, 127, 131, 133
Royal Theatre (Stockholm) 152
Royalty Theatre 18

Sansom, Laurie 12
Schauspielhaus (Hannover) 102
Sebold, Alice
　The Lovely Bones 6, 69, 74, **87–9**, 161, 162
Shakespeare, William
　Cymbeline 133
　Hamlet 5, 66
　King Lear 112, 113, 116, 121, 122
　Merchant of Venice, The 39, 43
　Winter's Tale, The 164
Shaw Theatre 25
Sierz, Aleks 123, 129
Smith, Andrew 122
Sokel, Walter H. 151
Sophocles 3
Spencer, Charles 1, 121, 165
Spink, Ian 102
Sprigge, Elizabeth 145
Stafford-Clark, Max 101
Stephenson, Shelagh
　The Memory of Water 6, **74–7**, 86, 104, 161
Stock, Gregory 115
Stoppard, Tom
　Arcadia 4, 6, 54, **55–64**, 74, 103, 162
Stothard, Peter 133
Stott, A. 28, 30
Strindberg, Anne-Marie 146, 147, 148

Strindberg, August 3
  Dream Play, A 7, 136, 137, 142, 144, **145–60**, 161, 162
  Easter 25, 149
  From an Occult Diary 137, 145, 146, 147, 148, 149
  Ghost Sonata, The 145, 162
  Letters 146, 147, 148, 149, 151, 152
  'Wonderland' paintings 142, 146, 150, 154
Swedish Theatre (Stockholm) 145, 149

Tate Modern 7, 138, 149, 158
Taylor, Don 128, 129, 130
Taylor, Paul 90, 91, 102
Thaxter, John 1
Thompson, Tony 78
Tinker, Jack 122
Törnqvist, Egil 156
Townsend, Mark 78
Traverse Theatre (Edinburgh) 96
Trewin, J.C. 13, 16

Tricycle Theatre Company 29
Tucker, Nicholas 139
Two Colour Theatre Company 5, 26

Vaudeville Theatre 74

Wardle, Irving 19, 21, 25, 26, 58, 100, 105, 113
Warnock, Mary 79
Wells, Holly 2, 74, 78, 79, 80, 81, 86, 90, 104
West Yorkshire Playhouse 3, 12, 18, 22
whodunnit 3, 4, 6, 9, 10, 11, 12, 14, 57, 61, 78, 79, 93, 94, 105, 111, 113
Woddis, Carole 90, 114, 129
Wright, Angus 157
Wright, Nicholas 136
Wyndhams Theatre 5, 51

Zeifman, Hersh 62
Zipes, Jack 78, 82, 84, 85

EU authorised representative for GPSR:
Easy Access System Europe, Mustamäe tee 50,
10621 Tallinn, Estonia
gpsr.requests@easproject.com

www.ingramcontent.com/pod-product-compliance
Lightning Source LLC
Chambersburg PA
CBHW020948230426
43666CB00005B/228